Libraries and Society

Libraries and Society

(Second Reivsed and Enlarged Edition)

PANDEY S.K. SHARMA

M.A., Ph.D. (RANCHI); B. LIB. SC. (DELHI)

M. LIB. SC., Ph. D. LIB. SC. (PANJAB)

ESS ESS PUBLICATIONS

New Delhi-110 002

First Published 1987

Second Revised and Enlarged Edition 1992

ISBN: 81-7000-133-1

Rs. 600/-

Published By:
Sheel Sethi (Mrs.) for **Ess Ess Publications**
4837/24, Ansari Road, New Delhi-110 002.

Composed at: Classic Computer Services
RZ-128/6K, Lane No.9, East Sagar Pur,
New Delhi-110 046.

Printed At: Printline, New Delhi.

Contents

Preface

To the Second revised and enlarged edition

The need for writing the second revised and enlarged edition of the book has been three fold:

1. Library-scene in the country has changed substantially since the first edition of the book was published in 1987. One of the major changes that took place, is in the field of public libraries legislation, as during 1988-89 three states viz, Haryana, Kerala and Manipur adopted library legislation. Updating and purging the text of the first edition was therefore called for.

2. The author received suggestions from many quarters to add a few more chapters with a view to increasing the utility of the book. Consequently, this second revised and enlarged edition has 6 more chapters, viz, (i) Library Legislation, (ii) Library Extension work, (iii) Library Publicity and Public Relation, (iv) Library Building, (v) Library Science Education and (vi) Network.

3. Otherwise also, the publisher intended to bring out second edition of the book, as copies of the first edition were exhausted.

I am immensely happy to give this revised and enlarged edition in the hands of lovers of libraries in the society who received the first edition cordially.

(Pandey S.K. Sharma)

Preface

(First Edition, 1987)

The present work is an attempt to throw light on the role of libraries in society and on related topics. This theme assumed great significance in western countries long back. In India also the feeling that libraries are the most economical and effective medium to provide life long education, adequate information and healthy recreation to one and all has been gathering impetus. As a consequence not only public interest in libraries has increased, but almost all the universities have incorporated a full paper on this subject in B. Lib. & Inf. Sc. course. The dearth of literature by Indian authors on this subject is, however, known to all. It is hoped that the present work will be of use to students and teachers of library and information science, and of interest to academicians and common readers.

There is nothing completely new under the sun. This book also does not claim to contain new ideas: It is concerned with compact presentation of the subject in simple language. The readers may however find the chapter on Library Profession interesting and thought provoking.

A

Libraries in Society

A0 INTRODUCTION

Libraries play a vital role in the overall development of the society. A whole book of quotations can be brought out by compiling what has been written and said in praise of libraries. In his book entitled "Public Library Services", Gerald Johnson writes, "The quickest and the easiest access to the world's best thought is through public library". There is no gainsaying the fact that a library houses the greatest thoughts of the world; for, books— a constituent of the library— are said to be the greatest creation of the humans, who are the greatest creation of the God. A library is thus a place where the greatest creation of the greatest creation are housed i⌒ an organised way for the use of one and all.

A1 CHANGING CONCEPT OF THE LIBRARY

Until recently the library was considered to be a "Store house for the recorded experience of mankind" [1] or "a place set apart to contain books for reading, study or refernece"[2]. The library was thus expected to collect, arrange and preserve reading material and make these available on demand. A library that performed these four functions was supposed to have functioned satisfactorily.

A library of any time and at any place would be expected to perform the four basic functions stated above. But in context of the present needs of the society it is not pertinent to restrict the activities of the library to these four areas alone. The activities or functions stated above, though are basic and fundamental, do not sufficiently highlight the role the libraries play in the society. As a matter of fact, these are traditional, derivative, and conservative functions of library. The library of yesterday opened its doors for the world; but the library of today not only opened its door more widely, but also has moved out of its four-walls to reach larger target groups. libraries of today are expected to do, and are doing much more than this and have assumed diverse dimentions. Wallace writes in this connection, about American public libraries, "Libraries have operated Railway Stations, housed red cross classes, sponsored concerts and dramatic productions, operated museums and even planetariums, held art shows, loaned umbrellas in rainy days and furnished high chairs for the infant"[3]. Such and many more other activities are being performed by the public libraries throughout the world in their endeavour to serve the society in a purposeful way. Kenyon Committee of U.K. recorded some sixty four years ago that a public library is "Centre of intellectual life of the area it serves"[4]. The library of today is thus an institution of complex nature as far as its operations, objectives, management, services and sources of finance are concerned. "It is concerned with the refreshment of man's spirit by the provision of books for relaxation and pleasure with assistance to the students and with provision of upto date technical, scientific and sociological information"[5]. The changed character of public libraries and the wide range of activities which these are performing today have made the library a social and cultural centre and a centre for satisfying the educational and informational needs of the society.

A2 LIBRARY : A SOCIAL ORGANISATION

Any organisation may be considered to be a 'Social Organisation' if it fulfils the following major conditions: (i) its origin and development is associated with the society and its objectves are social; (ii) it endeavours to inculcate (in the members of the society) religious, ethical, moral, intellectual and cultural values and side by side it teaches, directly or indirectly, right behaviour and conduct; (iii) it has the quality of adaptation to the prevalent social order; (iv) it keeps in touch with other social organisations and maintains a coordial relation with these, and (v) it strives to continue to ramain a live institution. Therefore, the library can be consider to be a social organisation if it possesses undermentioned qualities:

(i) Social orign and development
(ii) Social objectives
(iii) Quality of Adaptation to social order
(iv) Relation with other social organisations
(v) Liveliness

A21 Social Origin and Development

In order to determine whether or not the library is a socal organisation we shall have to find, if the library has its roots in the society. A society is a collective from of indivic uals, their activities and their beliefs. It is true that libraries of th: old days were not functioning as social institutions because in early times the library was considered to be the property of an individual or of a particular group. Then books and the library, were kept under locked almirahs. It reflects that the early libraries were not functioning as social organisations but as private property. But, there were sufficient, and justifiable reasons for this. In ancient times books were written by hand, and one or limited copies were available. It was an immensly difficult and costly affair to make multiple copies of manuscripts. Therefore, very rich people like kings and big Jamindars, could afford the heavy cost on reproduction, as well as on safety of books. Had the manuscripts were then kept open for the use of one and all, valuable records of cultural heritage of the society would have perished. At the same time, it is also not a fact that the kings and Jamindars maintained libraries for their presonal use alone and did not allow others to consult these. A few learned public were allowed to handle these carefully. But for the safe custody by the individual owners, this valuable cultural heritage would have 'died' in infancy. Here we may compare the ancient manuscripts with small seedlings and plants, which, when kept safely in conditioned environment, grow big and the society later reaps the benefits of their shadow and fruits. Likewise, the society could not have benefitted by the knowledge these valuale manuscripts contained, had these were not protected by the individual owners.

Advent of printing presses and developments that took place in the field of printing technology had great impact on book production. It made possible to make unlimited copies of a book. This contributed to growth of public libraries where books were kept for open use by the common man. Religion, which is social concept, also played significant role in making the library a social institution. Different religious organisations started distributing religious literature and establishing libraries for the propagation of their respective religions. In all religions and in all societies donation and charity are considered to be great virtues. Donation of books is also a regular form of donation. Buddhism considers it as a very/important act of donation. Many libraries and their collections were built up by the books donated by various individuals. The Emphasis of the rulers and the governments on public education, library oriented education, adult education and other such concepts laid marked stress on establishment and development of libraraies. Government is a bigger and more organised form of the society. Governments of different countries have also been engaged at various levels (national, state, district, municipal etc. level) in the establishment and development of libraries. In this way, every unit of society made consolidated efforts towards the origin and development of libraries. It can therefore be said that the library is a social organisation, as the society has been instrumental in its origin and development.

A22 Social Objectives

Documents are kept in the library for democratic use by all members of the society. The library aims at providing reading and other materials for ensuring healthy intellectual growth of all the members of the society. It's objectives are social and democratic i.e. society oriented . The Five Laws also lay marked emphasis on this objective. This also proves that the library is a social organisation.

A23 Adaptation to Social Order

The library has always been open and adapt to changing social order. It has never stuck to rigid and orthodox procedure and services. Rather, it has been changing with change in the society. Under changed circumstances, it adopted open access system, started public relation and extension activities, introduced computerization and engaged itself in fulfilling the intellectual, educational, informational, and cultural needs of the society. It is always willing to make earnest efforts to change with the society. Hence, it has the quality of adaptation to changing social order to the highest degree, which proves that it will continue to exist as a social organisation.

A24 Relation with Other Social Organisations

The concept of cooperation is inherent in libraries. The library is a firm believer of cooperation. On one hand libraries cooperate amongst themselves (through Inter-Library Loan, Cooperative acquisition, Cooperative Cataloguing, Network etc.). On the other hand, the library maintains relation and cooperation also with other social organisations such as educational, literary, cultural and service institutions.

A241. *Growing Organisation*

It is a scientific fact that only a growing and active organisation can survive. Growing indicates life and activity. The Fifth Law proves that the library is a growing organism and therefore, it is bound to exist in the society (for details see the Fifth Law discussed in this book under section C).

A25 Methods For Becoming Social Organisation

The Library of today is not only a study centre, but also a social centre. Libraries of all countries are functioning as social centres by extending their activities and services, such as organising exhibition, lectures, dramatic presentation, competition, reaching people through book mobile. The library of today is concerned with the provision of books for relaxation and pleasure with assistance to students and provision of up-to-date technical scientific and sociological information. All these factors, i.e. its origin, development, objectives, services, management and finance reveal that the library is a social organisation.

(for details see, chapter on **'Extension Work'**)

A3 LIBRARY: AN INFORMATION CENTRE

Human society has travelled a long journey from stone age to the age of technology. The age of technology, in which we are living today, and the technological revolutions that we are witnessing today are founded on the pillars of information. Our present society is thus information based society. It would be pertinent to mention here that information is being produced today with such an alarming speed which can only be imagined. There is vast ocean of information in every discipline. The world is delused with information. The more we learn, the more is left to be learnt. Every individual in the society—whether he is a student, a researcher, a specialist, a layman, a professional, an industrialist, a worker, a child or an aged person—needs information of one kind or the other. The flood of information has therefore to be controlled, analysed, and channelised so as to derive maximum benefit. This implies, taking steps to ensure that the available information reaches the right user.

And there can possibly be no better institution than a library for collecting, analysing, storing, and disseminating right information to the needy user on one hand and to find and locate right user for right information on the other hand. Libraries are thus indispensabale for the society for meeting its informational needs.

A4 LIBRARY: FOR BETTER CITIZEN

As stipulated by Unesco in its manifesto for public libraries, right of access to information is the basic right of an individual in a democratic society. Active and informed participation of each and every individual and group in the country's afair is essential for a real democratic set-up. A democratic society needs such citizen as are exposed to the environment around them and are well acquainted with the cultural, social, political, and economic heritage and development of the country. At the same time they should also be capable of analysing and discussing a given situation at a given time so that they could be able to take right decision at right time. Such decisions might range from ploughing fields to electing people's representatives at various levels. Citizen are therfore to be made knowledgiable both through formal and non formal education on continuing basis. Library is an agency which can serve this purpose most efficiently, effectively, and economically. Highlighting this role of libraries, Gaines says "to keep the society from being swamped by ignorance will require the utmost ingenuity and leadership from librarians as well as from educators, sociologists and politicians"[6] The role and responsibility of a library to make better citizen is more important and vital than providing facts and figures. Every society has realised this as will be evident from the *Kenyon Committee* report which put on roecrd "the public interest in libraries has greatly increased and we believe that there is now a far healthier belief in the value of knowledge and in the importance of intellectual life. The public library is no longer regarded as a means of providing casual recreation of an innocent but somewhat important character; it is recognised as an engine of great potentialities for national welfare, and as an essential foundation for the progress in education and culture without which no people can hold its own in the sturggle for existence"[7]

A5 LIBRARY : AN EDUCATION CENTRE

The library is the most effective and economic medium for spread of education and disemintation of information. Education is a process and from childhood to old age every one continuously passes through this process. In the whole life the human passes through or recieves education in two forms: formal education and informal education. The library plays vital role by helping the citizen pursue both forms of education. It is for this reason that the library is dubbed as "People's University".

A51 Library & Formal of Education

In formal education, men and women receive education of a specified level based on a specified syllabi. This form of education is imparted in academic institutions, such as schools, colleges, universities, research institutions etc.

The library does occupy a significant place in academic institutions. Eductionists and scholars hold that it is a "better proof of education to know how to use a library than to possess university degree"[8] The UGC (UK) maintained in 1921, "The character and efficiency of a university may be gauged by its treatment of its central organ, the library...An adequate library is not only the basis of all teaching and study, it is the essential condition of research without which additions can not be made to the sum of human knowledge"[9] The library has become still more important in academic set up due to change in the nature of education. During the past, formal education was based on dictation: the teachers used to dictate and speak and the students used to listen to. This system has been done away with in western countries and in India also we are following new methods with appreciable speed and success. The present-day education is no more an one way system is which the student had passive participation. In the changed system the student is expected to actively participate. The teacher mainly kindless the curiosity of students, makes them aware of basic facts, teaches them metholodgy and refers them to books to find detailed information for themselves which is discussed later in tutorials etc. *Parry Committee* wrote in this connection, "lecture and text book method is no longer regarded as the sole method for teaching",[10] and recommended, "If one of the main purposes of University education is to teach students to work on their own, reading by students must be preferabale to attendance at a lecture unless the lecture is superior in presentation or contents to the available literature"[11] Students are thus refered to books both by teachers and librarians. This leads to active participation of students in eudcational system. Education of today is becoming more and more library oriented which is evident from the fact that academic libraries of today are always full of students, researchers, and teachers alike. It has rightly been said, "a university is as good as its library".[12] The library is therefore indispensable for the society for meetings its educational needs.

A52 Library & Non Formal Education

Men and women do not cease to receive education after completing their formal education because the process of learning does not stop after school, college or university education. Education a the continuous process, and therefore, the human beings continue to recieve education before and after receiving formal education. Then, there are people who, for many factors, do not find opportunity to receive formal education. Formal education is like a pond of education with limited boundaries, whereas non formal education is like an ocean of education which knows no bounds. The library helps immensly in non-formal education and adult education.

A6 CONCLUSION

Libraries are indispensable for society. These educate, inform and convert an individual into a better citizen. There is no gainsaying the fact that the men and women who move and lead the world in any field are informed people and readers. A library is the most suitable place for such persons. It makes information available in a better, organised and more economical manner. The opening of more and more libraries may reduce the number of prisons, police stations and courts of law. These institutions will always be needed but in a library oriented society their number would certainly be less.

Further reading: Chapter on **Public Libraries**

REFERENCES

1. *The New Universal Encyclopedia,*. Ed. by John Hannerton (London, Educational Books) v 6, P. 5116
2. *The Shorter Oxford English Dictionary,* Ed. by C.T. Onions 3d ed. 2v. (Calcutta, Standard International Company, 1968), v, P. 1136.

3. Wallace, Sarah Leslie: *So you want to be a librarian* (New York, Harper and Row, 1963), P. 95.
4. Kenyon Committee (UK, Board of Education, 1924): Report on public libraries in England and Wales (1927), P. 3
5. Unesco Manifesto for public libraries, issued in 1949, rev. in 1972.
6. Gains, E.J. : *Intellectual freedom*, in A.L.A. Bulletin, Feb. 1966. p. 119.
7. Keynon Committee, *op. cit.*
8. Sir Cyril Norwood, as quoted by Robert Snenn, in *Test questions for school librry* (London, 1958).
9. University, Grants Committee (UK), *Report*, 1921.
10. *Committee on Libraries* (University Grants Committee UK) *Chairman*, Thomas Parry (London, Her Majesty's Stationary Office, 1967), *Report*, p.10.
11. *Ibid.*, p.11.
12. Hutchings, F.G.B. : *Librarianship* etc., (Kualalumpur, Oxford University Press, 1969). p.5.

B

Library Profession

B1 INTRODUCTION

Addressing the students of a library school Christopher Morlay gave them a quotation from Erasmss, "Assiduus sis in bibliotheca, quae tibi paradise locuest (may you be assiduous in your library which is for you a place of paradise)".[1] Libraries have been considered a place of paradise, a temple of learning, the heart of an university and so on not only for readers but also for the people who work in these. Working in a library means working with the people of all walks of life who want to read and do read. A librarian does not only come into contact with lovers of knowledge but also experiences the pleasure and thrill of providing right information to right person at right time. Librarianship thus can be a great profession for those who enter it with seriousness of purpose.

B-2. LIBRARIANSHIP FOR WHAT

The noted Sanskrit scholar Mammat has enumerated six purposes for adopting the pursuit of poetry or literature, *"Kavyam Yashase arthakrite, vyavahaarvide, shivettarcchhataye, Kantasammitopadeshyuje, sadyahaparinivritaye."* This means, there are six purposes of writing poetry : for name and fame (Yash), money (Arth), earning worldly wisdom and contact with people (Vyavahar), social well-being (Shivettarchhataye), delight of release (Sadyah parinivritaye), and communicating in soft and acceptable manner. (kantasammitopadesh). As a matter of fact, what Mammat said about the pursuit of poety is true to all pursuits and all professions, particularly service-oriented professions. Library profession can also be chosen for these purposes. Ranganathan has discussed the purpose of choosing librarianship as a profession in detail in his book

Preface to library science. He has discussed in detail as to for what one should choose librarianship as profession. According to him, one may do so for (i) personal profit, (ii) social well-being (iii) creative joy including delight of release, and (iv) fulfilment of nation's mission. The points mentioned by Mammat and later by Dr. Ranganathan are in consonance with one another and are of immense importance for the students of library and information science. These have been elaborated below.

B21 Personal Profit

Any one who chooses a profession normally chooses it for earning livelihood and for personal name and fame. Mammat has placed the purpose of name and fame at the first place and has enumerated the purpose of earning money as secondary purpose. One wants to earn name and fame also for the sake of his personal self. Dr. Ranganathan accepted in 1948 that (then) the librarians were miserably paid, but had forcasted that librarianship in India will soon become a highly paid profession. His blessing became true in his life time. As a result of his efforts, now librarians are considered to be at par in terms of salary and status with their counterparts in schools, colleges, universities and research institutions. Frequently we come across advertisements in newspapers wanting librarians in lucrative scales of pay. The pedestal of library profession and the status of librarians have also risen considerably. The profession of librarianship is bound to prosper more as far as personal profit is concerned, because the present society has entered the information age in which more and more librarians and information scientists will be needed.

B22 Social Well-Being

One may choose library profession for making contribution towards social well-being of the masses. Librarians can achieve this goal by providing information to various groups of readers including administrators, scientists, agriculturists, economists, engineers, and others, and thus can contribute towards the development of the nation. Dr. Ranganathan said in this context " I say that independent India cannot long delay realising the urgency for establishing libraries of the right sort manned by daring souls like you...She can not make progress without a public library system. When she realises and she will soon do so that her social betterment can not be achieved without libraries and the service of library science, then will her leaders and people appreciate the farsighted step which the Delhi University has taken...to introduce a degree course of library science".[2] Dr. Ranganathan spoke thus in one of the inaugural addresses delivered in the Department of libraray Science, University of Delhi in 1947. In his life-time he saw library profession growing into a fruitful profession. The country and her leaders realised the role which a library can play in social well-being of the nation and as a result we see numerous libraries of all tyes which were set up after independence.

B23 Creative Joy and Delight of Release

The profession of librarianship fills the professional with creative joy. Earning fame and personal profit also brings joy in ones life. This joy and happiness can be obtained through all the professions, but joy and happiness derived out of personal gains or profit are short lived. In addtion to this joy, a librarian drives personal pleasure and happiness also by serving a reader, by providing information to the needy, and thus by working for social well-being of the nation. Joy recieved out of such acts is everlasting and can be derived only in selected professions. Librarianship is one of such professions which brings to professionals everlasting happiness.

B24 Fulfilment of Nation's Mission

The fourth purpose of the pursuit of librarianship, according to Dr. Ranganathan, is fulfilment of nation's mission. Librarians have the potentials and capabilities to provide to the nation information needed by her for fulfilling her mission. "Whether a nation is destined to fulfil its mission by lifting library science to a higher potential or not and whatever be the field of knowledge towards which its mission gets gravitated, its fulfilment will have to depend on a long chain of events, personalities and institutions, one inevitable link of which should be its library system".[3]

B3 LIBRARIANSHIP FOR WHOM

B31 Difficult and Different Profession

Special type of manpower is needed for managing and organising a library. This is so because the profession of librarianship has distinct features. First of all, it is to be borne in mind that *Librarianship is a difficult profession.* To prove onself worthy of the profession of librarianship is much more difficult than to prove to be worthy of any other profession. For example, when one is appointed as a teacher in a particuair department, he has to prove his worth and ability to the teachers and students of his particular department alone. Students and teachers of other departments are not going to judge, apapreciate, or criticise him. But when he becomes a librairan, say in an academic institutions, all the teachers, students and administrators observe and judge him from their own different angles. And the librarian is supposed to come up to the expectations of all, proving himself competent on their standards. Of course, this job is not an easy job but, only by dint of his professional performances the librarian can make the library the heart of his institution and then he could become the most appreciated person on the campus. The second thing is that an aspirant for the profession should bear in mind that this profession is *different from other professions* in a peculiar way. In most other professions if the client is dissatisfied he would come to the professional time and again, but will cease coming to him when satisfied. For example, if a student is not satisifed (i.e., if he did not understand a particuair lesson) he would go to the teacher for learning again; if a patient is not cured he would come again and again to the doctor but would cease his visits when cured. Similarly, if the accounts people do not pass the bill or keep it pending, the claimant would approach them again and again, but after receiving the money he would not. On the contrary, when it comes to libraries, a satisfied reader would keep on consulting the library, but when dissatisfied he would stop his visits.

B32 Qualities of a Librarian

Discussing the qualities which a good librarian should posses, Wallace writes "... it goes without saying that there is not a single desirable personality trait which would not be desirable in a librarian".[4] Thus any good quality adds to the performance of a librarian and there is no end to such qualities. The following qualities must however be present in a librarian:

1. Organising Capacity
2. Love for books and readers

3. Service Minded
4. Soft spoken and tactfulness
5. Presence of mind and sense of humour.

B321 *Organising Capacity*

A librarian should be capable of organising men and material in his library in such a way as may be necessary for deriving maximum benefit for readers. To achieve this, a student of library and information science must be serious in studies so that he learns various techniques of organising knowledge in libraries. In libraries reading materials should be organised keeping in view the readers. A faulty classificatory arrangement and faulty cataloguing of books restrict the optimum use of a library. Secondly, right type of men (library staff) should be assigned a particular duty considering their skill and temperament.

B322 *Love for Books and Readers*

A librarian's foremost duty is to match right book with right reader and vice-versa. He should therefore have love for books and readers both. He should take keen interest in books and readers. He should try to search and discover the contents of each book of the library and also the needs of each reader of the library. Readers are like consumers and books are like consumer-goods. The librarian should know which consumer-good (i.e, book) suits which consumer (i.e., reader). This increases the use and popularity of the library. For this, the librarian is required to know the book and the reader by coming into close contact with them. He must also be a good reader. Each and every book acquaired in the library must be seen by him and he should know the contents of the book. Likewise, he should know the needs and interests of all the regualrly visiting readers. Some books as well as some readers are very shy. The titles of some of the books do not reveal the book's actual contents. Some times, a reader due to his shyness or complex character of library techniques, may not take much advantage of available materials. If the librarian remains in touch with books and readers he can help every book in finding its right readers. In the same way he can help each reader in finding his/her right book. Therefore love for books and readers is a quality that makes a librarian popualr and praiseworthy. Stressing this quality of a librarian Rose writes, "After all, if a person does not love books, why on earth should she, or he, wish to become a librarian? There is little enough in the way of financial reward, the hours are long, vacation short, and work hard....But a real love and knowledge of books...does constitute a passport to librarianship ... to that is added a genuine interest in people.."[5]

B323 Service—minded

A library is a service institution and librarianship is a service oriented profession. Power crazy and status conscious persons are therefore not suited to library pforession. Rather a librarian should be service-minded and should derive pleasure is serving people by trying to meet their library needs. A librarian should not wait for readers to come to him but he on his own should take all possible steps to ensure that educational and informational needs of his readers are fulfilled. This gives him immense and everlasting pleasure.

B324 Softspoken and Tactful

Service with smil and soft words does not cost anything but wins people. As is expectd from a service minded professional, a librarian should be soft spoken and tactful. He should serve the people with modesty and politness mixed with academic vanity. Daily he comes into contact with many types of people with varying intellectual levels and backgrounds. He should therefore be tactful in dealing with people. Speaking softly is a basic courtsey and a librarian cannot afford to lack in this quality.

B325 Presence of Mind and Sense of Humour

Presence of mind helps the librarian to serve readers in better way, and sense of humour makes his job easy and interesting.

B4 ASSOCIATION OF IDEAS AND LIBRARIAN'S PERSONALITY

B41 Association of Ideas

The theory behind association of ideas prescribes that some ideas are so closely united that when one's mind thinks of one idea or entity, it also automatically recalls other ideas or entities that have been associated with the former. For example, Kurukshetra and Mahabharata, Geeta and Krishna, Sita and Rama, Radha and Krishna. These pairs are so closely associated with one another that when we think of one of them, our mind automatically recalls the other. Likewise, if two or more friends are seen moving together daily, the sight of one will remind of the other. This is the theory of association of ideas. This theory is based on certain empirically derived laws which state the condition under which ideas are related and recalled in mind. When we meet or see one of the two persons whose acquaintance is known, our mind simultaneously recalls the other. Likewise, sketch of a man with flute and peacock feather reminds of Lord Krishna, of man with bow and arrow and wearing *pitambara* reminds of Lord Rama, of a man with *chakrà sudarshan* reminds of Lord vishnu and a man with *Jahnavi-phen lekheva yanmurdhanih shashinah kala* reminds of Lord Shiva. Therefore, on the basis of this brief description of association of ideas we can start with the presumption that when two ideas, things or entities are associated with one another, then our mind should automatically recall the other if one of them is present. In the same manner the mind should also attach the importance of one to the other because of their association. For instance Sita and Radha are respected, apart from other things, because of their association with Rama and Krishna respectively. This is association of idea. Till date it has proved to be universal, i.e., it has been working effectively in all the times and at all the places. Now let us see how effective the theory and its laws are in revealing the image of a librarian i.e., libraians' personality.

B42 Librarians' Personality

Experienced librarians have been able to discover two forms of librarians' personality, namely (i) imposed personality and (ii) actual personality.

B421 Imposed form of Librarians' Personality

Imposed form of librarians' personality is that which has been imposed on him/her by most of the readers including students, teachers, administrators and common men and women. In this form of his/her personality a librarian is a man/woman with grey or half-grey hairs, who, wearing a pair of spectacles, is sitting is a chair in a corner of the library-hall and is always busy in making entries in register, or filing cards, issuing and taking back books and performing like activities. In case he/she leaves his/her chair or counter, he/she shoud whirl inside the library hall like a drudge moving round a crusher. He/she has no right to move outside the four-walls of the library or to be associated actively and in a dignified manner with other academic, receational and cultural activities of the parent institution, same as the Shudras had no right in ancient India to read and learn the Vedas or to be associated with Vedic cer emonies. If he is attending to a reader, his gesture shoud be like that of the 'Maharaja' of Air India. This is a traditionally accepted and rather an imposed form of librarians' personality. Librarians have been held fastly to this form of personality to such an extent that it sometimes appears to be a difficult task to wipe out this image from the minds of others. Some librarians have accepted it as their destiny and have wrapped themselves in this form. There are still some others who try to displace this image but in vain. As a result, when a librarian tries to throw this cloak of imposed personality he/she is refused to be recognised. Grey or half grey hair, spectacles, the gesture of Air India's Maharaja and the image of a drudge have clung with the librarians' personality so tightly that a librarian's image is not formed without these components in the same way as no image of Lord Krishna is formed without flute and peacock feather, of Lord Rama without bow and arrow, of Bhim without a club, and of Lord Shiva without *Jahanviphen lekheva yanmurdhanih shashinah kala.*

B422 Actual form of Librarians' Personality

The former form of a librarians' personality is the negative and imposed from of his/her personality. In the real and positive form of his/her personality he/she is rational, logical, cautious, intellectual, and scholarly or almost scholarly person who is dedicated to a great cause and a dignified profession. At least half of the qualities of a sublime hero described by Dhananjaya should present in him. This is his real personality.

B43 Association of Ideas and Librarians' Personality

It is a fact to be accepted by all that the laws of association of ideas work more effectively in revealing the imposed form of librarians' personality, or in other words, these work less effectively in revealing the real personality of a librarian. This needs detailed discussion.

Much has been said about the importance of books and libraries. According to Sukarat, a religion without a book is not a religion. According to Johnson, if one wants to write a book he must read half a library. Radhakrishanan Commission on Education have

---

* "Neta Vineeto, Madhurastyagi, dakshah, priyamvadah, raktalokah, shuchirvagmi, rudhavamsh, sthiro, yuva, buddhyutsahsmriti prjna, Kalamansamanvitah, shoorodridhashch tejasvi, shastrachakshushch dharmikah".

given a library the status of the heart of a university. Today libraries have become part and parcel of an individual's day to day activities. Students, teachers, administrators, men and women, young and aged all come to library. Researches are conducted and completed in libraries. Students prepare for their examination and teachers for their lectures in the library. These activities cannot be performed in the biggest book shop of the world. Only a librarian can match the right book with the right reader and vice-versa. Some cows steal milk and then an expert in extracting milk from such cows can take the milk out. Books are milk-stealing cows in nature—some less, some more. Without the librarians' direct or indrect help a reader cannot utilise fruitfully the knowledge stored in many books. He is such an important man, attached to an importqnt institution like a library. Hence, if the laws of association work efficiently and in right direction, these should reveal the real image of the librarian instead of reflecting his imposed personality.

Many factors or reasons can however, be attributed to the ineffectiveness of laws of association in revealing the real personality of a librarian. Some of such factors have been explained below and some measures have also been suggested for creating proper atmosphere for enabling the laws of association of ideas to work in right direction:

1. Nature of Library Profession.
2. Dearth of Library Scientists.
3. Lack of Library Culture.

B431 Nature of Library Profession

The impression that mere association with an important institution like a library will make a librarian important is an illusion. It will have to be taken for granted that the importance of library will not be attached to the librarian until he stands for a cause and proves himself indispensable in academic set up. The second thing to be born in mind is that to prove onself worthy of the profession of librarianship is much more difficult than to prove to be worthy of any other profession. For example, when one is appointed as a teacher, say in Chemistry, he has to prove his worth and ability to other teachers and students of his department. None else is going to judge, appreciate or criticise him. The same is true of teachers in other disciplines including library and information science, as well as the persons engaged in other occupations. But when one becomes a librarian, say in an academic institution, the entire faculty, stu dents and administrators observe and examine him from their own angles. And the librarian is supposed to come up to the expectations of all of them, proving himself competent on their standards. Thus the job of a librarian is much more difficult than that of others. It should also be taken into account as stated earlier, that the profession of librarianship is defferent from most of the professions in the sense that in other professions the clientele or the user will cease his visits when satisfied but will continue to visit when dissatisfied. But in library profession the process is reverse. For example, if a student is not satisfied, he will come to the teacher again and again to understant the lesson; if a patient is not satisfied (i.e. not cured), he will come to the doctor again and again. So in other fields, the visit of the clientele will increase if he is dissatisfied. But in the field of libraries, a dissatisfied reader will not like to come to the library.

It is said that there is lack of proper environment for the libraries and librarians to work. As a result of this there may not be adeuate facilities, space, staff or finance for a library nor proper environment. But there is no way out for librarians other than to accept the limitations and prove their worth in these adverse circumstances. Battle and strike are not their weapons. It is neither proper nor effective. Their weapon can be modesty and politenes mixed with academic vanity. The situation reminds of the story of Hanumana and Surasa. When Hanumana was crossing the sea, Surasa wanted to swallow him. To evade this, Hanumana expanded his body but to his utter surprise he found that Surasa also expanded her mouth in equal ratio. Hanumana went on expanding his body and Surasa her mouth. Ultimately Hanumana realised that Surasa, with her demonic conjugation, is more powerful and capable of expanding her mouth upto any extent. So Hanumana adopted subtle form and escaped being swallowed. Librarians also cannot compete with others in power and strength. Therefore they should adopt Hanumana's way of becoming subtle, becoming humble, becoming ethical, but at the same time becoming indispensable. This can be partically achieved by following the code of conduct suggested by various schools of Indian philosophy.

B4311 The Three Fold Path: Library profession is the soul and the librarian is the body wherein this soul dwells.
The materialistic school of Indian philosophy named after **Carvak** does not believe in the soul and hence preaches adoration, grati-

fication and beautification of body. The 20th century world had adopted this philosophy. On the other hand, rest of the schools of Indian philosophy suggest that those who do not believe in soul and are pre-occupied with worldly affair are bound to suffer. This is equally true of those librarians who are more inclined towards themselves and have ceased making effort for the betterment of the profession. Our philosophers have suggested certain code of conduct after adopting which, whatever may be his profession or occupation, one can achieve the ture end of his life and can evade sufferings. The Buddhist school of Indian philosophy prescribes eightfold path, viz. right faith, right resolve, right speech, right action, right living, right effort, right thought, and right concentration. Other schools also, directly or indirectly, talk of these ways. For instance, the Jaina philosophy talks of only three ways, viz, right conduct (Samyag Charita) right faith (Samyag Darshan) and right knowledge and concentration (Samyag Jnana). These three include in themselves the other five too. Let us then discuss these three in context of library profession.

B43111 Right Faith: It concerns students of library and information science and junior librarians. It implies that the students and juniors should have faith in their teachers and senior professionals respectively. Seniors and elders in the profession are to be regarded as gurus. New entrants get practical training and working knowledge under their guidence and supervision. The story of Eklavya and Dronacharya is most frequently quoted to show the ideal relation which should exist between a student and a guru. Gurus and seniors of today, however feel that a student or junior of today, instead of giving his thumb to the guru, shows his thumb after the conclusion of the training or study. But this will ultimately boomerang. Those who are not respectful to their seniors should not expect respect and regard from their juniors. We may recall here the story of Ajatshatru and Bimbasara. King Ajatshatru jailed his father Bimbasara and mother Vasavi. Once he went to the dungeon where they were detained. He wanted to direct the guards to be more cruel to them. But as he reached there, a messenger from the palace came and informed him that the queen had given birth to a male child. Ajatshatru was so happy that he postponed rebuking his father and the guards and rushed to the palace to see the newborn. His happiness knew no bounds. Suddenly he was struck with two thoughts: first, that his father Bimbasara must have loved him and felt as happy on his birth as he did on the birth of his own son. Secondly, that following his own footsteps his son might one days jail him. These thoughts transformed him and he brought back his father and mother to the palace.

B43112 Right Conduct: Next to right faith comes right conduct. Right conduct can be of five types: Non-injury or *Ahima*, truth or *satya*, Non-stealing or *Astey;* Celibacy or *Brahmacharya*, and possessionless or *Aparigraha*. The Jainas call these "five vowes". Manu and Prashastapada have also enumerated these under "General Duties" or *Samanya Dharma*. Let us take these and interpret one by one in brief is conteat of library profession.

(a) *Non-injury:* Non-Injury implies that librarians should not injure books, readers and professional colleagues by thought, word, or deed. Propositions like "books are best friends' and comparison of books with brides waiting curiously for their briderooms, i.e. readers, reveal that books may be considered to be living entities. Living beings have desires which they want to fulfil. The third Law of Library Science (Every Book its Reader) supported by the first Law (Book are for use) postulates that a book may feel hurt if it fails to get its reader. To avoid such an injury to a book a librarian should apply his technical expertise and skill for ensuring better use of a book. Non-injury to books also implies that these must be protected from insects, dust, air, water and even from notorious readers who damage books in many ways. The concept of non-injury to readers has a direct relation with non-injury to books. If requirements of the Third Law are met, the requirements of the Fourth Law (Save the time of the reader) will automatically be met. So in one action two laws may be satisfied. Non-injury to reader also involves his initiation to the library if he is new to the Library. A new reader should be made to understand the arrangements of the library including various sections and techniques of finding books. If such an attention is not paid to a new reader he may feel chagrined. Non-injury to professional colleagues involves avoiding such practices as may cause alienation or ill-will among each other.

(b) *Truth (Satya):* The vow of truth postulates that a librarian should be true and sincere to his profession.

(c) *Non-stealing (Asteya):* Non-stealing is indicative of respect for property. Documents and library equipment are property of the library. Non-stealing implies that a librarian should have respect for these. The Yoga School of philosophy classes non-stealing under the 'Yamas' which are principles of self-restraint.

(d) *Celibacy and Non-Possession (Brahmachdrya and Aparigraha)* Celibacy involves control over sense. "Simple living and high thinking" is the principle behind 'non-possession'. These are general principles to be observed in every walk of life.

B4413 Right Knowledge and concentration (Samyag Jnan): Right concentration is necessary for attaining right knowledge of the profession. Faith in seniors and desire to know is not of much avail. A librarian's concentration must be like the concentration of a crane and not like that of an amateur shooter who may misfire. A crane never fails to catch a fish leaping on the surface of water. This is because a crane concentrates on the fish and watches its every movement. The same concentration should be applied in learning and practicing library techniques. The code of conduct referred to above may create proper environment for effective working of laws of association of ideas.

B432 Lack of Library Culture

Lack of library culture is also one of the most important factors owing to which the laws of association fail to work in right direction in revealing the real personality of librarians. Laws of association do not work in the absence of a particular culture. For instance those who are not aware of Indian culture and religion cannot co-relate flute and Krishna; club and Bhima; Sudarshan Chakra and Vishnu etc. Thus, a man who has been brought up in a society which lacks library culture cannot relate the importance of a library to the librarian. A very insignificant percentage of Indian population get opportunity to read formally. A few of those who read formally receive higher education, and a very insignificant percentage of those receiving higher education use libraries with zeal. Most of the students as well as the teachers use the library for convenience. They are interested mainly in text books and recommended books or at the most fiction, some times because these are available almost free in the library. All these show lack of library culture in our society. And culture cannot be inculcated in the mind of grown up people easily. The librarians shall have to make untiring efforts to build up library culture in the youth and the children. They must create such an environment in which library culture spreads and the seeds of law of association get favourable ground to germinate.

B5 CONCLUSION

Librarianship is a service oriented and modest profession. As Wallace has pointed out, "No library would promise an aspirant to the profession a garden of Edens. But you will find many fruits in it. There is no pavement of gold to make you rich but you can take from the trees comfortable living, generous fringe benefits, mental growth and achievement, interesting people, good friends, and endless possibilities for becoming a wiser, better, and more understanding human being"[6] Service mindedness is as important as is library education. Therefore the professionals should bear in mind that the success or failure does not depend solely on theoretical knowledge of library techniques but also on practical service. Library profession is like a coin of which teachnical knowledge and practical service are two faces or sides. Both the sides are equally important but when it comes to comparing the two it can outrightly be said that the service side is the 'head' side of the coin.

REFERENCES

1. As quoted by Wallace, *op. cit.*, p. 91.
2. Ranganathan, Preface, *op. cit.*, p.13.
3. Ranganathan: Preface., *op. cit.*, p.24.
4. Wallace, *op. cit.*, p.29.
5. Rose Emestine: *The public library in American life.* (New York, Columbia University Press, 1955), pp. 202-3.
6. Wallace, *op. cit.*, p. 91.

C

Laws of Library Science

C1 CONSTITUTIONAL LAWS Vs SUBJECT LAWS

By the term law is generally meant a rule or set of rules which has or have constitutional sanction. We also come across such expressions as canonical laws, divine laws, laws of motion etc. Such laws, even without constitutional sanction, are adhered to more rigorously in their fields of business or subjects. We may dub such laws "subject-laws" or "laws of subject". The only difference between constitutional laws and subject-laws is that the former is recognised and accepted to be binding on all sections of a community, society, or state, or nation, whereas subject-laws are recognised and accepted as binding on all the divisions, sub-divisions and branches of the subject. Therefore subject-laws also have a jurisdiction as have constitutional laws. Laws of Library Science are subject-laws and their jurisdiction is the subject of library and information science. These laws are therefore recognised and accepted as binding on all the branches of library science, viz. classification, cataloguing, reference service, bookselection, administration, organisation, bibliography and all other possible divisions and sub-divisions of the subject of library science.

C2 THE LAWS

When we say Laws of Library Science, we refer to the Five Laws enunciated by Dr. S.R. Ranganathan. Though conceived in 1928, these laws were first published in Ranganathan's book entitled *Five Laws of Library Science.*[1] These are us under:

1. Books are for use
2. Every reader his/her book
3. Every book its reader

4. Save the time of the reader
5. A library is a growing organism

C3 PHILOSOPHY OF THE FIVE LAWS

These five laws look very trivial, but embody deep thought. These are like pots containing oceans. Prior to their enunciation the subject of library science had no philosophy. These laws gave philosophical base, guaranting an everlasting future to the subject of library science, the profession of librarianship, and the use of libraries. Atherton suggests that Ranganathan deserves the Hall of Frame Award for enunciating the Five Laws alone.[2] Such philosophical contribution of Ranganathan made Eugene Garfield say, "Ranganathan is to library science what Einstien is to physics". On the same analogy and in Indian context it may be said, "Ranganathan is to library science what Panini is to Vyakaran and Manu is to Dharma Shastra.

C4 COMMAND OF THE LAWS

As stated earlier, the whole field of library science is the domain of the Five Laws. These have acquired the status of general normative principles. Ranganathan has discussed three types of normative principles : laws, canons and principles. There are canons and principles for each branch, eg. for cataloguing, for classification, etc. The Conons of cataloguing are recognised and accepted as binding on the branch of cataloguing only. Similarly the canons and principles of classification are to be satisfied in the branch of classification. These (canons and principles of classicfication) have no command over the field of cataloguing or any other field or branch. But the (five) Laws are accepted by all branches of library science and all the canons and principles of all the branches (classification, cataloguing etc) are required to satisfy the five laws and fulfil their demands. The subject of library science is like a state and the five laws are like the head of the state on whose authorisation and power the ministers and government servants (i.e. canons, principles, rule etc) run the state. The head of the state, though does not always interfere in running the state, but all the activities of all the ministers and government servants are performed to implement the expressed or unexpressed orders of the head. The five laws command such a power. In the event of controversy arising due to conflict between two principles, rules etc in any branch, an appeals is made to the five laws. They then take the command of the situation and solve the conflict.

C5 FIRST LAW

C51 Description

The, first law of library science is BOOKS ARE FOR USE. Enunciating the first law Ranganathan says, "How Simple, how trivial and yet how seminal."[3] Books are the creation of the greatest creation of the God, viz. the human being. A Book is a guide, a friend and a philosopher. An author writes a book to communicate his thoughts. Primary purpose of writing a book therefore is that the thought it contains should be communicated. To do so it is necessary to put the book to use. The first law, therefore, truly demands that all efforts should be made to ensure that every book kept in the library is used, because it is created for use.

C52 Neglect of First Law

Ranganathan wrote in 1931, "We shall find ample evidence of a deplorable neglect of this law".[4] The law is neglected when a barrier is created between the books and the readers. Keeping books in closed almirahs is one of such acts as reduces the use of books. Keping books in closed almirahs before the advent of printing press is understandable. But now such an act certainly amounts to deplorable neglect of the first law. Similarly, purchasing books with shabby format, keeping the library closed during the hours that may suit readers the most, opening the library at the isloated place, and unhelping attitude of library staff towards readers are some other acts that are detrimental to use of books.

C53 How to Ensure Use of Books

The first and the foremost duty of a librarian is to ensure proper use of a book available in the library. A library can ensure the maximum use of books by taking into account the following factors:

C531 Open access

Open access to books enhance their use. In this system every reader is allowed to go to shelves and choose the book of his interest. It saves time because a reader does not have to wait for the library staff to trace the desired book or its substitute. He may go to the shelves directly and find the book for himself. In case he does not find the desired book he can choose some other book to substitute the book which he was looking for.

C532 Location

There are two different views regarding location of a library. One view suggests that a remote and isloated place is the most suitable place for opening a library. According to the supporters of this view a calm, quite, and distantly located place is the right place for opening a library. Advocates of this view hold that a library is a place for serious study and therefore a lonely place which is far from the crowds is suitable for opening it. Then only selected few serious readers will come to consult the library and not all and sundry. The second view is that a library should be situated near a central place: if it is an institutional library, it should be situated in the centre of the institutional complex, or if it is a public library, it should be situated in the centre of the city. Supporters of this view hold that a library is not for selected readers alone but for all. Central location of a library promotes the use of books. Opening a library is like opening a shop. The fate of a shop can be imagined which is opened at a remote and isolated place. Such a shop will not invite many customers and will be closed one day or the other. Similarly, if it is decided to open a library at a far away place it will be used by chosen few only. Such a decision would amount to disobeying the instructions of the first law. An ideal place to open a sweet shop is near a temple, a betel shop near a hotel, and a coffee house near students' hostel. Only then more and more people would visit these places. Likewise, a shopping centre or the centre of the city, where people go by habit is the most ideal location for a library because it ensures maximum use of books, this satisfies the first law.[5]

C533 Library hours

The first law demands that a library should be kept open during the hours which suit its clients the most. This policy increases the use of book. For example, a public library must be opened in evening also so that people engaged in various occupations and students can use it after finishing their regular work every day. Similarly, an academic library should be kept open, in addition to normal hours, also when the students are free from class rooms. Hence, a library should remain open for as many hours as is possible and desisable. For example, it would be appropriate to open a university library till late night atleast during and before examinations.

C534 *Library building and furniture*

In order to promote the use of books it is advisable to have a functional building with provision for pleasant, natural and electrical, light, soothing interior, good-looking furniture, comfortable chairs and other such facilities. These increase the use of book. An unpleasant environment in the library dissuades the client from staying in the library and thus hampers the use of books. If a library can afford, it may go for linoleum flooring too.

C535 *Book selection policy*

The book selection policy of a library also has to give due care to the first law. Only such books may be purchased which are relevant to the needs of the clientle of the library. Secondly, books should be attractive in appearance i.e. its look etc. should be inviting so that the reader is tempted and picks it up. Paper, printing and presentation of books should also be such as fills readers with pleasure. These things increase the use of books.

C536 *Library Techniques*

Proper cataloguing and classification of books are essential for promoting the use of books. A badly prepared catalogue and wrongly classified book results in non-use of books or restrict their use.

C537 *Publicity*

The first law demands for wide publicity of each and every book in particular and of the library in general. There are so many ways of publicising a library and its stock. To mention a few, new addition to the library may be brought to the notice of readers by bringing out list of new additions and latest arrivals may be displayed for a week or so at a proper place. Abstracting and SDI service may also be of immense value.

C538 *Library Staff*

However big its building, however comfortable its furniture, however rich its book stock, a library cannot come upto the expectation of the first law unless its staff is attentive and cheerful, and cares for books and readers. Readers should not be looked upon as nuisance, but as a customer. Library staff should also render helping hand to the readers. Some readers are shy and need personal touch. Sometimes, owing to their shy nature or complexity of library techniques, many readers may not find the desired books. Library staff should therefore take keen interest in assessing the needs and requirements of their readers. These steps not only satisfy the readers but also enhance the use of books. An author writes a book to communicate his thoughts. The book is also a shy entity and it does not speak for itself. It reveals itself only when some one takes it in his hands. Books also therefore need the help of library staff so that these may reach the hand of right readers.

C6 THE SECOND LAW

C61 Description

The second law of library science is EVERY READER HIS/HER BOOK. It extends the message of the First Laws. The message of the first law is, "books are for use". The Second Law extends this message, and proclaims "Every Reader his/her Book", which implies "books are for use of all" or 'books for all'. Thus the second law stresses democratisation of the library where every reader has equal right to get the book of his interest. The first law is a revolt against the conservative concept of 'books are for preservation' and replaces it by the concept, 'books are for use." The Second law is also a revolt againt the feeling that books are for a chosen few and emphasises that 'books are for all.' The Second Law fixes some responsibilities or obligations of the state, the library authority, the library staff, and the readers. These have been discussed below.

C62 Obligations of the State

When we say "Every Reader His/Her Book" or 'books for all', the state or the government automatically comes in the picture. The state has certain obligations to its citizen and one of these is to provide to all equal opportunity to read. Unesco declares in its manifesto that the right of accress to information is one of the fundamental rights of every citizen. Concepts like universal availability of publications (UAP) also stress 'books for all' phenomenon. State has to play a vital role to achieve it. Ranganathan has discussed the obligations of the state under three heads: (i) Finance, (ii) legislation, (iii) coordination.

C621 Finance

Adequate finance is the first requirement for running a chain of libraries to serve the needs of all. It should be the duty of the state to provide it. The state may provide finance in two different ways: (i) by giving grant and (ii) by levying library cess. Ranganathan goes for the latter. In the first method, the state may allocate a fixed amount per year or during a plan for library development. In this method the state is not bound to allocate or relase a particular sum of amount every year. In the second method the state authorises local authorities to levy liberary cess as surcharge on certain taxes such as property tax etc. The amount collected thus is deposited in the Library Fund. The state normally contributes equal or more amount. We have 26 state and 5 union territories in India. Out of this eight states have enacted library legislation. In four states, namely Tamilnadu, Andhra Pradesh, Karnataka and Haryana provision for levying library cess has been made. In rest of the four states, namely Maharashtra, West Bengal, Manipur and Kerala the concerned state governments provide fixed grant for running library services. All other states are providing service without legislation and hence there is no provision for levying library cess in there states/-UTS. The two methods are means to provide finance for running public library service in a particulat state. Both of these have their own merits and demerits. In short, the second law insists that the state should make provision for sufficient finance for running library service.

C622 Library Legislation

In a democratic society every citizen has the right to read, and right of access to reading materials. The state should therefore make available to them facilities for reading throughout their life. This is the demand of the second law. This demand can be fulfilled to the highest degree by enacting library legislation by the state. Western countries realised this obligation of the state long back. For instance, U.K.

adopted library legislation as early as in 1850. India is lagging behind in this respect. After about 45 years of independence only 8 of our 26 states and 5 U.Ts. enacted library legislation. The second law emphasizes that the state should consider enactment of library legislation with a view to providing every reader his/her book, or in other words, books for all.

C623 Coordination

Coordination implies coordinating and linking library service at each level. It is usually found that all libraries or most of the libraries in a state function in isolation. Such a situation is against the spirit of the second law. It is, therefore, essential to coordinate libraries and their services at each level. Coordination among libraries ensures maximum utilisation of available resources of a country or state. Coordination among libraries may become easy to implement if desired so by the state. In such a system all the libraries, right from the national library to the State Central libraries, district libraries, subdivisional libraries, block libraries, and village libraries are linked with each other in the form of a chain. Book collection and service of one library are then made available to other libraries when needed. This ensures maximum utilisation of library resources and at the same time makes it possible for readers to have access to literary heritage of the country, available any where in the country in any library.

C63 Obligation of Library Authority

The second law has some thing to say to library authorities in respect of selection of books and staff. A library has limited finance. It has to select books within a particular financial limit. It is therefore desirable to assess and know the requirements of readers before selecting books. Then every reader gets his or her book. Similary, library authoritires should select staff for their library with professional competence and missionary zeal. It is not correct to think that any person can work in a library. Sometimes it is seen that those who were not found fit or acceptable to work at any other place were sent or transferred to the library. This voilates the demand of the second law and is fatal. Library staff should form a bridge between readers and books, but such staff members create barrier between the two. In stead of bringing right book to the right reader they separate the two by their unwillingness to work, lack of expertise and skill and other such disqualifications.

C64 Obligation of Library Staff

The second law lays marked emphasis on the role and obligation of library staff. With their professional competence and missionary zeal they can satisfy the demand of the second law. When a reader enters the library, the staff should approach him with helping hand. Many new readers need initiation in the use of the library.

C65 Obligation of the Reader

The second law expects the readers also to discharge some responsibilities. Readers should be willing to observe library rules. By doing so they help the library staff to help them. Besides, readers should restrain from cutting pages from books, hiding books, keeping books beyond due date etc. All such acts amount to keeping other readers away from their books.

C7 THIRD LAW

C71 Description

Third law of library science proclaims, "EVERY BOOK ITS READER". The demands and the implications of the third law are more rigorous than that of the second law. The second law, for instance, suggests that every reader should get his/her book(s). A reader can go to his book or can make a search for it. The second law is therefore fulfiled easily. On the other hand the third law suggests that every book should get its reader. This is much difficult to achieve. The reason is that a book cannot go to 'its' reader, nor it can make a search for him/her. Books are dumb and mute entities. Readers also "do not take to books easily"[6] The fact that a book cannot go to a reader, coupled with the fact that a low percentage of the literate population go to the library, makes the observance of the third law more difficult. Even in cent per cent literate society it becomes difficult to inspire people to come to the library. Explaining this phenomenon Dr. Rangnathan has given the example of a British town called Croydon. The town had (in 1930) cent per cent literacy. The town library was charging no membership fee or deposite money. The librry was highly publicised and well managed. Even then 40 percent of the poeple were not using the library. Ranganathan has narrated this in his book *Preface to library science.*[7] We can well imagine the situation in India where rate of literacy is much lower and people have diverse problems of life. It is therefore necessary to adopt measures to ensure successful implementation of the demand of the third law. The factors that may be kept in view in this regard have been discussed in succeeding sections.

C72 Nature of Books

Many books are like milk stealing cows. These conceal vast knowledge, but some times their titles are not expressive enough to reveal their contents. Similarly many books have composite and multifocal contents i.e. they deal with more than one subject. In such cases all the facts of the contents should be brought to the notice of the readers by making required number of entries in catalogue. The catalogue should otherwise also be complete and no book should go to the shelve without proper classification and cataloguing.

C73 Library Publicity

The third law makes it obligatory for a library to publicise its collection and services. There are so many ways to publicise a library; e.g. (i) The community may be made aware of the services of the library by arranging programme on the library on T.V. and publicising its activities in news papers, (ii) arrival of new books may be brought to the notice of the clientele by displaying them in the library, distributing the list of new additions, cerculating library bulletine, etc. (iii) abstracting and indexing services and other form of documentation services may be started (iv) suggestions from readers may be invited (v) literary talks, documentary film shows etc. may be organised in library on holidays, etc. Some one has rightly described a book as a bride, a reader as a bridegroom, and a librarian as a matchmaker. The librarians' duty is to make the match by inspiring the right reader to reach the right book. Publicity is one of the most effective ways by which readers are attracted to go the books kept on shelves.

C74 Open Access

Any type of publicity would not bring the desired result unless the library allows open access to books. In open access system readers are allowed to go to the shelves and see, choose and pick up any book of their interest. Library staff does not come in between readers and books unless asked for help. It is one of the most effective ways to ensure that maximum number of books are seen by readers. It also happens sometimes that the reader goes to shelves in search of one book and in the process of search selects many more books. But for the open access system such books would be naglected and would miss the attention of that particular reader. Open access system is criticised sometimes, mostly by the administrative people on the ground that chances of mutilation, misplacement and theft of books are more in this system. But the gains are still more. By adopting closed system many of the books would not come to the notice of 'their' readers as explained above and thus the third law would be voilated.

C75 Catch them young

Children are like unbaked earthen pots. Reading habit can be inculcated in them much easily. A child's mind is not rigid and can be moulded easily to adapt to new situation. Children like books. If they get interesting and healthy literature they will become good users of libraries and also advocates of libraries.

C8 FOURTH LAW

C81 Description

The fourth law demands "SAVE THE TIME OF THE READER". The law desires that a reader should not be delayed unnecessarily. Delay causes chagrine and the reader becomes dissatisfied. A dissatisfied reader ceases to come to the library. The profession of librarianship is different from other professions in many ways. For instance, if a student is not satisfied with the teacher (i.e., if he does not understand what has been taught) he would approach the teacher again and again; if one is not satisfied with the Accounts Officer (because his bill is not passed, delayed, or deduction made etc.) he would go to the Accounts Officer again and again, if a patient is not cured, he would continue to consult the doctor. Hence in case of other professions the dissatisfied client increases the frequency of visit but stops his visits when satisfied. But it is just reverse in case of library profession and its clientele. A dissatisfied clientele ceases to come to the library. Only satisfied clients continue their visits. It is therefore essential to keep a reader satisfied. And a reader is satisfied the most if his time is saved, i.e., if he gets the service in minimum possible time.

C82 Subjective v/s objective Time

Saving the time of a reader implies saving his subjective time as well as objective time. By Objective time is meant the *time actually spent* in waiting for a service or a book. And subjective time is the *time which a reader feels he has spent* in waiting for a service or a book. To make the concept clear let us take an example. A reader might have actually waited for a service for, say 10 minutes. If he was not well attended or he waited in idleness he may feel that he waited for half an hour for the service. Here subjective time becomes much more than the objective time. So at times the reader actually had to wait for 10 minutes but he feels that he waited for half an hour, when a reader waits in idleness, unattended and neglected he feel so. If he is well attended or if he feels that the staff is making sincere efforts to do his job, he may not feel even the actual time of waiting. It is therefore more necessary to save his subjective time of the reader (by paying attention and making him feel that his query is being looked into) alongwith the objective time. He may also be kept busy during the time of wait.

C83 Implication

The following measures may be taken for saving the time of the reader. Implications of the Fourth Law are as under:

C831 Location

A centrally located library saves the time of the reader. Conveyance is also available for a central place most easily. Central location of the library is, therefore, an ideal location from the view of the Fourth Law.

C832 Open access

In closed access system time is wasted unnecessarily whereas it is saved in open access system. For example, in closed access system the reader first gives the number or author/title of 'his' book to the library staff who, in order of the requisition, searches the book. If the book is not traced, the reader again gives another number etc. This process continues until a desired book is traced and given to the reader. This amounts to wasting the time of the reader which can be avoided by introducing open access system.

C833 Shelf arrangement, classification and cataloguing

Classification and cataloguing of documents should be done keeping in view various approaches of readers. Preparation of cross references and analytical entries play a vital role in fulfilling the requirements of the Fourth Law. Similarly readers prefer subject arrangement (i.e. classified) of books on shelves. Regular shelf reading and shelf rectification are also essential. All these things save the time of the reader.

C834 Issue and Return

The library should adopt such a system of issue and return of books as may save readers' time. For example, issue of book on register is time consuming and should be normally avoided. Issue of book in pass book, readers' card or readers ticket save substantial time. The library must also make provision for reservation of books so that a reader may not unnecessarily waste his time in searching the book every time.

C835 Documentation and SDI Service

Substantial time of readers is wasted in literature search even on most general or current topics. The library should therefore undertake comprehensive or selective, as the need be, documentation service including Selective Disseimination of Information (SDI) Service. This can be done by preparing and issuing list of additions, bibliography and abstracts of articles culled out from the periodicals received in the library and other such services such as SDI. On demand, bibliography on a specific subject may also be prepared for a particular reader. This saves his time.

C9 FIFTH LAW

C91 Description

The fifth law states 'LIBRARY IS A GROWING ORGANISM'. It means that the size, (i.e. collection and space), readers, and staff of a library grow. This however is the surfacial interpretation of the law. It is essential to know the biological aspect of growth before discussing the various dimentions and implication of the Fifth Law.

C92 Biological Aspects of Growth

Biological sciences have proved that:

(i) A living object or organism grows, or in other words, an object or organism that grows is a living object or organism.
(ii) A living organism which ceases to grow will decay soon.
(iii) There is a limit of aparant body-growth of a living organism. In other words, after reaching the optimum stage of growth the apparant body growth stops. But even then the object grows internally to keep the system alive.
(iv) In the process of (i) to (iii) above the object or organism after some interval, casts of old material and takes in view material.
(v) The two types of 'growth' as stated under (iii) above are known as *'growth by accretion'* and *'growth by replacement or renewal'* respectively. For example, the growth of a child is growth by accretion also: in it aparant growth takes place which is visible. On the other hand the growth of an adult is only 'growth by replacement or renewal' which is not visible, yet growth takes place in the body: new blood replaces old blood, new cells replace old cells etc. This is a continuing activity and life long process. Life comes to an end when this process stops.

Some biological facts have been given above to make clear the concept of 'growth'. These facts are true to every growing organism. For example, we can see a plant growing, it grows in two ways– externally and internally. After achieving its optimum external growth, it stops growing externally. It however continues to grow internally by replacement process in which new cells replace old cells, new leaves replace old leaves etc. Therefore 'growth' implies *child gorwth* and *adult growth* both, including casting off old material and taking in new material.

C93 Growth in Libraries

As stated earlier, the elements of growth in a library are its size (i.e. collection and space), readers, and staff. This also follows the established factors of 'growth' and therefore it should not be thought that the three elements of size, staff, and reader will continue to have 'child growth' for unlimited period. Referring to this fact, Dr. Ranganathan has propounded the pheomenon of the Fifth Law as, "The fifth law invites our attention to the fact that the library, as an institution, has all the attributes of a growing organism. A growing organism takes in new matter, casts off old matter, changes in size and takes new shapes and forms'.

C931 Collection and Space

Collection of a library grows and as a consequence grows its space. There is no contradiction to this statement. But no library of the world can afford to grow indefinitely and beyond limits. It would amount to wrong interpretation of the fifth law. Implication of the fifth law in this respect are as under:

C9311 Balanced Growth

Only balanced growth of library's collection should be allowed. In other words, the collection should grow in all areas or subjects keeping in view needs and requirements of the readers, as far as practicable.

C9312 Collection Versus Space

The collection of a library should grow keeping in view the space available at the disposal of the library. Space is always limited and even if it increases, it would increse to a limited extent. It is therefore necessary to be careful in inereasing the collection. In the context of a library, the collection is its soul and the space is its body wherein the soull dwells. The size of the body should essentially be much bigger than the size of the soul. It is rediculous to imagine a situation wherein the soul would grow bigger than the body. It would amount to torturing the soul. On this analogy it can be said that the size of the space must be bigger enough to house the collection and the collection may be allowed grow keeping in view the space.

C9313 Casting off the Old

Since growth in collection is unavoidable it is necessary to weed out old, obsolete, unused and torn books in order to provide space for the new additions.

C9314 Growth in National Library

The principle stated abaove however does not apply to the national library of a country or deposit libraries. Collection of such libraries would continue to grow by accretion (child growth). Such libraries always remain in 'child growth' stage. It is however necessary to take steps to preserve valuable materials from decay with the provision of lamination, deacidification etc. methods.

C94 Growth in Readers and Staff

The staff and readers of a library also grow with the growth in collection, size and services and also by replacement because of retirement, transfer etc. of reades.

C95 Impact on other Services

Growth in the three areas, namely size, reader and staff has impact on classification, cataloguing and circulation systems of the library the most. For example, when old books etc. are withdrawn, entries representing these in the catalogue should be taken out or marked appropriately. Similarly, the scheme of classification chosen for a library should be comprehensive enough to accomodate the increasing number of books and newly emerging subjects. Circulation system should also be chosen carefully keeping in view the fact that the number of readers will go on growing.

The fifth law is based on established biological facts. Its significance lies in the fact that it remedies the excesses committed by the other laws. For example, the second law would recommend unlimited growth of collection and space. The fifth law puts restraints on such excessess.

CX. CONCLUSION

The present state of libraries in the country is not much appreciable if considered from the point of view of the Five Laws. But if we compare the situation prevailing three-four decades ago, we will realise that much improvement has taken place due to efforts of individuals, library associations and the government. For example, most of the libraries now have adopted open access, classified arrangement on shelves, technical processing of documents etc. In consonance with the demands of the Five Laws, eight states have already enacted library legislation and others are in the process of enacting it. Though the process is slow, but efforts are still continuing. The Five Laws have revolutionised the field of libraries and gave a fresh fillip to the profession of librarianship. Bhattacharya has rightly said"... these Five Laws constitute fundamental contribution to the development of library science, documentation and information science. They are fundamental because they are relevant in relation to the past of these disciplines, they are relevant in relation to the present day developments of these disciplines, and they will continue to be so in relation to their future development."[8].

REFERENCES

1. Ranganathan, S.R.: *Five Laws of Library Science,* (Madras, Library Association, 1939—later Bombay, Asia Publishing House, 1963).
2. Atherton, Pauline A.: *Putting Knowldge to Work* (New Delhi, Vikas, 1978)
3. Ranganathan, *Preface, op. cit.,* p. 29.
4. Ranganathan, Preface. *op. cit.,* p. 26
5. *Ibid,* p.33
6. Ranganathan, Preface., *op. cit.,* p. 116.
7. *Ibid.,* p. 116.
8. Bhattacharya, G., Relevance of Ranganathan, In Mohanranjan; P.A., ed.: New trends in International Librarianship (New Delhi, 1984) p. 226.

D

Types of Libraries

Parry Committee on libraries (UK) talked about six types of libraries while discussing the functions and duties of the university library. These are (i) national libraries, (ii) special libraries, (iii) public libraries, (iv) libraries in instituion of higher education other than universiites, (v) libraries of ecclesiastic foundations, and (vi) university libraries.[1] Such libraries exist in almost all the countries all over the world. Libraries mentioned under (iv) and (vi)are mormally identified by a broader term, academic libraries, which may include school and college libraries also. Libraries of ecclesiastic institutions may also be grouped together with special libraires. Libraries can thus be grouped under following four broad categories:

1. National libraries
2. Public libraries.
3. Academic libraries.
4. Special libraries.

Brief study of each type is presented in the following pages.

D1 NATIONAL LIBRARIES

D11 Introduction

The feeling that there must be a place where the country's intellectual heritage may be collected, preserved and kept for use by the present and the coming generation, resulted in setting up national libraries in many countries. In France the library established by the King was declared national property in 1795 and was granted "the right to obtain deposit copies of all printed publications of the country."[2] Later, national libraries started collecting and preserving literature on their country, her people, language, culture etc., published anywhere in the world, and also important literature on other countries, subjects etc. This scope of a national library is the contribution of Anthony Panizzi, the well known librarian of British Museum, who pointed out that "the best collection of English literature and the best collection of literature on other countries"[3] should be the concern of a national library such as the British Museum.

D12 Definition

The definition of a national library, as adopted at the General Conference of Unesco in 1970, is as under:

> "Libraries, which irrespective of their titles are responsible for acquiring and conserving copies of all significant publications published in the country and functioning as a "deposit" library, either by law or under other arrangements. They will also normally perform some of the following functions: produce a national bibliography, hold and keep up-to-date a large and representative collection of foreign literature including books about the country, act as a national bibliographical information centre, compile union catalogues, publish the retrospective national bibliography. Libraries which may be called "national" but whose functions do not correspond to the above definition should not be placed in 'national library category."

Above quoted definition is comprehensive and clear. It explains with aptness the nature of a national library. It emphasizes that only the title or name of 'national library' does not give a library the recognition of a national library. A library, that claims to be national, whether the term national is in its title or not, must also perform certain functions which have been enumerated in the definition. A brief definition of the national library has been given by Natalia as follows, "library is called national when it is the official depository of printed works, a general access library, an information and bibliographical centre, and a centre of cordination, planning, and stimulating of the entire library system of the nation".[5]

D13 Functions

The definition adopted at the Unesco's General Conference (1970) incorporates some basic functions of national libraries. Functions of national libraries have also been discussed at various other platforms such as Unesco sponsord Seminar on National Libraries (1957), regional Seminar on development of National libraries in Asia and Pacefic Area (1964); Conference of Experts on National Planning and Documentation-service in Africa (1970) etc. The national library is expected to fulfil the following basic functions:

1. To acquire, store and organise the complete set of national printed output (due to literature explosion ephermeral materials are normally not acquired) and to serve as depository of these materials.
2. To acquire and conserve rare documents such as manuscripts.
3. To acquire, store and organise representative collection of other countries and on all subjects.
4. To provide access to its collection.
5. To provide bibliographic and other like services.
6. To publish retrospective national bibliography.
7. To provide leadership to the libraries of the country.
8. To provide training of library personnel.
9. To organise national and international exchange of publications.
10. To compile union catalogue.

D14 Some National Libraries

The *British Museum* which was founded in 1759, was national library of Great Britain (UK) until March 1973. Since April 1973 the *British Library* has assumed the status of National Library. The British Library was set up by an Act of Parliament on the recommendation of the Dainton Committee. British Library is not the name of one library but of a system of libraries which is comprised of many libraries and information centres viz (1) British Museum, (2) National Central Library, (3) National Lending Library, (4) National Lending Library of Science and Technology, (5) British National Bibliogrpphy, and (6) Office of Scientific and Technical Information. This is a new trend in the concept of national libraries. The *Library of Congress* which was founded in 1800 is the national library of United States. This is possibly the largest library of the world. Under Firemington Plan and its PL 480 scheme the library recieved literature from many countries which made it very rich, National Library of Medicine and National library of Agriculture also exist in USA. The

Lenin State library which was founded in 1925 is the national library of USSR. The National Library situated at Calcutta, which has a long history of changed names, is the *National Library of India.* The National library of India owes to Calcutta Public Library (opened in 1836) and Imperial Library, Calcutta (opened in 1891) for its existence. The Imperial Library was opened by Lord Curzon for the use of public in 1891 by combining a number of secretariate libraries. Later it was thought to merge Calcutta Public Library in Imperial Library which was made possible by enacting Imperial Library Act in 1902. On 30th Jan. 1903 this amalgamated library, which retained the name of Imperial Library, was opened for public, as notified in Gazette of India, "It is intended that it should be a library of reference, a working place for students, and a repository of material for the future historians of India in which, as far as possible every work written about India any time can be seen and read".[6] It may be observed that this notification in Gazette of India reveals that in 1903 the status of 'national library' was awarded by the British to the Imperial Library. After independence, the name Imperial Library was changed to National Library by an Act of Parliament known as Imperial Library (change of name) Act of 1948. In 1954 Delivery of Books Act was passed requiring publishers to send one copy of each of their publications to the National Library, and other two libraries in the country. The other libraires are Connemara Public Library (Madras), and Asiatic Society Library (Bombay). It was planned to start Central Reference Library at New Delhi, which was supposed to be the fourth deposit library. But due to certain problems it did not become feasible.[7] Since 1982 the Delhi Public Library was declared as the fourth depository library. On the recommendations of Jha Committee the National Library Act was passed providing for creation of National Library Board, Executive Council and a Director. Provisions of this act are however not in implementation except the appointment of Director. Besides the National Library, we also have subject national libraries in India, such as National Science Library (NSL), National Medical Library (NML) and National Agricultural Library (NAL).

D2 PUBLIC LIBRARIES

D21 Definition and Nature

It is understood that a library which is open for every one, irrespective of age, sex, occupation, affiliation and social or economic status is a public library. Unesco's manifesto for public libraries however makes it essential for a public library to fulfil the following conditions, (i) it should be established under the "clear mandate of law", (ii) it should be maintained "wholly from public fund", (iii) it should not ask for "direct charge" for any of its services, and (iv) it should be open for "free and equal use by all members of community". Explaining the nature of public library, the manifesto further explains as follows: "The public library is a practical demonstration of democracy's faith in universal education as a continuing and life long process in the appreication of the achievement of humanity in knowledge and culture. It is the principal means whereby the records of man's thoughts and ideas and, the experience of his creative imagination are made freely available to all... It is concerned with the refreshment of man's spirit by the provision of books for relaxation and pleasure, with assistance to the students and with provision of up-to-date technical, scientific and sociological information". Ranganathan also defines a public library as "a institution maintained for and by the community primarily for the social purpose of providing easy opportunity for self education throughout life of every person of the community".[8]

D22 Free For All Concept

Above quoted definitions of public library presented by Ranganathan as well as by Unesco emphasize that a public library is that library which is opened by the state with legislative support, maintained out of public fund, and the services of which are available to all free of charge. Ranganathan and Unesco are both the known spokesmen of legislative support for public libraries. Free public libraries were started in U.K. and U.S.A much earlier. For example, U.K. adopted library legislation is 1850. The need for free public library service was pleaded by Jevones even more than a century ago in his article "the rationale of free public libraries".[9] When it comes to providing free public library sevice in some poor countries, plea is given that the country is too poor to afford libraries: it is not proper to aspire to do so when it is difficult for the country to provide even the basic needs of food, cloth and roof to the masses. Supporters of this view forget that these three needs are basic not only for men but for animal as well. A sanskrit verse says, eating, sleeping, fear and to have sex are common in men and animals, it is only the intellect which differentiates a human being from an animal. Another sanskrit verse peoclaims that a man who lacks intellectual faculty is an animal without horns and tail. Such men can never prosper. Therfore if a country is too poor to afford free or almost free public library service to the masses it would continue to remain poor economically and intellectually also.

D221 The Middle Way

The situation explained above (i.e., to aspire for free pulic library service for all) is an ideal situation. In India libraries have adopted the middle way. Most of the libraries in our country would not fulfil all the four conditions laid down by Unesco. But still we have libraries with legislative support i.e. established under the clear mandate of law. Such libraries are fucntioning in the eight states which have adopted library legislation. In other states, though libraries have not been established with legislative support, in these states also we have government libraries which are maintained out of public money. Broadly speaking we have two types of public libraries in our country: (i) Government public libraires, and (ii) non-government public libraries. Government libraires, though may not be essentially established under the mandate of law but are run by the state out of public fund and are more or less free libraries. Some of these may be charging a nominal amount as membership fee or deposite money for borrowing material for home reading. But consulting reading material in the library is normally free of charge in these libraires. Libraries run by local bodies such as municipalities etc. may also be considered as government libraries because these are also maintained out of public money. Non-government libraries are run by variety of organisations, trusts, institutions etc. Among these a few are aided (i.e. receiving some aid or assistance from the government) and some are non-aided. To run their services these libraries normally charge some nominal amount from members, but consulting reading material (i.e. books, newspapers, magazines etc.) inside the library is free in most of these libraries. *We may therefore define a public library, in Indian context, as a library thrown open to the public free of charge or on a nominal charge for some specific service.*

D23 Functions of a Public Library

Much has been written on the function and objectives of public library. Some time ago a public library was considered to be a library to be used by the community in leisure for passing time for recreational reading. i.e. the study of fiction, drama, poetry, newspapers, popular magazines and like literature. The modern public library, however, is considered to be an intellectual power house, which strives to fulfil the educational, cultural, occupational and informational needs of all. To provide recreational material remains to be its one of the major functions, but it also provides to the public materials relating to their fields of formal study, specialisation, professions, activiites, and occupation. It also makes the people aware of economic, social, cultural and political development around them. Function of a public library, as discussed and enumerated by some learned bodies and library-scientists have been presented below:

D231 Unesco

Unesco, in its manifesto for public libraries makes it essential for a public library to perform the following functions:

> "The public library must offer to adults and children the opportunity to keep in touch with their times, to educate themselves continuously and keep abrest of progress in the science and arts. Its concern should be a living demonstration of the evolution of knowledge and culture, constantly reviewed, kept up-to-date and attractively presented. In this way it will help people form their own opinions, and develop their creative and critical capacities and powers of appreciation. The public library is concerned with the communication of information and ideas, whatever the form in which they may be expressed."

D232 American Library Association

American library Association, in its publication entitled *"Public Library Services; a guide to evaluation, with minimum Standards"* have prescribed the following functions of a public library:

(i) to facilitate informal education of all people in the community;

(ii) To enrich and further develop the subjects on which individuals are taking formal education;

(iii) to meet the information need of all;

(iv) to support the educational, civic, and cultural activities of groups and organizations; and

(v) to encourage wholesome recreation and constructive use of leisure time.

D233 Public Library Enquiry Committee (USA).

Public Library Enquiry Committee of U.S.A. have pointed out three broad functions of a public library as under:

(i) To gather resources in order to promote an enlightened citizenship and enrich personal life;

(ii) to provide reliable information to the community; and

(iii) to provide opportunities for self-education to children, young people, men and women.

D234 Roberts Committee[10]

The Committee to suggest Structure of Public Library Services in England and Wales (Roberts Committee) have enumerated the following major functions of a public library:

(1) "to supply to any reader or group of readers the book and related material for which they may ask;

(2) "Not only to satisfy, but promote the desire of books, consequently the provision of a children's library should be regarded as an integral part of the library service"

(3) To assist students and to hold exhibition, lectures, adult education classes.

D235 Functions in Detail

The authorities quoted above and in preceeding sections have dwelt extensively on the functions of a public library. Some functions have been commonly described by all. Wheeler and Goldhor[11] have also enumerated wide range of functions of a library. On the basis of their findings, the functions of a public library may be presented in detail as under:

D2351 Material Functions

The public library acquires, collects, organises, and makes available for use audiovisual materials to the public with an aim to:

(i) provide to them facilities for informal and life long self education;

(ii) provide to them facilities to support their formal education by collecting books and other documents on various subjects and courses.

(iii) provide healthy literature for recreation and constructive use of leisure time;

(iv) meet information need of the community;

(v) provide documents to support the civic and cultural engagements of the people; and

(vi) reach those who do not (or can not) reach it.

D2352 Service Functions

The functions of a public library are not confined only to collect, organise, and make available reading materials. The public library performs wider range of functions and activities in order to serve the community more effectively. Some of such service-functions are mentioned below:

(i) to provide guidance to readers in locating and using the document of their interest;

(ii) to promote the use of the library by inviting people, publicising the library's services and reaching the people at their door-steps. The tendency to serve only those who come or approach, results in a passive library. An active library reaches even those who do not or can not come to it; and

(iii) to serve as a social, cultural and intellectual power house for the community and for this purpose to employ efficient way of information retrieval, to organise extention activities, such as discussion on the current problems of the community, religious discourses after library hours, local festivals, book exhibition etc. It may be pertinent here to mention that some library scientists do not approve this role of the public library. For example McColvin, writes "it is bad for a library to associate itself with recreational activites as there is a danger of the public library neglecting its major task of providing books."[12] Similarly. Jast holds that the extention service, such as cultural and social, are nothing but the librarians" tresspassing on the ground of the educationists"[13]. These are however, conservative views expressed in the first half of this century and have become obsolete.

D236 Conclusion

A public library functions to serve all the individuals and groups including institutions, organisation etc. i.e., the entire community. It serves equally the least learned and the most learned; the child and the adult, the young and the old, the students and the scholars, the professionals and the non-professionals, the serving people and non-serving people, the technicians and farmers, and the user as well as the non-user. The non-users are those people who do not come to the library (those who have no reading habit etc.) or cannot come to the library (viz, aged, disabled, patients, prisoners etc.). They need the library the most. It is the duty of the public library to develop an understanding of the library requirements of this group and to plan its activities and functions keeping their educational, informational, recreational, and cultural requirements in mind.

D24 Place in Society

D241 Access to Best Thoughts

Functions enumerated in preceeding pages reveal that a public library plays an important role in all round development of the society. "The quickest and easiest access to the world's best thought is through the public library" (Gerald Johnson, in *Public Library Service)*. It plays an important role in a developing democratic society in particular. The progress of a country largely depends on education which she provide to her citizen from their childhood to old age. Active and informed participation of each and every individual and group in the country's affairs is essential for real democratic set-up. A democratic society needs such citizen as are aware of their environment and are well acquainted with the cultural, social political and economic heritage of the country. At the same time they should also be capable of analysing and discussing a given situation at a given time so that they could be able to take right decisions at right time. Such decisions might range from ploughing the fields to electing public representatives at various levels. In a developing and too big a country like ours it may not be possible to impart formal education to all due to many factors. Besides it, the citizen, who have recieved formal education, will also need continuing education for recreation, information and for enhancement of their knowledge. A public library can serve both the categories most economically, efficiently and effectively. As obsrved by Kenyon Committee in context of U.K., "The public interest in libraries have greatly increased and we believe there is now a far healthier belief in the value of knowledge and in the importance of intellectual life. The public library is no longer regarded as a means of providing casual recreation of an innocent but somewhat important character, it is recognised as an engine of great potentialites for national welfare and as an essential foundation for the progress in education and culture without which no people can hold its own in the struggle for existence."

D242 *Social Power House*

The functions of a public library make it an intellectual power house and 'a kind of social power station' as mentioned by Dr. Ranganathan. He writes, "a library is a kind of social power station where the minds of the members of the community are energised".

D243 *Social and Cultural Centre*

A public library is also a social and a cultural centre. In U.K. and U.S.A. the public library has already acquired this character. In order to become a social and cultural centre, the public library may organise exhibitions on painting, sculpture, local products etc. with the help of local artists, shopkeepers etc. Likewise classical plays, popular plays, plays on burning topics (e.g. bride burning, family planning etc.) may be staged and poetry and essay competition may also be organised. To quote an example, as early as in 1926 public libraries started staging the play entitled "Exit Miss Lizzie Fox" under the auspices of Indiana Library Assocation. Any of the following activities if adopted by a public library, would assign to it the character of a social and cultural centre:

(i) *Lectures:* On classical literature, popular literature of the region, religion, ethics, family welfare, childcare, family adjustment, bride burning topics etc.

(ii) *Exhibition and shows:* Exhibition of local products, flower, vegetable, carpentry etc., healthy child shows, cultural programmes, dance, drama, concerts etc.

(iii) *Competition:* Art competition, music competition, poetical recitation, essay competition etc.

(iv) *Functions:* On the occasion of national festivals, state level or local festivals, on the birth day of leaders, etc.

D25 Target Group

A public library's public (i.e. target group) is entire community. A community has been defined as a constellation of indiuduals, institutions, organisations and affilations, held together."[14] Thus, public of the public library may be identified as under:

D251 *The Family*

The family is the "First public" of the public library. The public library should therefore collect and provide literature to the family on home management, child care, gardening, married life, relationship in family, home economics, popular care of diseases, family welfare, etc. Everyone of the family in general and the children in particular should get the literature of their interest in a public library.

D252 The Student

The student is the "Second public" of the public library. The public library should therefore collect and provide to the student such literature as is of use to help him in carrying out formal studies. It is not essential to keep multiple copies of text books and maintain book-bank. It may also be appropriate to devise ways and means to ensure co-operation between the public libraries and other types of libraries functioning in the area.

D253 The Career Aspirant

The career aspirant is the "third public" of the public library. The public library should therefore provide to the career aspirant relevant material. This group (public) consists of students as well as non-students who want to prepare themselves for a particular career, occupation, vocation or competitive examination. The career aspirant should therefore be provided with such literature as may be helpful in (i) guiding him about admission to various professional and vocational courses (ii) finding jobs, getting scholarships and building career and (iii)preparing for various competitive examinations for jobs and study.

D254 The Adult Learner

The adult learner is the "fourth public" of the public library. This group may consist of neo-literate or persons interested in continuing education after completing formal education. Appropriate literature may also be provided to this group.

D255 Business and Industry

Some of the business houses and industries of the area may have their own library, but many of these may not have also. If the library is near an industrial area, it should also try to build up a general collection of material having some relevance to the industry owners, managers, and workers.

D256 Occupational Group

The Occupational group is the "sixth public" of a public library. This group consists of people engaged in various occupations e.g., service, agriculture, carpentry etc. If the community has sufficient number of members from one or more occupation, then the public library should provide literature relavant to their occupations.

D257 The Liesure-Time Reader

Majority of the readers of the public library belong to this group. Such readers want recreational literature. They also take interest in philosophy and literature of the country, state, or area. The public library should invariably have sufficient collection to serve such readers.

D258 Special Group

The "eighth public" of the public library belong to special groups, such as the handicapped, the aged, the prisoner, the petient, etc. They may be served by mail, mobile library etc. with special literature if need be (as in case of the blind, braille-book may be supplied).

D26 Conclusion

A Public library is a literary club, a cultural centre, a social power house, an information bureau, an intellectual place, and a place for recreation for all. It energises the mental faculty and multiplies the utility of material placed there. It is not for chosen few but for one and all. For example, one book placed in public library is used by thousands of people. Stanley Jevons, in his article captioned the *rationale of the free public libraries* (op. cit) has rightly said, "There is probably no mode of expending public money which gives more extraordinary and immediate return in utility and innocent enjoyment". It is less expensive than establishing a police station, a prison, a court of law and other such institutions. These will be reqired even after opening public libraries, but there is no gainsaying the fact that the number of such institutions may be reduced by opening more public libraries.

D3 ACADEMIC LIBRARIES

D31 Definition and Nature

An academic library is a library attached to an academic institution, i.e. an institution engaged in teaching and/or research and imparting formal education to students who aspire to complete a particular course under a prescribed syllabus. Schools, colleges, universities, and technological/engineering/medical institutions are some of such institutions. We thus have various types of academic institutions which may vary from one another in respect of courses offered by these. Since academic libraries exist to cater to the needs and requirements of their parent academic instution, these vary in shape, size, collection and services, depending upon the nature of the parent institution. For example, libraries attached to a school, college, and even to an undergraduate college, a post graduate college, a medical college, an engineering college would be different from the rest in respect of collection, shape, size, and services. However all academic libraries have common qualities in many respects. It is because all academic libraries exist to support the teaching and research programmes of their parent institutions. Besides having a good collection of reference books on variety of subjects, these emphasize on building up a strong collection concerning the courses offered by the institution.

D32 Need and Importance

Tremendous growth in student population; opening of new academic institutions including schools, colleges, and universities; introduction of new courses; rapid expansion of education; growing emphasis on qualitative education; and high cost of books are some of the factors which necessitate the establishment of a well equipped library attached with every educational institution. Libraries have become most important in academic institutions due to changed nature of education. During the past formal education was based on dictation. Teachers used to dictate and speak and students used to listen to and mug up. This system has been done away with in Western countries and in India also we are adopting new methods with appreciable speed. Present day education is no more an one way system in which students has passive participation. In the present day's system the teacher kindles the curiosity of the student, makes him aware of basic facts, teaches him methodoloy and inspires him to find details for himself from books-text as well as reference. Students are therefore referred by teachers to books which are available in library. This results in active participation of students in the process of learning. Education of today is becoming more and more library oriented which is evident from the fact that academic libraries are always full of readers.

D33 University Library

D331 Definition and Need

A university library is a library attached to a university. It exists to cater to the needs and requirements of students and teachers and to support the teaching and research programmes of the university. Libraries have become so much important for an university that the university can not exist without it. Tremendous growth in student population, opening of new universities, introduction of new courses, rapid expansion of education, growing emphasis on qualitative and purposeful education and rising cost of books are some of the factors which necessitate a well equipped library attached to a university. Libraries have become indispensable in a university due to the changed nature of education. During the past, university education was based on dictation: teachers used to dictate and students used to listen to or note. This system has been done away with as detailed in the preceding section. This fact in particular has laid down marked emphasis on the role libraries are expected to play in university education. Need and importance of libraries in an university has been realised and accepted by many authorities. For example, the Kothari Commission[15] recognises the library as the heart of the university. Similarly, the U.G.C. (UK) report maintained some seventy years ago, "The character and efficiency of a university may be gauged by its treatment of its central organ, the library."[16] The report stresses "An adequate library is not only the basis of all teachings and study: it is essential condition of research without which addition can not be made to the sum of human knowledge".[17] An eminent educationist Cyril Norwood in his speech at the Annual Conference of ASLIB (1936) said firmly, "it is a better proof of education to know how to use a library than to possess a university degree"[18] It is therefore an accepted fact that libraries are of paramount importance for universities. Some one has rightly said, "There are three distinguishing marks of a university— a group of students, a corps of instructors, and collection of books and of these the most important is collection of books'.

D332 Objectives and Purpose of Higher education and Universities

Before discussing the function of university library/academic library it is necessary to describe the objective and purpose of higher education to impart which universities exist. Today new type of student body enters a college and a university, new eduational technologies are being adopted and education has adopted new dimensions. It is therefore pertinent to know the objective etc. of university education. Some the most frequently quoted objectives and aims of a university are given below.

D3321 As Suggested by AIFECTO[19]

"The basic purpose of education is to create more efficient and productive citizens, aware of our glorious national heritage and the noble achievements of human civilization, possessing a basic scientific outlook and committed to the ideals of patriotism, democracy, secularism, socialism and peace, and the principles enunciated in the preamble of our constitution.

"Higher education has to produce capable leaders of society and economy for manifold activities committed to the aforesaid ideas.

"Higher education being integrally linked with the entire educational system should help in the betterment of the rest of the educational structure.

"Higher education should take note of academic excellence, progress of arts and science all the world over and ensure that our best talents make befitting contribution in this international endeavour."

D3322 As Suggested by Wilson and Tauber[20]

1. Conservation of knowledge
2. Teaching
3. Research
4. Publication
5. Extension
6. Interpretation.

D3323 As Suggested by Kern Alexander[21]

(i) To maintain, support, crictically examine and to enforce the existing social and political system;

(ii) To train students and faculty for leadership and superior service in public service, science, agriculture, commerce and industry;

(iii) To develop students to well rounded maturity-physically, socially, emotionally, spiritually, intellectually, and vocationally;

(iv) To develope, refine, and teach ethical and cultural values;

(v) To provide fullest possible realisation of democracy in every phase of living;

(vi) To teach principles of patriotism, civic obligation, and respect for the law;

(vii) To teach the practice of excellence in thought, behaviour and performance;

(viii) to develop, cultivate and stimulate the use of imagination;

(ix) to stimulate reasoning and critical faculties of students to encourage their use in improvement of existing political and social order;

(x) to develop and teach lawful methods of change and improvement in the existing political and social order;

(xi) To provide by study and research for increase of knowledge;

(xii) To provide by study and research for development and improvement of technlogy, production and distribution of increased national goods;

(xiii) To teach methods of meeting the problems of a changing environment;

(xiv) To promote directly and explicitly international understanding and co-operation;

(xv) To provide knowledge;

(xvi) To transfer the wealth of knowledge and tradition from one generation to another.

D-333. Functions of University Libraries

Universities of today, therefore do not only teach according to a prescribed syllabus. These are also expected to enable the students to learn how to investigate independently. To learn it, the students will need libraries. University libraries therefore do not only support universities by collecting books and other materials relating to syllabus but, at the same time, these are also expected to arouse and sharpen student's intellectual curiosity and mental faculty. University and college libraries therefore have great role to play in educational system. According to Ranganathan a Univeristy library must perform a set of five functions to justify its existence. Preparation, production, documentation, initiation of students and teachers, user education, and promotng use of the library, are some of the most important functions which a university library must perform. In sort the functions which a university/academic library is expected to perform may be enumerated as under:

(i) to acquire, process, organise and make available reading and other materials to students, teachers, and other staff members of the university so as to enable them to complete their reading, teaching, research, and other assigments.
(ii) In addition to the above, the university library is also expected to provide material to its users for (i) arousing their intellectual curiosity and sharpening intellectual faculty; (ii) stimulating imagination, reasoning and critical faculty. (iii) refining their ethical and cultural values (iv) making them aware of their environment and development around them (v) informing and guiding them with regard to their further education, profession or occupation.
(iii) To encourage the use of library by (i) initiating the fresh students and teachers, (i) taking up readers' education progrmmes, i.e. imparting instructions in the use of the library and issuing brochures etc. for this purpose.
(iv) To adopt new technology e.g. computerization in certain areas with a view to provide purposeful service in miniumum possible time.

D-34. Conclusion

Not only the task but also opportunities for university libraries are enormous. There may be students and teachers alike who are ignorant of most of the literature relating to their subject which may be available in the library. The university library and the university librarian have the responsibility to devise ways and means to ensure that these two (readers and books) come into contact with one another.

D4 SPECIAL LIBRARIES

D41 Introduction

There are four broadly accepted types of libraries, viz. national libraries, public libraries, academic libraries, and special libraries. The special library is distinctly different from the first two. But the special library and the academic library are so similar in nature that some times it becomes difficult to draw a line of demarcation between the two. For exmple, an academic institution may be a special type of institution e.g. engineering college, medical college etc. Then its library may appear to be a special library. Likewise, a special library may have collection on some specific academic area of study. Then this library may appear to be an academic library. It is therefore necessary to define the special library in order to differentiate it from other types of libraries.

D-42. Definition

A library is an organised collection of audio-visual materials maintained for the use of its clientele. Collection and clientele are therefore the two factors that may determine the nature (and therefore definition) of a particular type of library. Some library scientists base their definitions of the special library on collection factor. For example, Wright has defined the special library as "a library which is concerned almost exclusively with the literature of a particular subject or group of subjects-it also includes libraries with the collection of a particular form of material."[22] He has included academic libraries also in the fold of special libraries because some of these are "concerned with the literature of particular form or material". Wright's definition is not the sole definition based on "collection" factor.

If we go by the dictionary meaning of the word 'special' the above quoted definition would appear to be an appropriate definition of special library. The word special is used to denote some distinct or individual characterstic or to indicate a particular field of interest. The definition quoted above indicates and emphasises that a library with special interest in collection is a special library. Thus the definition appears to be appropriate. But if we analyse the definition in depth we may find it to be overlapping. It is so because then, some academic libraries and some public libraries may also fall under the category of special libraries. For examaple, the library of an engineering college or school of management which are obviously academic libraries, would then be categorised under special library. The same will happen to a public library with special collection, such as Khuda Bux Oriental Library or Adyar Public Library. Similarly, decipline-based national libraries such s National Medical Library would also fall under special library. It is therefore evident that the definition quoted above or any other definition based on 'collection' factor may lead to confusion. As a matter of fact, it is not the nature of collection but the nature of clientele that determines the type of library. The clientele of a special library do not normlaly consult the library for their individual requirements, but to discharge the duties assigned to them by their organisation. Secondly, all the users use the library for the common purpose of discharging their institutional responsibilities. On the other hand, the clientele of an academic or a public library use the library for their individual requirements and individual interests. It is therefore the clientele and not the collection that makes a library special. For this reason Ranganathan dubs a special library as a "specialist library". It may however be borne in mind that speciality of collection is also essential for special library. Fosket has given a comprehensive definition of the special library which takes care of the points discussed above. The definition is as follows: A special library "is one serving a group having an extra existence whose members direct at least some of their activities towards a common purpose. This excludes universities, whose members pursue their own purposes but the group served may be government department professional association, an industrial firm, a research association or institute or a similar organisation. Special libraries serve organizations with a clearly defined group policy, and the members of the group have indicated their acceptance of this policy by the fact of their joining which implies their recognisition of a common interest". A special library is thus an organised collection of special nature for the use of a group of clientele for enabling them to discharge and fulfil their official responsibilities and commitments. Libraries of government departments, industries, research institutions, and professional bodies/ associations thus fall under the category of special libraries.

D43 Main Features

On the basis of the above discussion, main features of a special library may be pointed out as under:

D431 Collection

A special library lays marked emphasis on *special collection*, i.e. collection in some specific field. The collection is built up keeping in view the objectives and policies of parent organisation. The collection may also fulfil research requirements of the organisation but does not aim at collecting documents relating to formal education.

D432 Clientele

A special library has *specialist clientele with common interest* i.e., all the clientele's interest and requirements revolve round achieving the objectives and goals set by the organisation under clearly spelt policy statements. The clientele normally have no individul interests or requirements, or atleast, the library is not set up with this objective.

D433 Service

Each special library is *unique library*. In the words of Mortimer Taube, "one of the great glories of special librarianship, one of the things that makes it special is that each special librarian creates his own organisation of information. He functions as a creater of special system for his own special purpose". Information needs of each special library is thus special or different from that of the information needs of another special library. Services of each special library are therefore, to be specially designed. Emphasis here is on information services which may be provided through documentation, Current Awareness and SDI services. These services also require advanced techniques of information storage and retrieval.

D434 Staff and Equipment

A special library requires highly skilled and professionally competent staff and advanced mechanical and electronic equipments so as to provide the desired service in the quickest possible time.

D435 Interest of Parent Organisation

For special library the interest of the parent organisation is more important than the interest of an individual, if any. Other types of libraries are also supposed to care for the objectives and policies of the parent organisation, but at the same time these give due watage to the individual requirements of the clientele. This is more true in case of a public library.

D44 Need

Above mentioned facts would reveal that a special library is 'special' in all respects.

The Need for the special library and the need to provide adequate library services to the specialist reader was felt at the advent of the 20th century. A group of American librarians, which met on July 2, 1904 at New Hampshire, gave the name of 'special libraries' to such libraries as were providing special materials to the specalist readers. It was truely felt then that special libraries will have to be built up and grown in order to meet the special needs of new clientele belonging to industries, various professions, business, learned societies etc. Since then, the need of special library is being increasingly felt owing to following major factor. (i) Universities of today, the government and the private sector have laid much emphasis on research in all deciplines in general and in the fields of sciences and technology in particular. Researches are conducted on a specialised topic for which the researcher in supposed to know the work already done and material already available in his field of research. It is therefore necessary to have special libraries or specialised collection in other types of libraries in order to fulfil the specialised research needs of the clientele and the parent institution.

(ii) There has taken place enoromous growth of information in all fields due to the advent of printing press which was invented in sixteenth century. Printed material had created a sensation about four hundred years ago. This is reflected in the statement made in the seventeenth century by Leibniz who said, " If the world goes on this way for a thousand years, and as many books are written as today, I am afraid that whole cities would be made up of libraries." Presently the world is witnessing the production of about 5 lakh printed books and about ten lakh periodical titles most of which are in various subject fields. Particularly in the field of science and technology the specialised literature is being produced at an alarming rate. Charles Bernier wrote in this context a decade ago: "To-day's scientific literature is so large that, one person can no longer read the output in one great branch of it, such as chemistry. If a chemist, fluent in 30 languages, started on January 1st to read all papers in his particular field for 40 hours a week, at a rate of 4 articles an hour, then by December, 31st he would have read not more than one tenth of the material published during that year". Thus the information explosion has made it essential not only to make all possible efforts to collect and organise the maximum number of available materials, but also to tell the needy as to what other material of his interest is available at what place and in what form. This can be achieved by establishing and strengthening special libraries.

D45 Some Terms and Concepts

Special libraries serve their clientele with the help of various types of services. Such activities and services are performed by a special library for specialist readers in the form of information storage and retrieval, and documentation service. Some of the most talked about concepts on which the services of a special library are based have been discussed below in brief with a view to present the basic elements of these activities.

D451 Document

The shorter Oxford English Dictionary (1986 reprint) gives general meaning of a document as "something written, incsribed etc., which furnishes evidence or information upon any subject, as manuscript, title-deed, coin, etc." S.R. Ranganathan has given more accurate and lucid definition of the term as" a record of work on paper or other material for easy physical handling, transport accross space, and prevention through time. It may embody macro-thought or micro-thought".

D452 Macro and Micro Document and thought

A macro-document embodies or contains macro-thought and a micro-document embodies or contains micro-thought. A macro document thus deals with a broad subject (macro-thought) and a micro-document with a narrow or minute subject (micro-thought). For example, a book is a macro-document as it dwells on a broad subject, and an article in a micro-document as it dwells on a narrow subject.

D453 Nascent Thought

Nascent means something which is in the process of development or has just begun to grow. Nascent thought therefore means new thought i.e., the thought which has just been expressed.

D454 Documentation

Some of the widely quoted definitions of "Documentation" as given by well known library scientists are as under:

(i) "Recording, organization and dissemination of specialised knowledge, or in other word— collecting organizing and providing micro-thought to the scientists and research scholars"

— Aslib

(ii) Documentation does, in fact, embrace the whole gamut of operations from the discovery of new knowledge through its publication, analysis, classification and arrangement to its arrival at the user, that it to say repoort writing, publication, abstracting, classification, indexing, presentation, and dissemination"

— Esncycobopedia of library and information Science

(iii) "The group of teachniques, necessary for the ordered presentation, organization and communication of recorded specialized knowledge in order to give maximum accessibility and utility to the information contained".

— Jesse H. Shera

(iv) "The designation of total complex of activities involved in the communication of specialized information, including activities which contribute special librarianship plus the prior activities of preparing and reproducing material and subsequent activity of distribution".

— Maurice Taube

(v) "Documentation is the complex of processes involved in pinpointed, exhaustive and expeditous service of nascent thought to specialists".

— S.R. Ranganathan

All these definitions stress that documentation is providing specialized information to specialists. Ranganathan has made one more thing clear that the specialised information genrally implies nascent thought and this is very important.

D456 Documentation Work and Service

Ranganathan has discussed in detail two aspects or facets of documentation. These are (a) documentation work and (b) Documentastion service. These include (a) collection, abstracting, indexing, and classifying special material and preparing documentation list and (b) serving the reader with the documents prepared for their specialised needs through information storage and retrieval including reprography. Such services are being provided in uncountable number of libraries and information centres and organizations.

D46 Conclusion

Different types of libraries, discussed in preceeding pages are in one way or other collection of similar nature. But at the same time these have some exclusive collection also which may not be available in other libraries. This necessitates cooperation and resource sharing among various types of libraries which has been discussed in the next chapter.

REFERENCES

1. *op. cit.*, p. 4.
2. Kent, Allen and Lancour, Harold, ed. *Encyclopedia of Library and Information Science* (New York, Marcel Dekker, 1972) v. 19, p. 94.
3. As quoted in *ibid*, v. 19 p. 94.
4. As quoted in *ibid* v. p. 19.
5. *Ibid*, v. 19 , p. 107.
6. As quoted in Kesawan, B.S., *India's National Library* (Calcutta, National Library, 1961), p. 14.
7. National Library Review Committee (1968) Chairman: V.S. Jha.
8. *Preface*, op. cit.
9. Jevones, Stanley: The Rationale of Free Public Library. In Contemporary Review, March 1881. Reprinted in Gerad, David: *Library and Society* (London, Clive Bingley, 1978).
10. Committee on the Structure of Public Library Services in England and Wales. Chairman: Sydney Roberts: Report. (London, Her Majesty's Stationary Office, 1959) pp. 8-9.
11. Wheeler, Joseph L. and Goldhor Herbert: *Practical Administration of Public Libraries*, (New York, Harper & Row, 1962).
12. McColvin, L.R.: *Public Library System of Great Britain*, p. 70.
13. Jast, L.S.: *The Library and Community*, p. 156.
14. McCormic, Peter J.: Identifying the library's public and community. In *The Library as a Community Information Centre*, papers presented at an Institute conducted by university of Illinois Library School, 1957) (Illinois, Union Book Store, 1959) p. 11.
15. India Education Commission, 1964-65, Chairman, L.S. Kothari: Report (New Delhi, Publication Division, 1968).
16. U.K., University Grants Committee: Report, 1921, *op cit*.
17. *Ibid*
18. As quoted by Robert Snenn. In Test Question for the School Library (London, 1939).
19. Extract from a note adopted by the All India Federatioon of University and College Teachers Organisation on code of professional ethics at its meeting held in Calcutta in November 1976. As quoted in Report of the Committee on revision of Pay Scales of Teachers in Universities and Colleges. *op. cit*.

20. Quoted by Wilson Louis R. and Tauber, Mourice F., *University Library—* Ed. 2. (New York, Columbia University Press, 1956) p.15.
21. Alexander, Kern: *College and University Library* (Chartollesiville,, Michie Co, 172), pp. 471-2.
22. Most of the quatations appearing in this section have been taken from Mukherzee, A.K. *Fundamentals of special librarianship and Documentation* (Calcutta, IASLIC, 1969) as quoted in the book under reference.

E

Resource Sharing

E1 INTRODUCTION

In ancient times bigness of collection was considered to be a significant factor in deciding the goodness of a library. A renound library was supposed to have good number of manuscripts and other reading material. This gave rise to the tendency of self sufficiency among libraries. But the modern library has realised that the goal or aspiration of self sufficiency is a delusion, like searching a lake in desert. Invention of printing press, opening of more and more academic and research institutions, spread of education and technological advances are some of the factors which have led to literature explosion. For instance, there were very few scientific journals in 17th century. Now we have more that 50,000 journals in the field of science and technology alone and the number is increasing every year at a compound rate.[1] In such a situation made more grave by many other factors, the goal of self sufficiency has become unrealistic and impracticable proposition even for the biggest library of the world. It is for this reason that someone had suggested that the slogan "No library can stand alone" should be adopted as the Sixth Law of Library Science.

E-2. DEFINITION

By resource sharing is meant an operation in which more than two parties agree to share voluntarily the fruits and cost of the operation, and in which a member has something useful to contribute to other members. It is also known as library cooperation. In the context of library, cooperation denotes sharing of resources. It means sharing of resource of a group of libraries. In nutshell it "denotes a mode of operation where library functions are shared in common by a number of libraries. The goals are to provide (a) positive net effect on the library user in term of access to more materials or services and/or (b) on the library budget in terms of providing level service at less cost, or more service at less cost, or increased service at less cost, or much more service at less cost than if undertaken individually. The goals should be realised without harm to the mission of the participating libraries."[2]

E3 NECESSITATING FACTORS

There are more than one factors that necessitate adoption of resource sharing or cooperation among libraries. Some of the major factors have been explained below.

E31 Literature Explosion

Tremendous growth of literature has made it impossible for a library to attain self-sufficiency. Exponential growth of library material available in the form of books, periodicals, research papers and non-book materials has made it beyond the control of a library to acquire all the materials which are being produced. About 20 years' ago Kent wrote that about two thousand pages of books, news papers, and other reading materials are being produced every minute in the world, and asserted, "If you attempt to keep fully informed of everything going on in the world-through reading, you would fall behind an estimated 1,051,2000,000 pages every solid year you would devote to reading."

E32 Readers' Demand

There had been tremendous increase in the number of users of a library and their varied demands. On one hand, governments' policy to increase literate population, mass education, and open learning and the changing nature of libraries (which are serving as a cultural, information, and community centre) have resulted in increase of readers population. On the other hand advancements in the entire field of knowledge and inter-disciplinary approach in education have resulted in diversified demands by various sections of readers to quench their thirst of knowledge and information needs.

E33 Limited Resources
A single library is not capable of meeting all the requirements of its clientete.

Limited resources of libraries in terms of money, space and manpower also stress upon the need for cooperation. Even the most resourceful library of the most affluen country can not afford to acquire, organise and put to use all the material that may be required by its clientele. Due to inflation, rising cost of books and space constraints a library cannot afford to buy all the available material. Annual subscription of Chemical Abstract went up from $. 12 in 1940 to over $ 4,000 in 1980. Similarly a study reveals that the average price of an US periodical has risen from $ 8.66 in 1968 to $ .27.58 in 1978.[3] These figures have been given here simply to substantiate the statement that prices of library material are touching sky and as a result buying power of any currency even in term of books and periodicals has drastically been reduced. Altredge and Atkinson have rightly observed in this context, "The increased cost of reading materials over past decade have far exceeded the general rate of inflation and the result had been a steady erosion of purchasing power for library."[4] Apart from finance, a library's space is also limited. It cannot therefore provide sufficient space for unlimited number of documents. It is necessary for library to impose restrictions on arbitrary growth of its collection even if it has finance to buy these. Similarly a library cannot employ any number of staff to organise and put to use unlimited number of documents because staff, like books, require finance and space both.

E34 Observation

An analysis of the situation as explained in the preceeding pages and above leads us to make the following observation:

E341. The laws like Every Reader his/her Book; and Every Book its Reader; and the concepts like books are for all; Free flow of information, Universal Availability of Publication (UAP) etc., make it obligatory on the part of a library to provide to its readers every reading material they are interested in;

E342. On the other hand the factors explained above, and the concepts like "maximum number of books at least cost" would make it impossible for a library to acquire, preserve and put to use all these materials to its readers out of its own resources.

E343. Even if a library can afford huge finance, vast space and array of staff it must avoide unnecessary duplication so that available resource may be utilised for some more fruitful purposes.

E343. These factors make it necessary that libraries should cooperate among each other to ensure proper ustilisation of their resources at one hand and for serving their clientele in a better way on the other hand.

E4 PREREQUISITES

The success of a scheme of a resource sharing depends to a large extent on the willingness of the member libraries to actively participate in the programme. Beside, the following elements are also necessary for the success of the scheme.

E41 Government's Sanction

Sanction of the government by enacting library legislation or by framing administrative rules makes a scheme of cooperation more successful.

E42 System of Libraries

A network of libraries is necessary for sharing of resources at all levels. This can again be done by the government.

E43 Memorandum of Understanding (MOU)

A code or Memorandum of Understanding (MOU) for sharing the resources is must for successful operation of the scheme. Such a code spells out the role, responsibility, rights, and duties of the participating libraries. It also contains provision as to which material is sharable and which is not and who will bear what cost.

E44 Bibliographical Tool

Preparation and updating of bibliographical tools like union catalogues and union list of holdings is also very much useful in this context.

E5 AREAS OF RESOURCE SHARING

Libraries may share their resource in many areas or fields. These determine the type of cooperation among libraries. Some of the areas of cooperation may be enumerated as under:

Shared or cooperative Acquitsition and storage.
Shared or cooperative technical processing.
Shared lending or inter library loan.
Cooperation in other areas.

E51 Shared Acquisition and Storage

Enormous increase in the field of reading material and rising cost of publications have made it difficult for a library to acquire all the documents required by its readers. Rapid and unchecked growth of collection creats problems for space also. It is therefore not possible for a single library to acquire and organise all the documents required by its readers. Codperative acquisition can solve these problems to a great extent. In cooperative acquisition programme a group of libraries join hands in procuring documents. The documents frequently required by the readers of each library are acquired by the library. Less used and very costly materials are however purchased by one specific library which lends these to other libraries when required by their readers. These libraries may also decide to procure documents on mutually agreed subjects in different libraries. Thus a particular library develops comprehensive collection on a particular field. This saves money, manpower, and space.

Similarly in cooperative storage programme depository libraries are set up at local and regional level where less used materials, such as old and bound volumes of periodicals and serials are deposited by the participating libraries. Less space is required for storing documents. For this purpose stacks with more height are installed and less space is left between two racks or shalves.

E52 Shared Technical Processing

Under the scheme of cooperative classification and cataloguing a group of libraries decide to cooperate in the technical processing of documents by cooperative and centralised methods. It is also known as centralised/cooperative processing of documents which has been discussed in succeeding sections. Shared processing implies classification and cataloguing of books at a central point or at various selected points by a central organisation or library for use of the recipient libraries. In other words, the operation envisages to render free or charged service to other libraries by a central organisation in centralised processing, or by a group of libraries which mutually agree to do so in specified areas in cooperative processing. Centralised service is being rendered in many countries in many forms and by many organisations including libraries and commercial organisations. Central organisation is the one which takes the responsibility of classifying and cataloguing all books or books in specified areas and sending the catalogue cards etc. to the concerned libraries. It is also responsible for formulating policies, distributing work among libraries if necessary, maintaining coordination among participating libraries, and ensuring smooth functioning of the scheme. It is also supposed to maintain a record of all the processed books in card form.

E521 Need for a Centralised Processing Scheme

Many factors will advocate for centralised processing of books. Some of these are as under:

(i) There has taken place over the years exponential growth of literature on widely increasing range of subjects. Besides, libraries also tend to acquire more and more books. Situation has become more grave as the strength of staff, particularly technical staff, does not increase to cope up with the increasing number of books added in a library. As a result either all the documents are not processed, or they are processed late resulting in fantastic delay in release of a book for use.

(ii) Owing to limited financial resources, libraries are not in a position to employ more number of technically qualified staff, which is essential for ensuring qualitative processing of books.

(iii) Many libraries in the country do not have technically competent staff to process the acquired books.

(iv) With reference to the books donated under various central selection schemes of the state or central government situation is much more grave. For instance, sometimes books gifted under such a scheme are processed very late or not processed at all in many of the libraries because of the fact that the libraries have insufficient number of technical staff who seldom find time to process the books received under the schemes after processing the books purchased directly by them and after performing other routine duties. This causes substantial delay in release of books for the use of readers.

E522 Advantages and Purpose

Advantages of centralised or shared processing are many and it serves various purposes. Some major advantages can be mentioned as under:

(i) *Economy:* It is the most economical form of processing. It not only saves money, but manpower and machinery too. Saving in term of money, manpower and machinery can be utilised for other services in the library.

(ii) *Elimination of Duplication:* It eliminates duplication of processing work in libraries.

(iii) *Quality:* It ensures qualitative cataloguing and classification at cheaper cost because at selected places expert cataloguers are engaged for cataloguing of books. They specialise the job of processing and also have fare knowledge of concerned subjects.

(iv) *Uniformity:* It ensures uniformity in inner and physical forms of catalogue etc., in the participating libraries.

(v) *Quantity:* Quantity of books processed is increased i.e., more books can be processed in less time.

(vi) *Union Catalogues:* It may be helpful in compilation of union catalogue, though it is not the purpose of shared processing.

E523 Disadvantages and Limitations

According to some library scientists shared processing has following limitations and disadvantages:

(i) It gives rise to unemployment of classifires and cataloguers because they will be required at the centralised or selected places mainly.

(ii) In case the centralised library or agency is not a copyright library, it becomes troublesome to operate the scheme. Because then in case the participating library acquires such a book which is not available with the centralised library, the participating library will either be required to process the book for itself or to send the book or details thereof to the central library. This is time consuming.

(iii) Libraries adopting different forms and type of catalogue and different schemes of classification cannot participate in it.

E524 Clarification

Limitations and disadvantages assigned to shared processing by its critics are more imaginary than real. It is also not correct to say that it creates unemployment of expert classifires and cataloguers. As a matter of fact, more and more number of cataloguers etc., with subject specialization will be needed by the central or selected agencies. On the other hand individual libraries would also appoint generalist classifires and libraries to adopt same form and type of catalogue and same scheme of classification. As a matter of fact, this is a prerequisite for adopting this scheme and therefore, it is unfair to criticise it on this ground. This amounts to criticising lemon by saying "It is not sweet" or sugercane by saying 'it is not sour'! Advantages of shared processing certainly have an edge over its limitations. It is therefore gaining popularity.

E525 Prerequisites

Following are the pre-requisites for starting a centralised cataloguing or centralised classification project:

(i) Sufficient number of libraries should be willing to participate i.e., take the advantages of the project.

(ii) Participating libraries must be using or willing to use same scheme of classification, same code of cataloguing, same physical form of catalogue, and same inner type of catalogue including same colour and type of cards etc.

(iii) Some sort of mechanism is essentially to be developed so as to ensure that the cataloguable documents acquired by all the participating libraries are seen by the central cataloguing agency to facilitate their cataloguing.

(iv) Collection of the participating libraries should be in similar subject in case of centralised processing.

(v) Delay in cataloguing of documents and irregular supply of entries for any reason may cause abandoning the scheme by participating libraries. Every care must be taken to ensure that delay does not take place.

(vi) Printing of entries should be economical and timely. The central agency must take care in determining policy, maintenance of records, distributing or supplying the entries among participating libraries and to coordinate with them.

E526 Forms and Services

Shared processing of books is not a new concept in the field of librarianship. For example, centralised cataloguing is being used in the world in various forms. There have been many experiments also in this respect. Some of the important forms of centralised cataloguing have been discussed in brief in the succeeding sections.

E5261 Cataloging-in-source

Cataloging-in source implies (i) pre-publication cataloguing of books and (ii) Printing of catalogue cards in books itself or providing printed catalogue card of the book alongwith the book. Cataloging-in-source was carried out by Library of Congress as an experimental project in 1958-59. It was concieved that if all the publishers send to the central agency (i.e. Library of Congress) final proof copy/sample copy of all their publications, it may be possible for the central agency to catalogue those books and send the entries to the publishers before the book was released by them. The concerned publisher then may print the main card of the book (publication) in the publication itself which may be copied by concerned libraries. America's Council of Library Resources gave a generous grant ($55,000) for this experimental project. Purpose of launching this project was as under:

(i) Availability of catalogue card together with books resulting in immediate cataloguing of books in libraries;
(ii) saving time, money and manpower; and
(iii) Standardisation of bibliographical data.

The experiment tried to ascertain (i) economic and technical issues involved, (ii) reaction of publishers and libraries, and (iii) if it would ensure standard cataloguing with the help of proof copies. Findings of the experiment were as under. These are also the major points of criticism against cataloging-in-source:

(i) According to prescribed time, Library of Congress was supposed to prepare and send the catalogue entry to the publisher within 24 hours of the receipt of the proof copy. It was difficult to maintain the time schedule.
(ii) Strict adherence to the prescribed time schedule increased the possibility of faulty or defective cataloguing.
(iii) In such a scheme cataloguing is based not on the actually printed-book but on its proof copy. Possibilities for making some changes in the title on any other vital information by the publisher can not be ruled out till the last moment before the book is finally printed. For example, index to a book is prepared or finalised normally after the text of the book is printed. Sometimes date of publication also needs to be changed at the

eleventh hour for many reasons, viz., delay in finalisation of index, delay in binding etc. Such situation may arise particularly when the book was likely to be released in the last quater of the year. Sometimes, publishers use to change the title at the eleventh hour. Such situations may result in defective or wrong cataloguing and that also permanently.

(iv) Most of the catalogue codes provide for preparation for entries of pseudonymous work under the real name of the author if possible, even if it is not printed on book (if it is possible to find the real name from other sources). On the other hand some of the authors many not like, for many reasons, to print their real name in the book. But in cataloging-in-source the real name of the author will become available in the entry printed in the book itself.

(v) Most of the cataloguing codes provide for giving year of birth of the author in the author/main entry for individualisation. Some authors, however, do not want their date of birth to be printed in the book. But if cataloging-in-source is adopted their date of birth will be printed in book (i.e., in the entry).

(vi) Needs of libraries vary form library to library: some libraries may require or desire to incorporate more information about a book in the catalogue card. But some other libraries (may be small) may be interested in giving smallest details or less information (for example shorter or broad class numbers, simple entries, less detailed notes or no notes etc). It is not possible to satisfy both the needs and requirements.

(vii) The Library of Congress realised that the project would cost it about three quarters of a million dollor each year which may not be easily recoverable.

Due to the reasons mentioned above the project received favourable response neither from publishers nor from libraries. It was found that in 481 cases entries provided in the books did not tally with the information given in books (for detail see Encyclopedia of Library and Information Science, Vol. 4, p. 235). These findings forced the Library of Congress to discontinue the project.

E-5262. Cataloging-in-Publication

It is a revised form of cataloging-in-source and was started as an experimental project by Library of Congress in 1971. If differed from cataloging-in-source in the sense that:

(i) Publishers were required to send only gally proof and not the final proof so as to ensure that they received back the catalogue entires before the book is printed without delaying its publication schedule;
(ii) Cataloguers were given ten working days' time for preparting and sending entries to publishers; and
(ii) Information of sub-titles, imprint, and collation were not included in the entries because these used to be changed by publishers at the last hour.

E5263 Prenatal Cataloguing and Classification

The concept of prenatal cataloguing (and calssification) is a contribution of S.R. Ranganathan. He conceived it in 1948 and proposed it as follows: Each publisher sends gally pooof of its publications to the National Library. The National Library classifies the book and sends to the publisher call numbers of the book immediately, and within resonable time the entry for the book. The publisher prints call number on the verso of the title page and spine of the book. The National Library completes cataloguing of the book before it is released for sale by the publisher. These are made available in printed or cyclostyled form to the publishing agency or interested libraries for their use. The concerned publisher may send printed cards alongwhith the book to interested libraries. According to Ranganathan this would save 79% of cost on cataloguing at national level. This scheme is yet to materialise. Merits and demerits of this scheme are almost same as cataloging-in-source or cataloging-in-publication.

E-527. Conclusion

There are no two opinions that shared cataloguing etc. in any form, and particularly in pre-publication form is most useful at idea level but practical difficulties are more. In India it is yet to be experimented.

E53 Shared Lending or Inter Library Loan (ILL)

E531 Introduction

Shared lending or inter library loan is one of the most discussed and popular types of cooperation among libraries. Inter Library Loan is perhaps the oldest form of cooperation among libraries. As a matter of fact 'inter library loan' was generally used as a synonym for 'library cooperation' and this connotation still persists in the minds of laymen. In this type of cooperation a group of libraries join together and agree to lend materials to one another for the use of the readers of all the member libraries.

E532 International Trends

Librarians and readers around the world have shown great interest in implementing the ILL operation, and as a result the system has been working successfully and satisfactorily in various countries. Apart from librarians and readers, national and international associations have also contributed a lot in the development of ILL. On International plane the names of IFLA, International Institute of Bibliography, the Institute for Intellectual Cooperation may be mentioned. Experience has shown that the countries that have developed lbrary system, national bibliography, and union catalogues, can implement the scheme smoothly. For handling or operating ILL in a systematic manner, a set procedure is necessary. In several countries ILL is being operated through regional library system in which the regional libraries are entrusted with "Location function" (i.e., to locate or trace the place of availablity of the desired document, and to prepare, maintain and handle tools, such as catalogues, bibliography etc. for ensuring rapid location of a document asked for). On the other hand, in many other countries the "location function" is being performed centrally by the national library of the respective country. For instance, countries like England, Sweden, and Germany are running ILL system through regional system or regional libraries. Countries like Australia, Newzealand, and South Africa have adopted centralised "location" procedure under ILL system. It may be pertinent here to mention the salient feature of the Regional System. In this system, the country may be divided into convenient regions in which regional bureaus or regional centres are created. Regional centres may maintain union catalogue for the documents available on ILL in the libraries of the particular region. Libraries in each region contact that regional centre in their region for identifying the location of a required document. If the location of the document is identified in the regional centre, it sends the requisition to the concerned regional centre, in which the document is located,. The book may be sent by the parent library through its region or directly to the borrowing regional centre or borrowing library as the case and decision may be. In case location of the document could not be identified in the concerned regional centre, the request is passed on to the national centre (normally, national library), which maintains a union catalogue for the whole country. The national centre may prepare, maintain and update the union catalogue for the country from the duplicate catalogues received from the regional centres. Regional library may prepare, maintain and update the union catalogue for their region on the basis of the duplicate catalogues received from the libraries of their region.

E533 Prerequisites

The success of a scheme of ILL depends to large extent on the willingness of the member libraries to actively participate in the scheme. Besides, the following elements are also necessary to be considered before implementing such a scheme.

(i) *Library system:* For successful implementation of an ILL scheme a library system and network of libraries is nearly necessary.

(ii) *Agreement:* There must be a well defined agreement among the member libraries about what to share, how to share, and the responsibility and function of each member-library should be spelt out.

(iii) *Bibliographic tool:* Bibliographic tools for running an ILL scheme involve (i) Preparation, maintenance and updating of union catalogues/regional catalogues, (ii) directory of participating libraries, (iii) subject bibliographies, and (iv) indexes of articles published in periodicals and like materials;

(iv) *Communication channel for locating and obtaining documents:* In Indian condition documents may be obtained and sent back by registered post. Local libraries may utilise the service of a messenger. It is a matter of discussion whether a proper channel for routing requests should be adopted.

(v) *Loanable and non-loanable materials:* This is very important factor and needs serious consideration. Normally, non-conventional reading materials, such as microfilms, records etc. are not lent in original. Loose issue of journals, rare documents, books sent or to be sent for binding, serials publications of current year, and books in much use fall under this catagory. Normally those materials are loaned for which there is no or less demand in the library. It is a matter of agrument also as to why a library should keep in stock unused books for the readers of other libraries? However, it is a proven fact that even in a library with good weeding out policy many of the books remain unused.

(vi) *Cost and payment:* Normal practice is that the administrative expenditure on ILL operation are to be borne by the concerned libraries. Such expenditure may involve expenditure on house-keeping jobs e.g., preparation of catalogues, bibliogrphy, correspondence with libraries. The cost of sending the book on loan to the borrowing library and returning the same back by registered post to the lending library is normally borne by the borrowing library or by the reader.

E534 Problems and Criticism

Below mentioned problems and criticism are assigned to a scheme of inter library loan. These deserve mention and consideration.

(i) As it requires two hands to clap, two (or more) libraries are needed to cooperate for implemention of (ILL). The general criticism of such a scheme is that in it the larger library becomes more a lending and less a recipient library. This may create apathy in larger libraries and the system may fail as a consequence.

(ii) Primary responsibility of a library is its own readers or members. A Library, therefore, can not afford to serve readers of other libraries at the cost of service to its own readers. Contrary to it, sending a book on (ILL) from one library to the other will mean non-availability of that book to the readers of the lending library.

(iii) Since the tendency of self sufficiency is hit at the root when ILL is adopted, the participating libraries or their administrators many become reluctant to enrich the collection of their library, thinking that it will be better to obtain many books on ILL when need arises. This may result in two-way catastroppe. First, the annual addition rate of libraries, particularly lower level libraries, may fall down and cause frustration among readers. Secondly, in case and for any reason the scheme fails, libraries may find it difficult to acquire many important books as most of them would go out of print.

(iv) It may appear that a better service could be rendered in a more economical way as substantial amount may be saved by not purchasing many books. However, the value of the money saved thus may be much less than the amount to be spent on the operation of the scheme i.e. in preparing and updating union catalogues, bibliographies and like materials, on correspondence, postage, and possibly for an extra hand.

(v) It may have two edged adverse effect on pricing and production of books: (a) less copies of a book will be sold, and (b) as a result of it, the publishers may decide to increase the prices of their books which will consequently result in (x) purchase of less number of titles in more money and (z) making it still more difficult for individual buyers to purchase books.

(vi) An average reader of a public library is normally not interested in serious or research literature. He therefore, may not like to wait for arrival of the book on ILL on payment. He may decide to quench his thrust with the documents already available in 'his library'.

(vii) To sum up, the system might fail because of any of the following:
   (a) Over use of and less compensation to larger libraries;
   (b) difficulties in preparing and updating bibliographies and catalogues;
   (c) lack of adequate fund for the scheme at each level;
   (d) non-cooperation of the readers due to delay in getting material by post etc.

E-538. Model Code

A well drafted code for inter library loan is necessary for the successful functioning of the scheme. Such a code normally stresses on the following factors:

(i) identifying the category of loanable documents,

(ii) identifying the category of non-loanable documents,

(iii) deciding period of loan,

(iv) deciding mode of transmission,

(v) deciding if loaned documents are to be consulted within the fourwalls of the borrowing library or if the reader of the borrowing library can take these to his/her residence,

(vi) deciding as to which library, lending or borrowing, will bear the cost of obtaining the documents, or if it is to be borne by the reader,

(vii) fixing the right of the lending library and responsibility of the borrowing library,
(viii) designing a standard requisition form,
(xi) any other aspect which may be decided by the borrowing and the lending libraries.

E54 Other Areas of Cooperation

There are many other area in which the participating libraries may decide to cooperate. Such areas are documentation services, cooperative binding, cooperative training etc.

E6 CONCLUSION

Cooperative programmes among libraries save cost, ensure maximum utilisation of available resources and increase the use of materials. We are living in the age of cooperation. No society and nation can exist in the absence of cooperation. Libraries are also social institutions and have come ahead to promote cooperative provrammes in their field. For instance IFLA, FID, UNESCO etc. have come ahead and developed many programmes of library cooperation. UBC (Universal Bibliographic Control) UAP (Universal Availability of Publications) UNISIST (Inter Governmental Programme for Cooperati on in Science and Technology), are some of such programmes which are the talk of the day. Resource sharing or cooperation is thus indespensable for libraries today.

REFERENCES

1. Price, D.J. Desola: *Science since Babylon* (Connecticut, Yalle University Press, 1961), p. 12.
2. Kent and Lancour, ed., *op. cit.*, V. 25, p. 295.
3. *Bowke's Library and book trade Annual* (New York, R.R. Bowker, 1979).
4. *Ibid.*

F

Library Movement in G.B. & U.S.A

F1 LIBRARY MOVEMENT

Explaining the concept of library movement Ranganathan says, "Library movement is not setting up of isolated libraries, big or small, primarily for collecting, arranging and preserving printed material. It is setting up and keeping in an effective state of action an integrated network of libraries– a library meaning an institution maintained for and by the community primarily for the social purpose of providing opportunity for self education, throughout life of every person of the community through the medium of thought presented in printed books– organised, served and administered without discrimination by persons who are adept in helping the retransformation of thought locked up in a static material state into one in dynamic mental state."[1] If we take into consideration this concept of library movement, it is evident that the movement was started in India in 1910 in the earstwhile state of Baroda. But in Great Britain and the United States library movement was started long ago which has been described in brief in following pages. Together with discussing library movement, an attempt has also been made to trace short history of development of libraries.

F2 LIBRARY MOVEMENT IN GREAT BRITAIN

Great Britain is one of the leading countries of the world in respect of library service. History of libraries and library movement in Great Britain may be described under following heads:

1. Subscription or commercial libraries.
2. Rural libraries.

3. Workers' libraries.
4. Scene after 1850.

F21 Subscription or Commercial Libraries

Subscription libraries which are also refered to as commercial or circulating or proprietory libraries are the earlier form of libraries in G.B. These existed mostly in urban areas. Allan Ramsay, a poet by hobby and bookseller by profession started in Edinburg a subscription library in the year 1725. By 1825 the number of such libraries rose in England to 1,500. Such libraries had in their stock scholarly, scientific and literary books also, but novels and receational literature occupied major protion of the stock. Books were available 'on rent' in one form or the other. Such libraries were popular, but their aim was to do business. Evaluating the performance of such libraries Davies writes, "The standard fare of the two hundered thousand who obtained books from circulating libraries was novels. The *Innocent Adultry* was read or atleast taken home twenty-times more often than Gibbon's *Decline and Fall of the Raman Empire.* Obviously commercial libraries were not what Petrerach and Chetman meant by the word library"[2] Davies has also quoted S.T. Coleridge saying, "For the devotees of circulating libraries, I dare not complement their pass time, or rather kill-time with the name of reading— we should therefore transfer this species of amusement-from the genuine reading to the comprehensive class characterized by the power of reconciling the two contrary yet coexisting propensities cf human nature, namely indulgence is sloth and hatred of vacancy".[3]

F22 Rural Libraries

History of library development in UK would remain incomplete without mentioning the name of Samuel Brown. This merchent of Haddington set up in rural areas from his own resources library of fifty books. A shopkeeper or a teacher acted as librarian of such libraries which Brown called Intenerating libraries. By 1830 he was able to set up 50 such libraries. Although an Act of Parliament was also passed as early as in 1708 which directed churches and clurgymen to set up village libraries in their respective area or villages, but the Act remained unoperative. In 1730 a village library was set up in Halton village by Sir John Cheshyre "for the improvement of learning, and that learned men may be encouraged to advance their knowledge".[4]

F23 Workers' Libraries

Circulating libraries and other libraries were mostly used by people belonging to the middle class. Workmen, such as factory workers, artisans etc., remained deprived of library facilities until late 18th. century. By the end of 18th century, libraries were opened in UK for urban workers. An example of such a library is "Birmingham Artisan Library" which was set up in 1795 with the purpose of "dissemination of knowledge among the working classes by the aid of book"[5] In 19th century many such libraries were opened, viz., the Sheffiled Mechanics' Library (1820) etc.

F24 Scene After 1850

Development of libraries in UK before 1850 may not be termed as library movement in true sense. Although the British Museum Act was passed in 1759 and the Museum Act was passed in 1845, these acts were directly concerned with setting up museums only. The year 1850 marked in U.K. the advent of free and tax-supported libraries. In this year U.K. adopted first public library act. Due to the efforts of William Ewart– a Statesman, and Edward Edward– a librarian, the Parliament appointed under the chairmanship of Ewart a Select Commitee to consider the relevance of introducing a bill authorising cities and borough to levy tax for the support of libraries. On the basis of the report of the select committee the bill was introduced and passed by both the houses of the Parliament and received Royal Assent on 14th Aug. 1850. This is known as Act of 1850. Numerous ammendments were made to this act, making it more liberal and more effective in providing useful library service in the country. Salient features of the act are that it provided for opening a library in a borough with a population of 10,000 or more persons. In 1855 this facility was extended to Perishes with a population of 5,000 or more persons, and in 1866 this limit was also removed. By the end of nineteenth century borough-councils and urban districts were also allowed to adopt and implement this act. The Library Association (LA) was founded in 1877 which is also a landmark in the history of library movement in UK. Another act was passed in 1919. The Act of 1919 empowered and authorised county councils also to adopt the provisions of the Public Libraries Act. This had a major influence on the provision of public library service in UK. These acts played an important role in creating library movement in UK, but setting up of libraries by voluntary efforts and public initiative also continued. The Government later set up committees on public libraries the report of which gave boost to public library movement in the country. For instance, the committee appointed in 1924 by the Board of Education (known as Kenyon Committee on public libraries in England and Wales) in its report of 1927 dwelt in detail on the functions which a public library should perform, and suggested means for improvement in library service. Similarly McColvin (1942) discussed in detail all aspects of a public library and made valuable recommendations for improvement of public library service. The Roberts Committee (Committee on the Structure of Public Libraries in England and Wales, 1957, Report 1959) is also worth mentioning here. Report of this committee led to the enactment of Public Libraries and Museums Act of 1964. This act vested in the Secretary of State power to superintend and promote public library services provided by local authorities such as boroughs, councils etc. Another important step taken in UK for improvement of library service is the enactment of British Library Act of 1972 which became effective from April 1973. The British Museum which was founded in 1759 was national library of Great Britain (UK) until March 1973. Since April 1973, after the promulgation of this act, the British Library has taken the responsiilities and acquired the status of national library. As per the provisions of this act, the British Library is not one library but system or complex of libraries which is comprised of British Museum, National Central Library, Nation Lending Library, National Lending Library of Science and Technology, British National Bibliography and Office of the Scientific and Technical Information. This is a new trend in the concept of national libraries.

F25 Conclusion

Library movements in UK reveals a commendable growth of libraries quantitatively and qualitatively both. Library service is provided now on the pillars of legislation and various reports and surveys have been infusing new blood in the system, enabling libraries to play significant role in providing reading facilities and information to interested users.

F3 LIBRARY MOVEMENT IN USA

History of library development in USA is long. Systematic development of libraries in U.S.A. may be discussed under following heads:

1. Colonial libraries.
2. Social libraries.
3. Circulating or lending libraries.
4. School-public libraries.
5. Tax supported free libraries.

F31 Colonial Libraries

In the seventeenth century many libraries were established in British colonies from Massachusetts to South Corolina to serve the colonies. These libraries were primarily of three kinds (i) Parochial (i.e., for the use of ministers); (ii) Provincial (i.e. for the use of general readers), and (iii) layman's (i.e., for the use of those allowed by the ministers). These libraries were however used only by wealthy persons and upper strata of the society.

F32 Social Libraries

Social libraries were set up in America in seventeenth century with a view to make library service (i.e., lending books) available to all those who were interested. Such libraries grew as clubs and set up as organisations for encouraging intellectual social and cultural life of the people. For setting social libraries a group of individuals deposited their personal books which they could spare. or/and by contributing to a common fund for opening a library. It is clear from the above description that there were two types of social libraries (i) *Proprietory* (based on joint stock in which each member owned some books, i.e. share in the property) and (ii) *Subscription* (based on payment of periodic or other contribution, fee or subscription). Most of such libraries had very few members i.e., below fifty and sometimes even twenty or so. Popularisation of circulating libraries led to the disappearance of social libraries, though the contribution made by these libraries cannot be under-estimated.

F33 Circulating or Lending Libraries

Circulating or lending libraries were business libraries. These used to lend books to any one who paid the required charge per book daily or weekly or monthly or annually. Since the purpose of running circulating libraries was to earn money, in these libraries mostly such books were kept as may be of general interest to the common man, i.e. popular reading material.

F34 School-Distric Public Libraries

In 1835 the New York legislature passed a law, permitting the voters in any school-district to levy a tax of $ 20 to begin a library and $ 10 each succeeding year to provide for its growth".[6] This type of libraries were free public libraries housed in school-buildings.

F25 Tax Supported Free Libraries

In 1848 the state legislature gave the city of Boston permission to levy taxes for runing a public library and general court of Massachusetts promulgated a law for Boston Public Library. The Boston Public Library was organised in 1852 and was opened to the public for free use in 1854. This step gave boost to the concept of tax supported free libraries in America. Another significant development in the field of library movement in America is the establishment of American Library Association in 1876. In 1948 with the efforts of the Association, Public Library Demomstration Bill was introduced in Congress, but could not be passed. The year of 1956 can be accepted as a turning point in the history of library movement in America. In this year Library Services Act was adopted followed by new Depository Act (Public Law or PL 87-579) of 1962. The Library Services Act of 1956 (federal act for development of library service in America) laid more emphasis on providing qualitative library services in rural areas. The public Law 480 (1954) had already authorised Library of Congress to purchase foreign publications from respective countries by utilizing the US owned fund in the concerned countries. Next significant development in the history of federal support for library movement in USA is the enactment of Library Service and Reconstruction Act of 1964. It provided funds for grant to states on matching basis for providing and extending library service in those areas that were less served or neglected. In 1970 the federal Government established, by enactment of a law, a National Commission on Library and Informtion Science (NCLIS). It is composed of 15 members including professional librarians and social representatives. It has many committees to assist it. Main purpose behind setting up the Commission was (i) to advise the Congress, the President, state and local etc. agencies on matters relating to library development, (ii) to undertake surveys and studies in assessing library needs of the nation, (iii) to apprise the adequacies and deficiencies in the existing library service, and (iv) to prepare plans for improving library services with a view to meeting library needs of the nation.

F4 CONCLUSION

In the foregoing sections we have discussed in brief library movement in U.K and U.S.A. which reflects the keen interest of the people and the government which they evinced in library development and library service. In the next chapter an attempt has been made to describe development of libraries and library service in India.

REFERENCES

1. Ranganathan: *Preface, op. cit.*, p. 148.
2. Davies, W.D.: *Public Libraries as Cultural and Social Centre.* (Metuchen, Scarecrow Press, 1974), p. 3.
3. *Ibid*, p. 3-4.
4. As quoted in *Ibid.*, p. 5.
5. *Ibid.*, p. 7.
6. Gates: *Introduction to Librarianship, op. cit.*, p. 79.

G

Library Movement In India

G1 ANCIENT AND MEDIAEVAL PERIOD

G11 Ancient Period

In India, since the ancient times libraries have been functioning as light houses for those who wanted to read and to extend the boundaries of various disciplines. References are available to prove that Nalanda University (in Bihar) had its own multistoried library in 600 A.D. with massive collection of manuscripts. The collection of the library was housed in three buildings, each having nine floors and three hundred rooms. This library was opened by the then emperor of India, king Devapal. The library was open for any body who was a konwn scholar and took interest in reading , interpreting and even copying the documents kept in the library. Chinese traveller Whuen Sang is known to have consulted this library in the seventh century and to have taken from there hundreds of treatises to China and Japan. This library ws completely destroyed by Bakhtiar Khilaji, who iinvaded India in 1205 A.D. and burnt the library. The library kept on burning for about six months. Faheyan has given a detailed account of the library. Taxila and Vikramshila (Bihar) universities of ancient India also had valuable libraries. Vikramshila University had massive collection of manuscripts on tantras and Taxila university library had rare collection of manuscripts on agriculture and archery. History also tells us that the great Sanskrit poet Banabhatt, who composed his famous work Kadambari, managed the palatial library of king Bhoja.

G12 Mughal Period

The Mughals had also set up royal and pomposh libraries during their regime. There were also libraries attached to academic insti tutions (madarsa). The first Mughal emperor Babar was a voracious reader, prolific writer and a great lover of manuscripts. His successors were also lovers of books and libraries. Humayun set up in Agra Fort a library which was managed by Lal Beg. Similarly Akbar also set up a library under the management and control of Sheikh Faizi. Although printing press was invented by then, Akbar took deep interest in manuscripts and appointed caleographers (Katibs) for copying good manuscripts. He also got translated in persian the famous Hindu epics, namely, the Mahabharata and the Ramayana. He converted the library of Agra Fort in a rich library. Other mughal emperors also took keen interest in libraries and books. Important features of mughal period libraries weré magnificent buildings, rare manuscripts, and scholar-librarians.

G13 Other Rulers

Other rulers and kings also patronised libraries. Among them the names of Mahararja Sawai Man Singh of Jaipur and Maharaja Ranjit Singh of Punjab will be remembered with appreciation in the history of library service in India. Maharaja of Tanjaur, who started the famous Saraswati Mahal Library can also be grouped with them.

G14 Observation

The libraries of ancient and mediaeval India were managed and patronised by emperors, kings, big capitalists and jamindars. Therefore, although these libraries housed valuable collections in magnificent almirahs kept in palatial buildings, these could not play a vital role in providing continuing education to the masses. As a result of this, the common masses of the country remained deprived of library service until the advent of the British on Indian library scéne.

G2 19th CENTURY: ADVENT OF THE BRITISH

G21 Description

The British were the first to set up public library-like institutions in India. The Britishers came to India primarily for establishing trade and for this purpose to secure raw materials from the vast and unexploited natural resources of the country and then to market their finished goods among the teeming millions throughout their colonies. There were however, people among them who were interested in the upliftment of the rich cultural heritage of India. Such Britishers first of all set up public library-like institutions in Bombay, Calcutta, Madras and other parts of the country. In Gujarat, Maharashtra, and West Bengal a number of libraries were opened by or with the encouragement received from the Britishers. The Bengal Royal Asiatic Society set up a library in 1784 and the Bombay Royal Asiatic Society in 1804. The Calcutta Public Library was set up in 1835. This library later grew in the Imperial Library (1903) and National Library (1948). In the other part of the country i.e. west authorities were also considering to start a network of public libraries. For this purpose the Government set up a committee in Bombay in 1939 under the chairmanship of A.A.A. Fyzee which also contributed to the development of public libraries. The committee in its report submitted in 1940 recommended building up of a strong network of public library system in the state with a state central library, district libraries, talluka libraries, block libraries etc. linked with each other in the form of chain. Some of the important libraries set up in 19th century in India are Andrews Library, Surat (1850); Gaya Public Library, Gaya (1855); Long Library, Rajkot (1856); Connemara Public Library, Madras (1860); Government Library, Junagarh (1867), Adyar Library, Adyar (1886); Dahi Laxmi Library, Nadiad (1892).

G22 Observation

Libraries set up during this period by the British or with thier support, due to many factors, were used mostly by the members of the upper class and the elites of the society. The lower strata of the society could not make use of these libraries. It will however have to be admitted that these libraries opened the portals for setting up libraries for the common man. The common man, inspired and enlightened by the education imparted by the British, became interested in books and libraries.

G3 20th CENTURY: LIBRARY MOVEMENT

G31 Imperial Library Opened to Public

The first three decades of the twentieth century will be remembered as golden period in history of public library movement in India. In 1903 the reading room of the Calcutta Public Library (renamed then as the Imperial Library) was opened by the British for the common man. Later, this library became the National Library of India. The National Library of India is located in Calcutta. The library has a chequered history and its name was changed many times. Its origin can be traced in the Calcutta Public library, started in 1835. In 1891 with the efforts and patronage of Lord Curzon was established by amalgamating secretariat libraries. Later, in the year 1902 the Calcutta Public Library was merged with the Imperial Library by enacting the "Imperial Library Act (1902). On 30th Jan. 1903 the Inprial library was opened for public use which was also notified in Gazette of India. A few lines of the notification read as follows: "It is intended that it should be a library of reference, a working place for students, and a repository of material for the future historians of India in which, so far as possible every work written about India any time can be seen and read".

This reflects that in the year 1903 the British government in India for all practical purpose had given the Imperial library the status of India's national library. In Indipendent India the Goverment of India renamed this library as National Library by enacting Imperial Library (change of name) Act of 1948. Again, the government of India enacted in the year 1954 the Delivery of books Act according to which it was made obligatory on the part of each publisher to deposite one copy free of charge to each of the three libraries namely National Library, Calcutta; Connemara Public Library, Madras; and Asiatic Society Library, Bombay. Vide this Act, these three libraries are given the status of Depository Library. In addition to it, it was also proposed to start the fourth Depository library is Delhi under the name "Central Refrence Library". But the Central Reference Library was opened in Calcutta on the National Library's campus, but the status of a Depository library was not given to it. This status (i.e. the fourth depository library) was given in 1982 to Delhi Public Library. Besdies the national library of India, we have in our country subject-national labraries also such as National Science Library, National Medical Library, National Agricultural Library.

G32 Library Movement in Baroda

The erstwhile state of Baroda and its ruler Maharaja Sayaji Rao

Gaekwad III will be remembered with respect for starting and giving a concrete shape to library movement in India. M.S. Gaekwad III is the first Indian ruler to declare and implement compulsory elementary education in the year 1907. The Maharaja wanted to take his subjects from darkness to light by opening free library service in his state. He invited an American librarian, William Allenson Borden, to give shape to his dreams and appointed him as Curator of libraries of his state. By the year 1910 Borden, who was the like deciple of the like mentor-Melvil Dewey, was able to organise a network of free library service in the state. The network consisted of central library, district libraries, talluka (subdivisional) libraries, city libraries and village libraries. Mobile library service was also provided. There were also special libraries such as cinema libraries, manuscript libraries, and libraries for women and children. The Curator of Libraries was assisted by Assistant Curator, Inspectors etc., in managing library service. Library fund was available to the libraries. Apart from government libraries, there were also aided libraries assisted by the government on matching basis. Main objectives behind setting up a well knit library-system was to provide free public library service to one and all. Those who were not in a position to reach the libraries were served by moblile libraries and circulating libraries. We thus find that most of the functions which a public library is supposed to perform according to Unesco's manifesto were performed by the libraries of Baroda in 1910. Such a fresightedness is rarely seen. M.S.Gaekwad III and W.A.Borden had such a foresightedness. They were ahead their times and will always be remembered as pioneers of library movement in India. Due to the sad demise of the Maharaja (1933) the library movement in Baroda suffered a great set back. It was unforturnate that W.A.Borden had also left for America earlier. Though his work was carried forward successfully by T.D.Wakins and M.M.Dutt, the loss caused by Maharaja's death was irrepairable.

G33 Contribution of S.R. Ranganathan

In the third decade of twentieth century Shiyali Ramamrita Ranganathan appeared on the scene like a radiant luminary. Though he worked in the libraries of academic institutions, he made significant contribution towards public library movement in India. Owing to his efforts and the inspiration received from him four states, viz. Madras (Tamil Nadu) Andhra Pradash, Mysore (Karnataka), and Maharashtra passed and enacted library legislation in their states in 1948, 1960, 1965, and 1967 respectively. Ranganathan, besides preparing Model Library Bill and Development Plan, also prepared draft library bills for almost all the Indian States.

G34 Role of the Central Government

The government of India took keen interest in providing public library service to the massess. During the first Five Year Plan (1951-56) the Government included the scheme of improvement of public library services alongwith Community Development Programme. It was visualised and proposed under this plan to set up a national central library at central level and central libraries at state level (i.e. one in each state). Delhi Public Library (1952) and INSDOC (1955) were set up during this plan with the joint efforts of and assistance of Government of India and Unesco. Delivery of Books Act was passed in 1954 and later ammended in 1956. It prescribed that every Indian publisher will send free of cost one copy each of its publications to each of the three libraries in Calcutta (National Library) Madras (Connemara Public Library), and Bombay (Asiatic Society Library). Delhi Public Library became fourth depository library in 1982. In this plan period the Government- on the recommendation of the seminar on Role of Libraries in Social Education, held in New Delhi in 1955- set up an Advisory Committee for Libraries (1957) under the Chairmanship of Shri K.P. Sinha. The Committee had following terms of reference:

- (i) to enquire into the present reading needs of the people, how and what part the existing library set-up plays in meeting the needs;
- (ii) to enquire into the reading tastes of various sections of the people, what agencies are there to provide suitable literature and how the reading taste and literature can be improved;
- (iii) to recommend the future library structure in India.
- (iv) to recommend the form of co-operation between libraries and social education set up;
- (v) to go into the question of training of librarians and the condition of thier service; and
- (vi) to make recommendation of the administrative and financial measure, necessary to support the future set up of public libraries in India.

The term of reference shows that the government had in view the over all development of public libraries, their network, their services, their linkage with other institutions, providing the use of books, inculcating reading habit in masses, training of library staff, and matching finance to support libraries. Sinha Committee submitted its recommendations in 1959 during the Second Five Year Plan (1956-61). It was published in 1961. It recommended an integrated library system in states, linking state central libraries with the National Library at one end and with district, subdivision, block, panchayat and village libraries at the other end. During this plan period a sum of rupees 140 lakh was alloted by the Central Government for public library development, besides alloting rupees 10 lakhs for setting up a Central Institute at Delhi for training of librarians. The committee also recommended setting up an independent Department of Social Education and Libraries at the centre and a State Library Authority in each state. It strongly recommended imposing library cess for proper financing of public libraries and asserted that it is the only reliable source of library finance. It further recommended that the state governments should supplement the amount collected as cess. Major recommendations of the committee are as under:

(i) in states, library cess may be levied at the rate of 6 paise per rupee on property (urban) tax;
(ii) the government may grant a sum equal to the amount collected as cess;
(iii) a separate departement may be set-up for libraries including social education; and
(iv) each state should have a public library system under the control of a State Library Authority.

During the Third Five Year Plan (1962-67/69) the central government felt, "An adequate system of library is an essential part of any well organised system of education, Steps will be taken to set-up or develop all the four national libraries at Delhi, Bombay, Calcutta, and Madras. There are also provisions to strenghen libraries at the state headquarters and for increasing the number of libraries at district and Talluka level."

The Fourth Five Year Plan was implemented in 1969-74. The Planning Commission had, however, started preparing draft plan much earlier. While preparing proposal for the Fourth Plan, the Planning Commission set up in 1964 a 'Working Group on Libraries' under the chairmanship of V.K.R.V. Rao. The group formulated over-all policies, priorities, and programmes of public library development and estimated the cost on it (during the fourth plan) to the tune of Rs. 30.99 crores as detailed below:

	Cateogory of library	Expenditure in Rs
1.	State Central Libraries	3,10,00,000.00
2.	District Libraries	10,00,00,000.00
3.	Block Libraries	13,75,00,000.00
4.	Branch and Subdivision Libraries	1,00,00,000.00
5.	Model Public Libraries	60.00,000.00
6.	Union Territories/other areas	1,60,00,000.00
7.	Training of Library personnel	40,00,000.00
8.	Library Division at centre and state Library Directorates	44,00,000.00
	Total	30,99,00,000.00

The Working Group recommended: (i) Creation of separate division/ branch for library affairs, (ii) Setting up a Directorate of Libraries in each state with a qualified Director, (iii) Constituting an All India Library Adisory Council with Union Minister of Education as Chairman, and (iv) establishment of three model public libraries in the country on the pattern of Delhi Public Library. The Group also prepared a Model Public Library Bill which was circulated by the government to the states for adoption. During the Fourth Plan period Raja Rammohun Roy Library Foundation was also set up (1972) as an autonomous organisation under the Department of Culture, Ministry of Education (now Ministry of Human Resource Development) for the development of public libraries in the country. The Foundation works in collaboration with State Library Planning Committees working in each state. Detailed description of the Foundation have been given in the appropriate chapter. The planning Commssion has also set up working Group on Libraries for Eight plans

G4 LIBRARY DEVELOPMENT IN STATES

In the field of library service in India nothing probably is more difficult than to ascertain and describe the present situation of library development in states owing to non-availability of a consolidated picture. An attempt has however been made below in this direction on the basis of information gathered from various sources. There are at present 26 states and 5 Union Territories in the country. All of these have their own library system, structure, and pattern of financial assistance. Eight of the states have enacted library legislation and rest are providing public library service without legislation. A brief description of existing situation can be discussed under the following heads;

(i) States with library legislation, and
(ii) States without library legislation.

G41 States with Library Legislation

The concept of legislation for libraries is a contribution of S.R. Ranganathan to Indian public libraries. He conceived the idea of library legislation more than sixty years ago. He drafted a Model Libraries Act which was discussed and approved at the first All Asia Conference held at Varanasi in 1930. According to M.A.Gopinath, "This Model Act is the seed out of which library legislation grow in India." The patrons of library legislation plead for its enactment and adoption by each state on the grounds that it (i) makes provision for essential financial support on gradually increasing basis; (ii) ensures proper and systematic development of public libraries on uniform pattern; and (iii) shields the growth of libraries against administrative and political changes.

In India, so far eitht states have enacted and adopted library legislation. These are, Tamil Nadu (Public Libraries Act of 1948); Andhra Pradesh (Public Libraries Act of 1960); Karnatka (Public Libraries Act of 1965); Maharashtra (Public Libraries Act of 1967) West Bengal (Public Libraries Act of 1979). In Haryana Kerala and Manipur also Public Libraries Acts has been passed in 1989, 1989 and 1988 respectively. In the succeeding pages an attempt has been made to describe public library situation in these states.

G 411 Andhra Pradesh

G4111 Introduction: Andhra Pradesh is one of the leading states which have developed a network of public libraries and built up a sound system of library services. Evidence is available that in this

In between are regional libraries, district central libraries, and branch libraries. A village library is also a branch library with part time workers. Library system in the state has been oragnised on the lines of the recommendations made by th Sinha Committee. Under the provision of the Act, a Directorate of Public Libraries was set up in 1961 to ensure the smooth functioning and administration of public library sytem in the state. Until 1967 the Director of Public Instruction remained the ex-officio Director of Libraries. In 1967 an independent Director of libraries was appointed. The Director of Libraries controls the entire library system in the state. He is Head of the Department of libraries, is under the direct control of Education Secretary and Controls the entrire public library system in the state. He is also the ex-officio Secretary of the State Library Committee of which the "Minister for Public Libraries" is the Chairman. This Committee, which advises the government on all matters relating to public libraries in the state, is composed of both official and non-official members. There are also *Zilla Granthalaya Sansthas* (District Libray Committees) in each district. The Librarian of the concerned *Zilla Granthalaya* (District Library) functions as ex-officio Secretary to the district library committee. District library committees control, supervise and manage libraries in their respective districts.

G4113 Pattern of Financial Assistance: The State Government bears major portion of expenditure on public libraries. In 1984-85 finance of libraries was approximately Rs. 356.03 lakhs out of which a sum of Rs. 152.12 lakhs was collected as cess and the state government gave a grant of Rs.204.91 lakhs. Public libraries in the state are financed from three sources viz., (1) Government grant (2) amount collected as cess by *Zilla Granthalya Sansthas* and (3) Library's own resources. For the purpose of receiving grants libraries are categorised under three catregories as under:

(A) The purely government libraries receive full financial assistance from the state government. These are State Central Libray, Regional Libraries and Moblile Library, Eluru.

(B) Libraries below regional level i.e. District Central Libraries, Branch Libraries, Village Libraries, Book Deposit Centres, and Mobile Riksha Libraries are partially financed by the state government fund and partially by the Library Fund maintained out of the amount collected as library cess. Pattern of assistance for these libraries is as under:

(i) The State renders full financial assistance to these libraries towards the salary of staff.

(ii) For other purposes, such as acquisition of books maintenace of Library etc. Finance come from Library Fund. In accordance with the provisions of the Act the Zilla Granthalaya Sansthas have been empowered to collect library cess on property tax in the form of surcharge. The amount received so is deposited in the appropriate account known as, 'Library Fund'. Donation from the public and regular and special grants from the government are also received. All these are deposited in 'Library Fund'. Amount accumulated so is spent on collection building, maintenance etc., of libraries of this category.

(C) Panchayat libraries, libraries managed by cooperative societies and private libraries are aided libraries. These receive grants from State Government, Zilla Granthalaya Sasmthas and also have their own resources.

G4114 Services and Other Activities: Public libraries in the state also act as cultural and recreational centres. Some of the libraries are equipped with film projectors and other audio-visual equipments. Literacy programmes, lectures, conferences, book exhibitions and group discussions are also frequently organised. The state has also brought out a bibliography of Telugu Books published with the help of National Library, Calcutta. Union catalogue of Telugu books and district catalogues of book are also compiled. Annual administration report of the Department is also brought out annually which provides elaborate information and statistics on library services. Since March 1973 the Director of Public Libraries has also been made ex-officio Registrar of Publications for implementing the provisions of the Registration of Books Act of 1867. One copy of every document published in the state is deposited by the publishers to the State Central Library under the provision of this act. Refresher courses for librarians of regional libraries and district libraries are also organised from time to time . The Department has also established links with schools. A scheme has been introduced to supply books from District Central Libraries to school student with an intension to inculcate reading habit among school children. State Central Library, Regional Libraries and some branch libraries maintain an exclusive text book section. These sections cater to the needs of college students as well. There are 22 branch libraries exclusively for women and 50 libraries with independent section for women readers. Children libraries are present in almost all the districts and many libraries have separate children section. The State Central Library has an impressive section and collection for the blind also. (For salient features see H432.)

G412 Haryana

Haryana is comparatively a smaller state. Public Library service is available in this state through the State Central Library (Ambala Cantt) and district libraries which have been set up in each district. These function under Department of education. esides, there are Municipal libraries set up by each Municipality. In 1989 Haryana Legislature passed Public Libraries Bill, the details of which is given in section H438.

G413 Karnataka

G4131 Introduction: The state of Karnataka is one of the leading states which has build up developed system of public libraries. Libraries existed in this state in ancient and medieval period. The Kings, ruleres, scholars and temples had rich collection of manuscripts. Later the Britishers established libraries in 19th century in Belgam, Dharwar and other places. In 1913 Sir M. Vishavashraiya recommended for the establishment of public libraries in the state which gave a momentum to public library movement in the state. The Karnataka Library Association was formed in 1929 but could not do much for the development of library Association. On the occasion of all India Congress Committee's at Belgam in December 1924 a national level Library Conference was organised to impress upon the public and the government the importance of public libraries. Karnataka is one of the eight Indian states which have adopted library legislation. Mysore Public Libraries Act was enacted in the year 1965 for establishing and maintaining a network of public libraries both in urban and rural aeras of the state. The act came into force with effect from 1st April, 1966.

G4132 Administration and Organisation: Under the provisions of Act Central Libraries have been set up in the state at state level, city level, and district level. Besides these there are many hundred branch libraries and grant-in-aid libraries. Apart from these there are village and other libraries. As prescribed under the act, City Central Libraries should be set up in all towns with a population of one lac and above. Likewise Destrict Central Libraries should be and have been set up in all the districts. Some of the district head-quarters have both City Central Libraries and District Central Libraries. In such cases District Central Libraries serve as administrative units. There should be a branch library for every 25,000 population under CCL and for every 5,000 population under DCL. Besides it,there is provision for setting up service stations for the population of 2,000-5,000 people. Mobile libraries are also working. The State Central Library renders centralised services to readers and libraries through (i) Copyright collection, (ii) State Library for blind, (iii) Bibliographic Bureau (iv) Bureau of Inter Library Loan, (v) Bureau of Technical servcice etc. The State Central Library, Bangalore is at the apex of library system. There are however no divisional libraries in the state and the City Central Libraries are directly under the supervision and control of State Central Library. District Central Libraries and other Subunits are also supervised and controlled by the SCL. Branch libraries are functioning under the CCLs and DCLs. In order to implement the provisions of the act a separate Department of Public Libraries has been set up at Banglore. The Director is Head of the Department of Public Libraries. He is the chief executive of public library services in the state. The State Library Authority manages the State Central Library and advices the government on matters relating to libraries, including administration. Local Library Authorities, such as District Library Authority and City Library Authority manage and Control public libraries in their areas.

G4133 Pattern of Financial Assistance: The State Central Library is financed from the goverment funds. Libraries at district and city level, including branch libraries are financed from 'Library Fund'. Under the provision of the act library cess is collected, for running these libraries, in the form of surcharge on property tax/land revenue. This surcharge is collected by the local body of the concerned district/city and deposited in Library Fund. The State Government supplement this amount. Aided libraries receive grant from government and Taluk and village libraries receive from the state government. Actual receipt and actual expenditure of the Department in 1985-86 was Rs. 2,32,10,89 and Rs.193,07,430 respectively.

G414 Kerala

Kerala Public Libraries Act was passed in 1989. Details and salient features of the Act is given in Chapter H. Existing library situation in the state has been discussed below:

G-4141. Introduction

The state of Kerala came into being on November 1, 1956. It was formed by integrating Malabar area of Madras State and the erstwhile states of Cochin and Travancore. Libraries have been set up in the state through individual initiative and public donation since the 19th century. The present State Central Library was set up at Trivandrum in 1847 due to the efforts of Public Library Society. It was handed over to the Travancore Government in 1898 and was given the status of State Central Libary in 1959. Other important libraries set up in nineteenth century are Kottayam Pubic Library, Kottayam (1858); Public Library, Eranakulam (1870) and Suganposhini Vayanasala, Vinchiyoor (1884). During 1917-18 the Travancore Government formulated rules for grant-in-aid for libraries to manage the affairs of 27 developed libraries under Education Department which existed in the state at that time. In the Cochin state the Government took initiative in starting libraries in village as early even before 1930. According to a report there were about 350 libraries in Travancore area in 1948-49 and about 250 libraries in Cochin area in 1946. Likewise in Malabar area (state) also about 500 libraries had been set up by 1955-56. The Kerala Library Association was formed in 1945 and started functioning under the name "All Travancore Granthasala Sanghom". It adopted the name of "Kerala Granthasala Sanghom" in 1956 and made significant contribution since then towards the development of library service in the state. The Association started functioning with 47 memberes in 1945 and now its membership has been increased to more than 3,000 libraries. S.R. Ranganathan and the Kerala Library Association made some concrete efforts towards enactment of Library legislation, S.R. Ranganathan prepared draft library bill for the state in 1946 and 1949, both on the request of the Government. The first attempt could not succeed owing to political change. The second attempt was hampered by the Kerala Library Association (Kerala Granthalaya Sanghom) as the Association felt that in the bill drafted by Ranganathan the activities of the association have been pruned. The state however, passed and enacted library legistation in 1989 (Salient features of Kerala Public Libraries Act have been given in Chapter H, Section 437).

G-4142. Organisation and Administration

The present state of Kerala was formed in 1956 by intergration of (i) Malabar region which was part of Madras state and (ii) the erstwhile states of Travancore and Cochin. Organisation structure and administrative set up of public libraries in the two areas/region are different from the another. In order to manage, administer and run library service in Malabar region a Local Library Authority was constituted under the provisions of Madras Public Libraries Act (1948) in 1951. The Authority was empowered to levy and collect library cess as surcharge on property and house tax and the State Government contributed an amount equal to the amount collected as cess. After the reorganisation of states and after the formation of the present constituent state of Kerala the state government split Malabar region into three revenue district, viz., Calicut, Cannanore and Palghat. Consequently three Local Library Authorities were constituted in 1959, one for each revenue district. These three authorities used to collect cess and organise library service in the area or district. In Travancore and Cochin area library service was under the Kerala Granthasala Sanghom (Kerala Library Association). Section 37 of the Kerala Public Libraries Act (1989), has provision that the Sanghom will be dissolved once the act is implemented, and its powers and liability will be vested in the State Library Council. As per the provisions of the Act, there shall also be constituted District Library Councils, and Taluk Library Unions for the purpose of organizing and administrating library service in each district and taluka respectively. These are also possibly yet to be constituted. The state central library at Trivandrum is run by the state Government. Rest of the libraries including a district central library function under the concerned library authority. There is no government—Taluka or Block level libraries, although taluka is covered by a library set up by voluntary organisations and local bodies. Branch or village libraries are also run. In all there are more than 4000 libraries in the state.

G415 Maharashtra

G4151 Introduction: In the state of Maharashtra, temple, other religious institutions, rulers and scholars must have their own libraries, but the concept of modern public libraries in the state is the contribution of Europeans, particularly the British. They established in Bombay a branch of Royal Asiatic Society (Now the Asiatic Society) in 1804 with a rich library. In 1830 the Bombay General Library was established.The library was open to all responsible citizen irrespective of caste, creed and religion. By the start of 20th century many significant libraries were set up in this area. Many Indians also took interest in establishment of libraries and reading room. V.G. Ketkar, D.W. Joshi, L.R. Phadnis, Justice M.R. Ranade, N.C. Kelkar, D.R. Gadgil, Vinayak Rao Bhuskonte, H. Deshpandey are some of the worth naming personalities. The Maharashtra Library Assosiation which was founded in 1920 has also been instrumental in spreading library movement in the state. Appointment of a Library Development Committee under the chairmanship of A.A.A. Fyzee by the Congress Ministry of Bombay in the year 1939 is a landmark in the history of library movement in this part of the country. The report of the committee, though considered late, (the report was submmitted in 1940 but considered after the country got independence) forms the backbone of library service in the state. Major cecommedations of the committee are (i) establishment of Central Library at Bombay and Regional Library at Pune, (ii) establisment of one library in each district and each Taluka, (iii) encouragement to local initiatve by the government by recognising private libraries for giving financial assistance subject to the condition that these libraries will allow free use of books etc. to all and sundry. The Government accepted and implemented the recommendations of Fyzee Committee and appointed a Curator of libraries to look after library service in the state. This arrangment worked till 1967. In 1967 the Legislative Assembly passed a Public Library Bill at its Nagpur session on 17-11-1967 and the Government enacted it. It came into force w.e.f. Ist May 1968. The act provides for a public library system on uniform pattern in all parts of the state. Salient features of the Act are as under:

(a) Establishment of a separate Department of Public Libraries (under Education) with a professional Director heading it.

(b) Establishment of State Central Library and Divisional Libraries at Government's expenditure.
(c) Constitution of a State Library Council to advice the Government on matters relating to library service and development.
(d) Constitution of District Library Committees in each district for advising the Government on Metters relating to public library development and service.
(e) Making it obligatory on the part of the State Government to provide every year an amount not less than 25 lakhs for the development of public libraries, besides administrative and establishment expenditure. No provision for collection library cess.
(f) There has been improvement in library service in the state, both qualitatively and quantitatively. Due to the encouragement received from the provision of the act number of aided libraries (run by voluntary organisations) have been increased. In

1981 total number of recognised public libraries were 2674 against 1499 in 1979 and 669 in 1970. This shows that library moverment is spreading in rural area fastly. Libraries have been set up in all the districts. These is no State Central Library but the Asiatic Society Library, which is also a depository library functions as State Central Library.

G4152 Administration and Organisation: Director of Libraries is the Head of the Department of public library services. He is responsible for planning, maintainance and organisations of public library services in the state. There is one Assistant Director in each of the 5 divisions to assist the Director. The Government has set up a State Library Council to advise it on matters relating to public libraries, with Minister Incharge of Education as the Chairman, Director of Libraries as Member Secretary. Representatives of State Library Association and Local bodies are also on the Council. At district level District Library Committees have been set up for each district under the provision of the Act. The Chairman of the Education Section in *Zilla Parishad* (District Board) is the chairman of the District Library Committee and Education officer of the District is Member Secreatry.

G4153 Pattern of Financial Assistance: Under the provisions of the Act the State Government is obliged to provide a sum not less than

25 lakhs for library development. This does not include administrative and establishment expenditure. Libraries upto divisional level are fully financed by the Government and for all practical purposes these may be termed as "Government Libraries", Libraries below divisional level have been set up by private initiative. These receive grant in aid on the Condition that they shall provide free library service and allow free access to the library for all. For receiving grant from the Government a library must be a 'recognised' library, which means it must get itself registered under Registration of Society Act 1860 or Bombay Public Turst Act 1950 under a local body such as Municipality, Grampanchayat etc. For receiving grant-in-aid such libraries have been grouped under A-D catagories on the basis of book stock, membership etc. as per the following table:

Category	Booksd	Periodicals	Newspapers	Members
A	15000	50	15	300
B	5000	15	5	100
C	1000	5	3	50
D	100	5	3	25

Libraries of these four categories receive 75% of the admissible expenditure incurred by them in the previous year subject to a maximum of:

Category	Districts	Taluka	Others
A	Rs. 30,000	Rs. 16,000	Rs. 12,000
B	Rs. 16,000	Rs. 12,000	Rs. 8,000
C	–	Rs. 6,000	Rs. 4000
D	–	–	Rs. 1,000

In addition to this, grant for building, for running circulating libraries, incentive grant for reaching higher category etc. are also made available to libraries. The Government on the recommendation of the State Library Council, also gives grant for such special purposes as organising functions, seminars, celebrations etc. Regular grant-in-aid is also given to State and dirtrict level library associations.

G4154 Services: Library service has been extended in the state to rural areas by establishing conventional, mobile, and circuating libraries etc. Book exhibition and special functions are also organised by the Directorate and the libraries. Bibliography of Marathi Books has also been compiled. Care is taken to preserve and extnd the use of manuscripts and rare books. The Directorate also sponsors training programmes for librarians (certificate level). Some of the libraries have been supplied with a jeep to facilitate the work of circulating library centres.

For Salient features of the Act, see Chapter H.

G416 Manipur

(For salient features of the Act, please see Chapter H

G-417. Tamil Nadu

G4171 Introduction: The State of Tamil Nadu came into being in 1947. Prior to 1969 it was known as Madras State. On 1st January 1969 its name was changed to Tamil Nadu. It has a rich tradition of libraries. Saraswati Mahal Library was set-up by the Maharaja of Tanjaur at Tanjaur as early as 1800 A.D. The Government Oriental Manuscript Library was set-up at Madras in 1837 and Adyar Library, Adyar (Madras) in 1886. These libraries, which were set-up as manuscript libraries, are still the pride of the nation. In 19th century some other libraries, keeping printed books were also opened, such as Madras Literary Society Library (1818), and Connemara Library, which named after the then Governor of Madras, became the State Central Library under Madras Public Libraries Act. It is also necessary to mention the role of Madras Library Association in developing library movenment in the State. The Association was founded in 1928 with K.V. Krisnaswami Ayyar as President and S.R. Ranganathan and S.M.Fossil as Secretaries. They toured the area extrensively and popularised library movement though library exhibitions and other methods. The Association also organised travelling library services, and library services to prisons, hospitals etc. Owing to the efforts of the Association and its office bearers, especially S.R. Ranganathan, Madras Public Libraries Act was passed and enacted. It became effective from 1st April, 1950. Tamil Nadu is the first Indian State to pass and adopt library legislation. The Association and its office bearers had to struggle a lot for its adoption They started their effort in 1929 and as early as in 1931 they had submitted to the then Governor a draft Bill. Since then they never looked back until the Goverment enacted Library Act in 1948. Thus the Act is the fruit of the seed which bore result after 19 years. Library Associations and their office bearers in other states without library legislation should receive inspiration from the efforts made by the Madras Library Association and should not be disheartened if their first or successive attempts have not received desired attention of the concerned Goverments.

G 4172 Organisation and Administration: The State has a well knit system of libraries. The State Central Library (Connemara Public Library) is at the apex. It also receives one copy of each book pubished in India under Delivery of Books Act and one copy of each book published in the State under the provisions of the Madras P.L. Act. Next in the chain are district libraries, branch libraries and village libraries. A district library may obtain books from the State Central Library and the branch libraries from district libraries. The State has a Directorate of Public Libraries headed by a director who is the Executive Head of library services under the general control of the Education Department. The Director of Libraries superintends, directs and runs public library service. Library Committees have been set up for managing libraries at each level. There is one local Library Authority for the city of Madras, and one Local Library Authority for each revenue disrict, except Kanyakumari District. It consists of representatives of elected bodies, such as Municipalities, Panchayats etc. and some members nominated by the Government. The Members elect Chairman from amongst themselves. There is one District Lirary Officer in each district attached to the Authority. With this group, the Local Library Authorities run library service through Disrict Central Libraries and its service points, e.g., Branch Libraries etc. There are now 15 Local Library Authorities one in each district (The Act is not effective in Kanyakumari District and Shencoltah Taluk of Taruhelveli district), 15 District Central Libraries and about 1500 Branch Libraries. A branch library can be opened with a ful-time librarian in a village with a population of 5,000 and above. Delivery stations can be started in a village with a population of 1,000. These will be looked after by a school teacher or anyone else. interested in the job, on part-time basis. Some honorarium is paid to such service minded persons. It is learnt that some school students may be engaged for taking books to the doorsteps of the citizen. These boys are authorised to collect a nominal monthly charge for this service and to keep the collected amount with them. Besides these, there are mobile libraries, libraries for special category, and aided libraries also.

G4163 Pattern of Financial Assistance

(a) The State Central Library and Kaurmani Nilayam Library, are Government libraries and are fully financed and maintained by the Government.

(b) Libraries under Local Library Auttorities are financed and maintained from Library Fund. Each Local Library Authority is empowered under the Act to collect library cess in the form of surcharge on property tax or house tax. The sum collected thus is deposited in Library Fund. The Government gives matching grant equal to the amount collected as cess.

(c) Aided libraries receive grants from time to time depending upon their stock, staff and services.

G418 West Bengal

The State of West Bengal has a rich tradition of public libraries. Europeans were the first to set-up public library-like institutions in Calcutta, though entry in these was slightly restricted. East India Company opened a library in its factory at Hooghly in seventeenth century. Christian Missionaries also had their own libraries. Some important libraries opened in 19th century are (i) Library of Asiatic Society of Bengal, (ii) Rajnarayan Basu Memorial Library (1851), (iii) Hooghly public Library (1854), (iv) Uttarpada Public Library (1858), (v) Konnagar Public Library (1858), (vi) Joynagar Public Library(1859), (vii) Krishanagar Public Library (1869), (viii) Srirampur Public Library (1871), (ix) Chandannagar Public Library (1873), Shivpur Public Liibrary (1874), (xi) Baranagar Public Library (1876), (xii) Bagbazar Library (1883), (xiii) Bansbedia Public Library (1891) etc. West Bengal Library Association was formed in 1925 and since then it has been instrumental in developing library movement in the State. Mainly due to the efforts of the Association library legislation was passed and enacted in the State in 1979. Salient features of West Bengal Public Libraries Act (1979) is as under:

(1) no provision for levying library cess.

(2) provision to create a Directorate of Libraries with a professionally qualified Director, who will manage the Central Library and its branches, and shall also superintened and direct library service in the state.

(3) provision for constituting State Library Council with Minister in-charge of library services as Chairman and Director of Library as Secretary. This will act as an Advisory Committee on Public Libraries and will render adivise to the government on all matters relating to library system, development and organisation.
(4) provision for constitution of Local Library Authority in each revenue district with Destrict Magistrate as Chairman and District Library Officer (professional) as Secretary.
(5) provision for appointing District Library Officer in each district.
(6) modification of Press and Registration Act of 1867 with a view to ensure the deposit of one free copy to the State Central Library by the publishers.

Library services in West Bengal fall under Education Department. A separate Directorate of Libraries has been created.

There is no provision for collection of cess by Local Library Authorities. The Government Libraries are fully financed and managed by the State government. Grants are released to libraries according to their categories e.g. Sponsored Libraries, District Libraries, Town/ Block Libraries, Area Libraries, and Rural Libraries.

G-42. States without Library Legislation

There are no two opinions on the importance of library legislation. It is certainly important for uniform, systematic and successful growth of public library service. Most of the Indian States are deprived of an act relating to libraries. This however, does not mean that (i) proper growth of libraries is "not possible" in the absence of legislative support; and (ii) no effort has been made towards drafting and passing library bill in many of the States. As a matter of fact some of the States are carrying library service satifactorily without library legislation. But things can certainly improve with legislative support, particularly in a developing country like ours where due to political and administrative changes instablity prevails in many quarters. Even in advanced countries, public library legislation has played significant role in systematic development and balanced growth of public librariies. An attempt has been made in the following pages to describe public library situation in some of the states which are running library service without enactin library legislation

G-421. Assam

G-4211. Introduction

In the state of Assam the first public library, namely the Government Public Library was started by the British Government. In 1956 it was merged with the State Central Library. All Assam Public Library Association (Sadau Assam Puthibharal Sangha) was formed in 1938 on the initiative taken by Kumudeshawar Barthakur. However, public library service in Assam was started in real sense during the first Five Year Plan. The Assam Government took steps to organise library service in 1954-55 on the lines suggested by Sinha Committee. A State Central Library was established in Shillong, the then capital of Assam. By the end of 1955 seven District Libraries were established. The State Central Library of Assam was shifted to Gauhati in 1974, the then capital of Assam. It has a branch now in the present state capital, Dispur. The state has not enacted a legislation in respect of public libraries, although attempts were made several times in this direction. For instance, on the request of the Assam Library Association Dr. S.R. Ranganathan prepared a Draft Public Library Bill for the State which was discussed, approved and recommended for acceptance of the Government by the Assam Library Association at its Eighth Conference held at Gauhati in 1964 J. Sarmah and R.L.Mittal also prepared and sent to the government an other draft Bill in 1971. Enactment of library legislation in the state has been recommended from various plateforms but the government has not taken any decision in this respect. The Government, however recently (1984) created the post of a Director of Libraries under the Education Department.

G-4212. Organisation and Administration

The State Central Library at Gauhati is at the apex of the state's library system. Next in the link are District Libraries and Subdivisional Libraries. There are also book mobiles with about one hundred service or book deposite centres. The Director of Libraries is the overall Incharge of the libraries under Education Department. The State Central Librarian was functioning almost as the Director before the post of Director was created. The libraries in the state are however not under administrative control of one department. For instance, there are labraries (village) set up and administered by Community Development Offices/Blocks, and private libraries set up and administered by trusts/institutions.

G-4213. Pattern of Financial Assistance

Government libraries, i.e., State Central Library with a branch, District Libraries, Subdivisional Libraries and Mobiles Libraries with 100 deposit centres are financed by the Government. Libraries have also been set up in villages under Community Development Programme of the government. Libraries run by trusts etc. are aided libraries receiving varying amount from the government as grant.

G-4214. Services

Public libraries in Assam, particularly the State Central Library, are rendering commendable service even in the absence of library legislation. The State Central Library has separate childern's section. It has been publishing Assamese Section of Indian National Bibliography and has published bibliography on libraries of the state and nearby areas. Book Mobile services are also organised. Almost all of its districts and subdivisions have been covered by library service, though it will take some time for the government to extend required library services to villages and blocks. Book collection of district level libraries is impressive (ranging from 20,000 to 70,000), but the subdivisional level libraries have small collection (ranging from 5,000 to 20,000).

G 422 Bihar

G-4221. Introduction

Bihar is one of the Indian states which is famous for her cultural and literary heritage. Nalanda, Vikramshila and Taxshila had magnificent libraries. Good collection of manuscripts was made in Bihar even before the dawn of Christian era. Besides, there were good collections of manuscripts etc. of kings and landlords. The first public library-like institution was set up in 1855 in Gaya. On the visit of Sir Federic James Halliday, the then Lieutenant Governor of Bengal, the citizen of Gaya decided to establish a public library by public donation and contribution. The Union Club and Library was set up in Hazaribagh, and Bihar Hitaishi Pustakalaya in Patna City in 1882 and 1883 respectively. Most important year in the history of library development in Bihar is 1891 when the Khuda Bux Khan Oriental Public Library of Patna was opened to the public. The library was previously owned by Maulavi Muhammad Bux Khan. After his death he left behind splendid collection of manuscripts. During the first half of 20th century many good public libraries were opened by private and collective initiative. Importing among these are Nagri Pracharini Sabha Library, Arrah (1901); Manu Lal Library, Gaya (1911), Bhagwan Pustakalaya, Bhagalpur (1913); Town Hall Municipal Library, Muzaffarpur (1919); Bihar Hindi Pustakalaya, Bihar Sharif (1920); Sinha Library, Patna (1924); Ram Mohan Roy Library, Chaibasa (1929); Hind Library, Giridih (1936) etc. Bihar Library Association was founded in 1936. It changed its name to Bihar Rajya Pustakalaya Sangh in 1955. The first Conference of the Association was held at Gaya in 1937. Kumar M.N. Deb Ray Mahashaya presided over. The Conference desired the Association to prepare a draft scheme for development of libraries in Bihar. The scheme was prepared and submitted to the Government in 1938, recommending setting up of a chain of libraries from State Central Library to village libraries. Later, All India Library Conference was held at Patna in 1940. This Conference also stressed that the government should accept the recommendations of 1937 Conference. Many attempts were made in future also but of not much avail. In 1973 R.S.P. Singh prepared and submitted to the government a draft bill. In 1976-77 Bihar Government invited the comments of P.N. Kaula on the draft library bill. No progress had been made in this direction. Bihar is one of the three Indian states in which the State Central Library (Sinha Library) is not a government library but managed by a trust/-body. The other two states are Madhya Pradesh and Gujarat. There are about 5000 libraries which receive full or partial assistance from the government. These have been set up by the government or trust/institution/agencies at various levels such as state library, divisional libraries, special or distinguished libraries, district libraries, subdivisional libraries, block libraries, and village libraries. There are some unaided libraries also.

G 4222 Organisation and Administration

There is no library system in the state. Every library functions in isolation or as an independent entity. Therefore the State Library (Sinha Library) is not functioning as the State Central Library. Public library service in the state is looked after, controlled and administered by the Education Commissioner. The Director of Higher Education is incharge of library services. The Education Department has created a separate office of Superintendent of Libraries in order to coordinate library services at various levels and to see that the decisions of the Government in the field of public libraries are implemented. Shri N.P. Gaur, the former Librarian of Sinha Library and a librarian of International repute, writes in this context, "The Superintendent of Libraries for Bihar, who is Chief Executive administering the public libraries in the state, has ever since the creation of this post— more than 20 years (now 40 years) ago (in 1950-51)— been a non pfofessional, without any library or entation. Further, this post has always been treated as a transit camp for a class one officer of the Education Department, who had, in most cases, been on his way to some stable assignment." The position is still the same. The government has not framed rules for running libraries. Decisions on specific issues are taken when situation arises. At state level the "State Library Planning Committe" with its three subcommittees (Planning, Book Section, and Distribution) made vital recommendations on the matters relating to library development. The Education Commissioner is ex-officio Chairman and the Superintendent of Libraries is ex-officio Secretary of the Committees In each district,- there are library committees headed by the District Megistrate and District Education Officer as Secretary. At Subdivision level also there is a Subdivisional Committee. District Education Officers send their recommendations to the Superintendent of Libraries who obtains the orders of the Education Commissioner through the Director of Higher Education and Joint Secretary Education.

G-4223. Pattern of Financial Assistance

The state normally spends about 20 lakhs rupees on public libraries. The entire expenditure on salary of staff, purchase of books and periodicals, furniture, maintenance etc. is borne by the state government for State Central Library, divisional libraries and a few district libraries. Rest of the libraries including the remaining district libraries, all subdivisional libraries, block libraries and all village libraries are aided libraries and receive assistance in the form of books, furniture, and a nominal amount. The Management Committees of these libraries are expected to run library service out of their own resources, which is supplemented partially by the insufficient government grant. Small libraries situated in a subdivisional or district town also are known as village/rural libraries. So the term rural/village reveals the status of a libraries for the purpose of receiving grant under various schemes.

G-4224. Library Service

As mentioned in the preceding pages, every library in the state works as independent entity. The government naturally, keeping in view the meagre assistance to these libraries, can not pressurise the aided libraries to provide a standard and fruitful library service. The government does not seem to have taken major step in this direction. For instance, there were 5 Government district libraries out of 17 districts in 1970. These were fully financed by the Government. Each Government district library was provided with a mobile library van for circulating books in the district. If we consider the present position we shall find that though the number of districts have increased from 17 in 1970 to 39 in 1990, yet there are still only 5 Government district libraries in the state. In rest of the districts some private libraries have been given the status of district library and such libraries receive a nominal grant in form of books, furniture and meagre assistance against salary for one-two staff. Mobile vans were also withdrawn from the 5 government district libraries long back. It shows that in Bihar library service has practically declined.

G-423. Gujarat

G-4231. Introduction

The state of Gujarat came into being in 1960, comprising of (i) erstwhile Baroda and Saurashtra states (ii) Kuch region, and some area of former Bombay state. It has a rich tradition of public library service. Gujarat Vidya Sabha Library was founded as manuscript During 19th century many important libraries in the state. These are Raichand Deep Chand Library, Baroach (1855): Long Library, Rajkot (1856); Government Library, Junagarh (1867); Town Library, Rajkot (1868); Aparao Bholanath Library, Ahmedabad (1873); Barton Library, Bhavanagar (1882); Dehi Laxmi Library, Nadiad (1892) etc.

Gujarat is the first Indian state to have a fully developed public library system. Maharaja M.S. Gaekwad III of Baroda, who had declared compulsory elementary education in his state in 1907, brought an Americal Librarian, namely William allenson Borden. A State Department of Libraries was created and Borden was made its Director. By the year 1910 he organised free public library service in the state with a well knit network of public libraries which included conventional libraries, mobile libraries, and cinema libraries. Motibhai Amin, a school teacher, who took interest in public library development was made incharge of rural library service under Borden. The work of Borden was continued by N.M. Dutt, T.D. Wakins etc. Library development in the state received a set-back in the year 1933 when the enlightened ruler passed away. Gujarat Library Association was formed in 1939. On the request of professionals of the state, S.R. Ranganathan prepared draft library bill for the state twice in 1944 and 1964. The state of Gujarat is carrying the tradition of Maharaja Sayaji Rao Gaekwad III even without library legislation. It has set up State Central libraries (two : one at Ahmedabad in Gujarat Vidyapeeth and other at Braoda), district libraries in all the districts and subdivisional (Taluka) libraries in many of the talukas. Many villages are covered by library service. There are three main agencies engaged in providing library service (i) State Government (ii) Autonomous bodies and (iii) Voluntary agencies. Municipal corporations Municipalities and other local bodies are also running commendable library service. For instance, the Municipal Library of Ahmedabad can be compared with any public library of similar status in the country in respect of collection, maintenance, building, and services. It is much better than many of our state Central libraries even so far as service, collection and building is concerned.

G-4232. Organisation and Administration

Gujarat is one of the three Indian states with more than one State Central libraries. One is library of Gujarat Vidyapeeth which is an aided library and also functions as a public library. It has been given the status of State Central Library. The second Central library is at Baroda and a branch has been set up at Gandhinagar, the capital. District libraries have been set up by the government in all the district headquarters. Many of the Talukas (subdivisions) have government libraries. Some District libraries are provided with mobile library vans for catering to the needs of the district and for extending library service to the masses. Government also give grants to voluntary libraries. Library service is the responsibility of Education Department under which the office of Curator of Libraries look after library service. Labraries run by the state government are state central libraries, district libraries which are one in each district, and, tluka libraries. Libraries have also been set up in tribal areas. The Central Library at Baroda receives Gujarati and other books published in the state as it is a depository library. Rest of the libraries are aided. There are district branch libraries, town libraries, women libraries, children's libraries, and village libraries. The Curator of Libraries controls government public libraries. Grants to aided libraries are also supervised by the Curator's Office. The libraries of local self government such as, Municipal Libraries are administered by the concerned municipalities. Aided or grant-in-aid libraries are administered by their parent organisation/trust etc. Curator of Libraries is assisted by four regional officers designated as Assistant Curator of Libraries. Each Assistant Curator looks after the libraries in four to five district. The librarian of Central Library of Baroda assists the Curator of Libraries in technical matters.

G-4233. Pattern of Financial Assistance

Government Libraries such as, Central libraries, district libraries and taluka libraries are fully financed by the government. Municipal libraries are fully financed by the municipalities and are also aided libraries. Other grant aid libraries run by the voluntary organisations receive partial financial assistance. Assistance to such libraries is made available by the government on the basis of population being served by the libraries, subject to the condition that at least 25% of the expenditure is to be borne by the organisation running the library. In other words grant may be made available to these libraries to the maximum of 75% of their total approved expenditure. Grant is given only to recognised libraries. Recognised libraries are those that are registered under the Public Trust Act.

The state of Gujarat has expanded library service from state capital to village level. Mobile service, special libraries for women and special libraries for children also exist. The State Government and library Association also organise from time to time conferences and training programme for libraries. The two states library associations, viz. Cujarat Pustkalaya Mandal and Granthalaya Seva Sangh are making sincere efforts to propagate library movement in the state also popular.

G424. Madhya Pradesh

G4241 Introduction

In the state of Madhya Pradesh the rulers of the princely state had their private libraries, but the first public library was opened in Indore in 1954. Among other old libraries of the state the name of Madhav Pustakalaya of Gwalior (1899) and Yuvaraj Sarwajanik Pustakalaya of Ujjain (1914) can be enumerated. These libraries were set up by voluntary efforts. The first government library of the state is the central library of Gwalior which was set up by the Britishers in 1927. In 1946 S.R. Ranganathan prepared draft library bill for the central provinces but nothing came out of it. The matter was also discussed at the Eighth All India Library Conference held in Nagpur in 1949 and at Madhya Pradesh Library Conference held at Bhopal in 1957. The Madhya Pradesh Library Association was formed in 1957. and the 1957 Conference was organised by the Association as its first conference. The state however could not adopt library legislation as yet. It has a State Central Library, but it is not fully owned by the government. The state is providing library service through Regional, District, Subdivisional and village libraries etc.

C4242 *Administration and Organisation*

Library service in the state is scattered in the absence of library legislation. Administrative supervision finance and maintenance of public libraries is the responsibility of three different departments in the state as indicated below:

(i)	Library service in urban area	–	Department of Education
(ii)	Library service in rural area	–	Department of Panchayat and Social Welfare
(iii)	Library service in tribal area	–	Department of Harijan and Tribal Welfare

So far as urban libraries are concerned district level libraries and administered by the concerned District Education Officers under the overall control of the D.P.I. The state has a Chief Librarian also who inspects Regional Central Libraries and District Libraries and provides technical assistance/advise to public libraries as well as school and college libraries. Libraries in rural areas and libraries in tribal areal areas are looked after by different departments as indicated above.

G4243 Pattern of Financial Assistance:

State Central Library, regional central libraries and district libraries are fully financed by the Government. Rest are aided libraries.

G-425. Meghalaya

History of libraries in Meghalaya may be traced back to 1903 when the earstwhile state of Assam established a Government Public Library in Shillong. Later the Government of Assam established in 1954 a State Central Library at Shillong and a Government Public Library at Omalgama. Shillong was then part of Assam. The State of Meghlaya came into being on 21st January, 1972. Assam State formally handed over the Government Public Library to the Government of Meghalaya on January 19, 1974. The State Central Library of Meghalaya has now emerged as a worth seeing library with beautiful building, magnificent collection and useful service. The State also runs district librâries and mobile libraries.

G-426. Punjab

During the past many libraries were set-up in Punjab (undivided) due to the encouragement and patronage of the Britishers and kings, philanthropists and library professionals. Maharaja Ranjit Singh, Dayal Singh Majithia, Lala Lajpat Rai, Sir Ganga Ram, Asa Don Dickinson, R.C. Manchanda, G.L. Trehan and R.L. Bhatia played significant role in spreading library movement in the state in undivided Punjab. Maharaja Ranjeet Singh had set-up many libraries in his State, in 1896 Dayal Singh Majithia set-up a turst for running a public library and established Dayal Singh Library in Lahore (then in undivided India) in 1908. This was later shifted to Delhi. It is one of the eminent public libraries in Delhi. Sir Ganga Ram and Lala Lajpat Rai also set-up libraries in Lahore in 1920s. Punjab Library Association was formed in 1916 by Asa Don Dickinson, an American librarian who was invited to organise Punjab University Library at Lahore.

Public libraries function in the state under various departments. For example, Director of Public Instruction (celleges) under the overall control of Education department manages State Central, special and district libraries. Muncipalities and Panchayats also run libraries under their direct administrative control. Likewise there are public libraries run by Public Relation Depatment and by private institutions. The budget of Department of Education for public libraries in the year 1986-87 was Rs. 5 lakhs.

G-427. Rajasthan

G-4271. Introduction

The State of Greater Rajasthan came into being in 1950. On Novermber 1, 1956 it was given the name of Rajasthan. Rajasthan has a rich tradition of library service. There were manuscript libraries of Jain monks even in fourteenth century, but these cannot be considered public libraries. Maharaja Sawai Jai Singh, who founded Jaipur city, was a great lover of books. He also had his private library, housing a good cellection of manuscripts and printed books. Other rulers of various States of Rajasthan also set up libraries, such as Rajgranthalaya (Govrnment Library), Udaipur; Anoop Sanskrit Library and Palace Library at Bharatpur and Jodhpur etc. Modern library service in the State is a contribution of Maharaja Sawai Ram Singh II who established Maharaja Public Library at Jaipur in 1866. Thus dawn of library service in the State can be dated back to about half a century ago than that of dawn of library reevice in the erstwhile Baroda State. Maharaja Sawai Ram Singh invited a British Librarian, Sir Frank Alexander to organise library service. Printed catalogues of books kept in the library were also brought out many times since 1883. The Maharaja Sarvajanik Pustakalay/Public Library functions now as the district library of Jaipur. Sir Mirza M.Ismail, The Dewan of Jaipur State also made singnifiant contribution to the grtowth of this library. During early 20th century many public libraries viz., Sethia Jain Library (1913), Bikaner; Abhay Jain Library (1921); Bikaner; Sammati Library (1920) were set-up. Rajasthan Library Association was formed in 1962. The Association has generally taken interest in promoting library movement.

G-4272. Organisation and Administration

Public library in the State, till 1954 were looked after by the Department of Art and Culture. Presently these are functioning under the control of Education Department. The Deputy Director of Social Education, under the control of Director of Education, Bikaner, is the incharge of public library services. The State Central Librayry is at Jaipur. The librarian of States Central Library inspects divisional/district libraries. There are also aided libraries and municipal libraries.

G-4273. Pattern of Financial Assistance

All the govrnment libraires, viz., State Central Library, divisional libraries, district libraries and Tehsil Libraries are fully financed and maintained by the State Government. Other libraries are grant-in aid. In the seventh plan the State planed to spend 13.5 crores on development libraries, including an establishment of a Directorate of Libraries, but it remained a dream only.

G-428. Tripura

G-4281. Introduction: The State of Tripura attained full statehood on 21st January, 1972. During past the kings of the erstwhile Tripura State established a few libraries. One of such libraries is Birchand State Central Library. This library was set-up by Maharaja Bir Chandra Manikya Bahadur in 19th century. In 1953 it was taken over by the Government and in 1973 it was made State Central Library. Presently the State is rendering library service through State Central Library, district libraries, sub-divisional libraries, and block libraries All these are Government libraries and one moblie library is also being run by the Education Directorate.

G-4282. Organisation and Administriation: Director of Higher Education is the Chief Administrator of library services. Under his supervision the Head Librarian (of State Central Library) supervises and inspects the work of lower category libraries. A mobile library with its three units is managed by Social Education Section unde the control fo Director of Higher Education. This service has been provided with a view to cater to the needs of villagers.

G-4283. Pattern of Financial Assistance: All the libraries are Government libraries. These are naturally fully fianaced by the Government. State's bubget on public library is normally Rs.6 lakhs.

G-4291. Uttar Pradesh

G-42921. Introduction: The State of Uttar Pradesh has rich tradition of libraries. Many important libraries were opened in the nineteenth century. Some of these are, Raja Rampur Library, Rampur; Nagri Pracharnini Sabha Library, Varanasi; Allahabad Public Library, Allahabad; Canerchia Library, Varanasi; Bharti Bhawan Library, Allahabad etc. Interest of the British in library development is reflected in the following circular issued on 19-4-1869 (as mentioned by Sohan Singh in History of Adult Education during Biritish Period): "With a view to encourage village and other teachers to imporve ihemselves by private reading out of school hours, the Director wishes that each Deputy Inspector should have a library of useful and interesting vernacular books to be lent to teachers to read. With the sanction of the Chief Commissioner, he, therefore, proposes to grant Rs. 50 per annum to each Deputy Inspector to purchase books". Sohan Singh, while mentioning the development of libraries in Uttar Pradesh, during British period writes: "The Government of Uttar Pradesh gave as much attention to the spread of literacy as to... a system of libraries and reading room. On the first literacy day (1938) 768 libraries and 3,600 reading rooms were opened in rural areas. The number of libraries was increased to 1,000 in 1940-41 and 1,040 in 1941-42. 40 additional libraries were opened for women in 1940-41...Besides the libraries opened by the Govrnment, grants were given to about 500 private libraries in rural areas". The Teachers Handbook of Social Education (1953) brought out by Government of India indicates: "The 104 village libraries and 3,600 reading rooms, established in the pevious period (1939-42) carried on their work. The libraries continued to issue from 16 to 17 lakhs of books in a year including half a lakh to women... In 1942-43, the Government started a Central Lending Library at Allahabad." After inpependence the Uttar Pradesh Government reported "For the maintenance of literacy the Government of Uttar Pradesh had earlier established 1,0040 libraries (which inculded 40 libraries for women) and 3,600 reading rooms. Again in 1950 the Panchayat Raj Department set-up 6,796 reading rooms and 3,754 librares. There were also 277 Rural Development libraries." (from All India Report of Social Education for 1947-51) The Department of Education, Government of Uttar Pradesh also set-up a Government Central Provincial Library in 1949 at Allahabad and authorised it to receive books under Press and Registration Act of 1867. This library was made Central State Library of Uttar Pradesh in 1958. Eight District Libraries were opened during second plan period in Agra, Almora, Bareilly, Gorakhpur, Jhansi, Kanpur, Mathura and Meerut. Three more District libraries were opened in Pithoragarh, Uttarkashi and Varanasi in the third plan period. By the end of fifth plan, there were 54 District libraries. In Uttar Pradesh libraries are looked after and run by various departments. The Sinha (Advisory) Committee reported the picture in 1957 as, "At least 7 Departments, namely, The Education Planning and Development,Social Welfgare, Panchayat Raj, Harijan Sahayak, Information and Labour are interested in libraries in Uttar Pradesh". The Department of Education however, has been the major Department so far as library service is concerned. Uttar Pradesh Library Association was founded is 1937. In spite of many efforts made by the professionals and U.P.L.A. the Government could not take decision about enacting library legislation in the State due to which library service in this vast and populated State is not very encouraging. Library services are under various Departments, but major public library service is run and maintained under the over-all control of the Education Secretary An Officer on Special Duty (Libraries) controls, superivises and inspects public libraries. The State Central Library is at Allahabad and not at the state headquarter. There are District librararies out of which some are Government libraries and some are aided libraries. Town libraries and village libraries are also aided. Eduction Department also renders assistance to Education Extension Libraries (housed in primary schools), which are bout 1400.

In Uttar Pradesh praise worthy development of public libraries has taken place.

G-43. Analysis of the Situation

We have different types of libraries in the States and Union Territories; viz., State Central Library, Divisional Libraries, Village Libraries, Branch Libraries, mobile libraries ect. As far as State Central or State Library is concerned, all the States and Union Territories except Delhi, Lakshadweep and Sikkim have set-up State Central Library in their respective States. Two State Central Libraries viz., Connemara Public Library (Madras) and Asiatic Society Library (Bombay) are Depository Liibraries also under the Delivery of Books Act. One State/ Union Territory normally has one State library, but Dadra and Nagar Haveli, Gujarat, and Jammu & Kashmir have two State Libraries each. In three States, viz., Bihar (Sinha Library, Patna). Gujarat (Gujarat Vidyapeeth, Ahmedabad) and Madhya Pradesh (Maulana Azad Library, Bhopal) the State Central Libaries are not Government libraries, but run by trusts/autonomous bdies. Some of the Indian states have set-up Divisional Librearies which are supposed to enjoy higher status than that of

District Libraries. These are also known as Regional Libraries. Divisional/Regional Libraries have been set-up in the States of Andhra Pradesh, Bihar, Dadra & Nagar Haveli, Gujarat, Jammu & kashmir, Madhya Pradesh, Maharashtra and Rajasthan. These may be called upgraded district libraries. District libraries have been set-up in all states, but not compulsorily in all districts. Some of the district libraries and majority of libraries below district level in the country except in the South, are aided libraries. The same is the case with Sub-divisonal Libraries which are known as Taluka libraries in the South.and Tehsil libraries in the West are aided libraries.

Facts presented above will reveal that most of the states except Sikkim and Lakshadweep have set-up State Central Libaries. District Libraries have also been established in most of the district headquarters with a few exceptions. The district level libraries are not in all cases Government libraries. Most of them are aided libraries. Pattern of library organisation below district level is not uniform. In South, we find Branch Libraries, in the West Taluka Libraries, in the North Tehsil libraries, in the East Sub-divisional libraries. Branch Libraries do not conform to any particular geographical entity or area. A Branch Library may be located in Panchayat headquarters or in Block headquarters, in an urban Centre or in a village. District Library Authorities may plan and establish Branch Libraries in different localities. In some States, particularly in the Northern and Eastern India, the State Governments are taking initiative to extend library services to sub-divisional level. But in those states where library services have developed considerabl, such as West Bengal, Kerala etc., libraries have grown mainly by private initiative Once established the State Governments have come forward to help the libraries with some financial assistance. Hence we see many grant-in-aided libraries in these States. It is difficult to identify these libraries with any geographical unit such as Sub division and block. There is another categorisation of public libraries viz. Urban/Town and rural. Municipal libraries may be classified as urban libraries. Rural libraries in may areas are organised by voluntary organisations.

H

Library Legislation

H1 DEFINITION

By library legislation is meant a legislation enacted and enforced by a state for running and maintaining public library services within its terretorial jurisdiction. Library legislation is therefore an instrument for development of public libraries in a planned manner.

H2 NEED

The following facts emphasise the need of library legislation

H21 Planned Development

Explaining the concept of library movement Dr. S.R. Ranganathan emphasized the fact that library movement does not imply the opening of small and big libraries here and there; it insinuates a well knit network of libraries in which libraries of various level are connected with each other and are run in a planned and coordinated manner. This is not possible in the absence of library legislation. Taking this fact into account the Second Law of Library Science makes it the obligation of the State to enact library legislation. Unesco Public Library Manisfesto also stressed the need of library legislation by emphasizing that a public library should be "established under the clear mandate of law, so framed as to ensure nation-wide provision of public library service". The Sinha Committee (Advisory Committee) set up by the Government of India in 1957 (Report, submitted in 1959 and published in 1961) recommended the enactment of library legislation by each state. Recommendations of Chatopadhyay Committee (Committee on National Policy on Library and Infor mation System) set up by the Government of India in 1986 also emphasize that each state should enact library regulation.

H22 Financial Support

In a democratic society every citizen has the right to get lifelong information free of cost. Right to get information is treated as universal right. Second Law of Library Science makes it a duty of the State to provide books for all. In order to achieve this objective it is essential to arrange for sufficient fund for smooth and even running of public library service. This can be done only through legislation. Fund for library can be collected through two major means (i) by levying library cess, and (ii) by receiving library Grant. In the former method, the government (Central/State/local self) levy library cess (i.e. surcharge on property tax, excise duty etc.) for running public library service. It is different from usual library grant which is allocated by administrative dicision, which may vary or get reduced in each successive year. On the other hand if some amount is collected through library cess, or a certain minimum amount of grant is prescribed in the Act, the finance cannot be reduced by administration's decision.

Both the methods of raising fund for library service are useful. However, there are different groups advocating different pattern or method. One group is against levying library cess on the ground that the public is already heavily burdened with various taxes and therefore levying library cess will be opposed by the society. However, the Advisory Committee after considering this aspect in depth, concluded that the fear of opposition by the society is imaginary. In three States of India, Tamilnadu, Andhra Pradesh and Karnataka, library cess is being levied since 1948, 1960 and 1965 respectively but this has never been opposed by the members of the society. Rather, when people know that the library is being run out of public money by levying cess, the use of library increases. Recently the Haryana Public Libraries Act (1989) has also made provision for collection of Library Cess. In brief it may be concluded that what-ever may be the pattern for arranging fund, enactment of library legislation ensures certain, and sound financial footings for smooth running of public libraries.

H23 Level of Service

As a result of enactment of legislation, level of library services may be elivated, because after enactment, standard for different items and services can be prescribed and implimented.

H24 Co-ordination, Co-operation and Balanced Crowth

Library legislation is also essential for ensuring co-ordination and co-operation among libraries which are important for balanced growth and optimum utilization of resources. In the absence of legislation each library is bound to work in isolation. this situation is against the spririt of the Five Laws and also it is detrimental to optimum utilization of resources, i.e.books, manpower and money.

(See also, Chapter G, Section 41)

H3 QUALITIES OF GOOD LIBRARY LEGISLATION

An Act or library legislation should have the following major provisions

- (i) Provision for effective administration and guidance of libraries
- (ii) Provision for constituting Library Authority and committees/ sub-committees at various levels for various matters
- (iii) Distinct provision for powers, jurisdiction and responsibilities of each committee etc.
- (iv) Provision for strong financial support for running library service
- (v) Provision for opening new libraries by the Government and also for encouraging autonomous institutions, societies etc. to open libraries for public use through the government's financial support or aid
- (vi) Provision for coordination and cooperation among libraries
- (vii) Provision for extension service
- (viii) Provision for a separate Directorate of Libraries with full time professional Director
- (ix) Provision for education, training, promotion and betterment of service conditions of library staff.
- (x) Provision for a cadre for library staff

H4 LIBRARY LEGISLATION IN INDIA

In strict sense, by library legislation is meant an Act enacted for providing library service to people. If we go by this connotation of the term "Library-Legislation", in India the first library legislation was enacted in 1948 in Madras (i.e. Tamilnadu). However, while discussing library legislation in India in its historical perspective, connotation of the term may be widened by taking into fold other Acts also which have bearing on books and libraries. Similarly, such an historical account should also refer to Model Library Bills or Acts which provide a model for the makers or architects of library bills

H41 Acts with bearing on books/libraries

In this background, the Press and Registration of Books Act of 1867 may be considered to be the first legislation having bearing on books and libraries. Main purpose of enacting this legislation by the British Government in India was to scan and examine the literature printed in the country with a view to know the reaction of Indians about the British Raj. The Act made it obligatory on the part of each publisher to deposit with the state complimentary copy of each of their publications. Even today this Act, with modification is in vogue in many states, though the purpose now is different i.e. to preserve the national heritage of books. The Imperial Library Act of 1902 may be considered to be the second library legislation in the country. The Imperial Librtary (Change of name) Act of 1948 is a similar Act by enacting which the name of the Imperial Library was changed to 'National Library'. Delivery of Books Act (1954) and later Delivery of Books and Newspapers Act may also be enumarated in this category. (For details see Chapter 7).

H42 Model Library Act/Bill

In India the concept of library legislation is the contribution of Dr. S.R.Ranganathan. In the year 1930 he prepared a draft of a Model Public Libraries Act and presented it at the First Asia Conference at Varanasi in 1930. M.A. Gopinath has written that it was the seed of library legislation in India. Public Libraires Act of Tamilnadu, Anddhra Pradesh and Karnataka are based on this Model Act. Dr. Ranganathan modified his Model Act in 1972. The second Model Public Libraries Bill was drafted in 1963 by a committee set up by the Ministry of Education, Government of India under the Chairmanship of Dr. D.M. Sen. This Bill was released in 1965. The third Model Public Libraries Bill was prepared by the Working Group of

Planning Commission.

H43 Public Libraries Act: Salient Features

In India so far eight states have passed libraries legislation as indicated below:

S. No.	State	Name of the Act	Year of Encatment
1.	Tamil-Nadu	Tamil Nadu Public Libraries Act	1948
2.	Andhra Pradesh	Andhra Pradesh Public Libraries Act	1960
3.	Karnataka	Karnataka Public Libraries Act	1965
4.	Maharashtra	Maharashtra Public Libraries Act	1967
5.	West Bengal	West Bengal Public Libraries Act	1979
6.	Manipur	Manipur Public Libraries Act	1988
7.	Kerala	Kerala Public Libraries Act	1989
8.	Haryana	Haryana Public Libraries Act	1989

Salient features of these Acts are given as under:

H-431. Tamil Nadu Public Libraries Act (1948)

Orignally the Act was named as Madras Public Libraries Act. Tamilnadu State was established in 1947 but then its name was Madras. On 1st Jan. 1969 its name was changed to Tamilnadu. Accordingly, later the name of the Act was also changed as Tamilnadu Public Libraries Act.

H-4311. Salient Features

Salient features of the Act are as under:

(i) Constitution of State level Library Committee with the Education Minister of the State (as Chairman) and many other members, alongwith the Director of Libraries (as Secretary).

(ii) Appointment of Director of Libraries (and distinct listing of his/her powers and responsibilities) who will work under DPI

(iii) Provision for constitution of Local Library Authority at different level, such as one for the city of Madras, and one each for each district; and vesting the authorities with varying powers and responsibilities for providing library service

(iv) empowering local bodies, such as municipal cooperations, Municipal councils, District Board and Panchayat Board to levy library cess, collect it, and send it to the relevant Authority for depositing in Library Fund.

(v) Making it a duty of the State to contribute an equal amount (i.e. amount collected through library cess) to Library Fund.

(vi) Implementing the provisions of Press and Reistration of Books Act of 1867 with modification by making it obligatory on the part of publishers of the state to deposite five copies, free of cost, of each of their publications.

(vii) Provision of promoting and encouraging trusts and societies etc. to run public libraries and for this purpose to give financial assistance to them.

H-4312. Criticism

The Act has, however received critisim on the follwing issues:

(i) Absence of provision for a State Library Authority

(ii) Director of Libraries works under DPI

(iii) Less representation of public/common man on Local Library Authorities

(iv) Asking five copies of each publication from a publisher free of cost

H432 Andhra Pradesh Public Libraries Act (1960)

Andhra Pradesh was constituted in 1956 by joining the earstwhile Hyderabad state and a portion of Tamil Nadu. A.P. Public libraries Act was enacted in the year 1960. Before its enactment public library service in this State was run in some areas under Tamilnadu (Madras) Public Libraries Act (1948) and in some other area under Hyderabad Public Libraries Act (1955). Andhra Pradesh Public Libraries Act combines the fetures of both of these Acts. But this act also has some advancement over the Tamil Nadu (Madras) Act. For example, it is the first Act in which, following the recommendations of Sinha Committee (Advisory Committee) a provision has been made for setting up a seperate 'Department of Libraries'. In the year 1970 the State Govt. constituted a review committee under the Chairmanship of Justice Goplarao Akbote for evaluating the existing provisions of the Act and for suggesting measures for improvements. One of the main recommendations of the Review Committee was that the Minister Incharge of Library Services i.e. Education Minister should be responsible for running library service in the state and he should also function as State Library Authority.

Salient features of the Act are as under:

(i) Vesting the responsibility for running library service in the Minister-Incharge of Library Service, and provision for his functioning as State Library Authority also.
(ii) Giving the Directorate of Libraries the Status of independent Department. As compared to the Tamil Nadu Act in which the Directorate of Libraries functions under the Directorate of Public Instruction, it is certainly an improvement.
(iii) Provision for State Library Committee with Minister Incharge of Libraries, as Chairman and Director of Libraries as Secretary. It is an advisory committee for advising the Government on matters of library developmet and library policies etc.
(iv) Provision for District Library Samstha for each district. The Samstha shall also maintain Library Fund and the amount collected through Library cess and generated through other means shall be deposited in the Library Fund.
(v) Provision for Library Cess and making it obligatory on the part of the Government to deposit an equal amount (i.e.equal to the amount collected as Library Cess) in the Library Fund.
(vi) Implementation of Press Registration of Books Act (1867) with modification, vide which the publishers, of the state are required to send copies of their publication free of cost.

H-433. Karnataka Public Libraries Act (1965)

Enacted in 1965, this act came into force w.e.f. April 1, 1966. Salient features of the Act are as under:

(i) Provision for State Library Authority. This is the First Library legislation in India to make this provision. Tamilnadu Act lacks this provision completely. Andhra Pradesh Public Libraries Act has indirectly provided for it by vesting the Library Authority in the Minister-Incharge for libraries. In this respect Karnataka Act is ahead its predicessors.
(ii) provision for setting up a Directorate of Libraries Headed by a Director of Libraries (previously headed by State Librarian)
(iii) Provision for a seperate Cader of Librarians in the State
(iv) Provision for Local Library Authorities, such as City Library

Authorities (for cities having a population of one lakh and more) and District Library Authority for each district.

(v) Provision for levying Library Cess on urabn property and automobile etc.

(vi) Provision for maching grant (equal to the amount collected through Library Cess) by State Government.

(vii) Provision for Special Library Service for the blind.

(viii) Implementation of the provisions of the Press and Registration Act (1867) in modified form.

H434 Maharastra Public Libraries Act (1967)

The Act was passed at the Nagpur Session of the Maharashtra LegislativeAssembly on 17.11.1967 and came into force w.e.f. 1.4.1968. Salient features of the Act are as under:

(i) Constitution of State Library Council under the Chairmanship of the Minister for Education

(ii) Provision for a Department of Libraries headed by a professional Director

(iii) Constitution of District Library Committees for each district.

(iv) No provision for Library Cess. Instead, provision for fixed amount of grant by the Goverment for running library services.

H-435. West Bengal Public Libraries Act (1979)

The Act was passed in 1979 owing to ernest efforts of Bengal Library Association made since 1925. Salient features of the Act are as under:

(i) No provision for Library Cess. Instead, provision for a fixed amount of grant by the Government for running library service.

(ii) Provision for setting up a Directorate of Libraries headed by a Director.

(iii) Constitution of 'State Library Council' under the Chairmanship of the Minister Incharge for libraries.

(iv) Constitution of District Library Committee in each district

(v) Appointment of District Libary Officer (professional) in each district.

(vi) Implementation of the provisions of the Press and Registration Act (1867) with modification.

H-436. Manipur Public Libraries Act 1988

The act to provide the establishment and maintenance of public libraries in the state of Manipur was passed by the State Leilsture in 1988. Important Provisions on some vital matters have been reproduced below from the Act.

THE STATE LIBRARY COMMITTEE

Constitution and Composition of the State Library Committee and its functions:

1. As soon as may be after the commencement of this Act, the State Government shall, by notification, constitute for the purchases of this Act a committee to be called the State Library Committe.

2. The Committee shall consist of-

a. the Minister in-chare of Education, who shall also be the Chairman of the Committee;
b. Commissioner/Secretary to the Government in the Education Department;
c. the Director of Public Libraries;
d. the Chief Librarian of the State Central Library;
e. one person elected by the syndicate of Manipur University;
f. one person nominated by the Manipur Library Association;
g. two persons nominated by the State Government from amongst the members of the District Library Authorities;
h. one person co-opted by the Committee;

3. The Committee shall advise the State Government on all matters arising under this Act and shall exercise and perform such other powers and duties as may be prescribed.

8. Control of the State Library Committee by the State Government: If, at any time, it appears to the State Government that the Committee has failed to perform its functions or has exceeded or abused any of the powers conferred upon it by or under this Act the State Government may communicate the particulars thereof to the Committee, and if the Committee omits to remedy such failure, excess or abuses or to give satisfactory expression therefor within such time as the State Government may suspend dissolve or supersede the committee and cause all or any, of powers and functions of the Committee to be exercised and performed by any reason or agency for such period as they may think fit or direct that it be reconstitued.

DEPARTMENT OF PUBLIC LIBRARIES

9. Constitution of the Department of Public Libraries and appointment of the Director thereof and his duties: For the purpose of this ACt, the State Government shall constitute a separate Department of Public Libraries and appoint Director to be the Director of Public Libraries in-charge of the department. The Director so appointed shall subject to the control of the State Government-

a. Supervise the State Central Library and the branches of such library;
b. superintend and direct all matters relating to public libraries;
c. declare, in accordance with the rules made under this Act, What libraries are eligible for aid from the State Government and supervise and direct all matters relating to such libraries;
d. direct and control the work of all District Library Authorities under this Act in the manner prescribed;
e. submit to the State Government through the State Library Committee every year, a report on the working of the libraries under this Act in the preceding year;
f. submit reports to the committee on the working of libraries, whenever necessary;
g. perform such other duties and exercise such other power as are imposed or conferred on him by this Act or the rules made thereunder.

THE DISTRICT LIBRARY AUTHORITIES

10. Constitution and incorporation of District Library Authorities.

1. For the purposes of organising and administering public libraries in the State, there shall be constituted a District Library Authority for each district.
2. Every District Library Authority shall, by the name of the area for which it is constituted, be a body corporate having perpetual succession and a common seal with power to acquire, hold and dispose of property, and to enter into contracts and may by the said name, sue and be sued.
3. It shall be the duty of every District Library Authority to provide Library service in the area of its jurisdiction.

11. Composition of District Library Authorities: (1)The District Library Authority for each district Library Authority for each district shall consist of the followin member, namely:

a. four members nominated by the State Government from among the citizen of the district who have rendered eminent service to the cause of education or public libraries or a person of social eminents.
b. two members elected among themselves by the members of the governing bodies of the public libraries (other than those referred to in sub-clauses (a) and (b) of clause (9) of section (2) in each revenue division in the district;
c. Two members elected from among themselves by the board of municipalities or by the Small Town Committee in the district;
d. two members nominated by the district branch of the Manipur Library Association;
e. the Librarian, District Library who shall be the Secretary of the District Library Authority;
f. the Distirct Eduction Officer of the district.

(2)Every District Libraryt Authority shall elect one of its members to be its Chairman.

12. Term of Office of members of a District Library Authority: (1) Every members of a District Library Authority other than ex-officio members, shall hold office for a period of three years from the date of his nomination or election, as the case may be.

(2) A member nomianted or elected in his capacity as the holder of a particular office shall, if he ceases to be the holder of that office cease to be a member of the District Library Authority.

13. Filling up of casual vacancies of the members of the District Library Authority: A vacancy occurring in the office of a nominated or elected member of a district Library Authority before the expiration of his term shall be filled by nomination or election as the case may be, of another person so nominated or elected shall hold office for the remaining of the term of his predecessor.

14. Powers and functions of District Library Authorities: A Distirct Library Authority may-

a. provide suitable lands and buildings for public libraries and also the furniture, fittings, material and conveniences requisite therefor;
b. stock such libraries with books, periodicals, newspapers, manuscripts, maps, works and specimens of arts, and science, lantern slids, films, cinema projectors, recorders and the like;
c. employ from time to time, such staff as it considers necessary for such libraries;
d. with the previous sanction of the State Government, shift or close, any public library mentioned in sub-clause (a) of cluase (8) of section 2, or discontinue aid to any other public library, the payment of which is regulated by the prescribed Library Grant-in-Aid Code;
e. accept any gift or endowment for any purpose connected with its activities;

Provided that no gift or endowment of an immovable property shall be acceepted without the previous sanction of the State Government;
f. provide for lectures and the holding of classes and conduct other activities connected with public library service including social eduction;
g. with the consent of the management and the previous sanction of the State Government acquire any library on such conditions as may be approved by the State Government;
h. distribute grants for public necessary to carry out the provisions of this Act.

15. Scheme to be submitted by District Library Authorities: (1) As soon as possible after a District Library Authority is constituted and thereafter as often as may be required by the Director, every District Library Authority shall, and when ever it considers it necessary so to do, a District Library Authority may prepare a scheme for establishin libraries for spreading library service within its area in such form and manner as may be prescribed, and submit it to the Director for sanction. The Director may with previous approval of State Government sanctioned it with such alteration, if any, as he may think fit after giving the District Library Authority an opportunity to make its representations, if any, in respect of such alterations and the District Library Authority shall there upongive effect to the scheme so sanctioned by him.

(2)The Director may, with previous approval of State Government, on application by the District Library Authority concerned, modify and scheme sanctioned under sub-section (1) or replace it by a new scheme.

16. Executive Committee and sub-committees of District Library Authorities: (1) A District Library Authority may appointment an Executive Committee Consistin of such of its members as it may deem fit and deleate to such committee any of its powers or functions under this Act except the power to borrow money, to dispute of immovable property, and to pass the budget account and the audit and annual reprots.

(2)A District Library Authority may also, from time to time, appoint sub-committees to inquire into the report or advise on any matters which it may refer to them.

17. Act of District Library Authorities not be invalidated by informality etc.; no act of Distirct Library Authority shall be deemed to be invalidated by reason only of the existence of any vacancy in, or any defect in the constitution of that authority.

18. Vesting of Properties in District Library Authorities: (1) All property acquired or held in any area by the District Library Authority for the purpose of any public library defined in subclause (a) of clause (8) of section 2 shall vest in the District Library Authority of that area.

(2). Any immovable property required by the District Library Authroity shall be deemed to be land needed for a public purpose within the meaning of the Land Acquisition Act, 1894 (No. 1 of 1984) and may be acquired under that Act.
19. Power of District Library Authorities to make bye-laws: (1) Subject to the provisions of this Act and the rules made thereunder, a District Library Authority may make bye-laws, generally to carry out the purposes of this Act.

(2) in particular and without prejudice to the generality of foregoing power, such bye-laws may provide for all or any of the following matters namely,

a. the admission of the public to the public libraries in its area on such conditions as it may specify;

provided that no fees shall be chared for such admission;

b. the guarantee or security to be furnished by persons desiring to use such libraries, against injury to or misuse, destruction or loss of the property of such libraries;
c. the manner in which the property of such libraries may be used and the propection of such property from injury, misuse, destruction or loss;
d. the authrority to be exercised by its officers and servants in the matter of exlcusion or removal from any such library; of any person who contravenes does not comply with the provisions of this Act or the rules or bye-laws made thereunder;
e. the conduct of meetings of the District Library Authority and the procedure to be followed in regard to the transaction of business at a meeting

Provided that a District Library Authority shall not have power to make any bye laws affecting a public library mentioned in sub-= clause (2) or sub-clause (12)of section 2.

(3). The Director may with previous approval of State Government modify or cancel any bye-law made by a District library Authority under sub-section (2):

Provided that before modifying or cancelling any bye-law, the Director shall give the District Library Authority concerned a reasonable opporunity to make its representations in the matter.
20. Control of the District Library Authorities by the State Government: If, at any time, it appears to the State Government that a District Library Authority has failed to perform its functions or has exceeded or abused any of the powers conferred upon it by or under this Act, State Government may communicate the particulars thereof to the District Library Authority, and if the Distirct Library Authority omits to remedy such failure, excess or abuse or to give a satisfactory explanation therefor within such time as the State Government may fix in this behalf, the State Government may suspend dissolve or supersede the Distirct Library Authority and cause all or any of the powers and functions of such Authority to be exercised and performed by any person or agency for such period as they may fit or direct that it be reconstituted.

FINANCE AND ACCOUNTS

21. Library Fund: (1) Every District Library Authority shall maintain a fund called the Library fund from which all its payments under this Act shall be met.

(2) These shall be credited to the Library fund the following sums namely:

(a). Contributions, gifts and income from endowments made to the District Library Authority for the benefit of public Libraries,
(b). Special grants which the State Government may make for any specified purpose connected with libraries and social education;
(c). Fund and other amounts collected by the District Library Authority under any rules of bye-laws made under this Act.

(3)The State Government shall contribute annually to the Library fund maintained by every District Library Authority.

22. Maintenance of Accounts: (1) An account shall be kept of the receipts and expenses of each District Library Authority.

(2) The accounts shall be opened to inspection, shall be subject to audit, and shall be dealt with in all other respects in such manner, as may be prescribed.

H-437. Kerala Public Libraries Act (1989)

The Kerala Public Libraries Bill was presented at and passed by the eighth Kerala Legislative Assenbly (Bill No.12). Salient features of the Bill Act, as culled out from the bill ducoment, can be presented as under:

Short title, extent and commencement

(1) This Act may be called the Kerala Public Libraries Act, 1989.
(2) It extends to the State of Kerala.

Kerala State Library Council

As soon as may be after the commencement of this Act the government may, by notification constitute a Library Council for the state to be called the Kerala State Library Council which shall be a body corporate by the name aforesaid having perpetual succession and a common seal with power...

The State Library Council shall consist of sixty six members, of whom sixty one members shall be elected by the general body of the District Library Councils, one each from a Taluk and five members nominated by the Government".

(3) There shall be an Executive Committee for the State Library Council consisting of twenty-five members of whom fifteen shall be elected by the Government and five officials namely, the Secretary to Goverment, Higher Education Department, the Secretary to Goverment, General Education Department, the Secretary to Goverment, Finance Department, the Secretary to Government Cultural Affairs Department and the State Librarian of the Trivandrum Public Library.

(4) The Executive Committee shall meet at such times and at such places as the President of the State Library Council may decide and exercise such powers and functions as may be prescribed.

(5) The members of the Executive Committee shall elect a President, Vice-President, Secretary and Joint Secretary from among themselves to be the President, Vice-president, Secretary and Joint Secretary respectively of the Kerala State Library Council.

(9) *Powers and functions of the State Library Council*– (1) Subject to the other provisions of this Act and the rules made thereunder, the State Library council may,–

(a) advise the goverment on all matters connected with the administration of this Act;

(b) Co-ordinate the working of the District Library Councils and the Taluk Library Unions;

(c) Supervise and direct all matters relating to library service in the State;

(d) in consultation with the government establish one or more State Libraries at such place or places in the State as may be considered.

Provided that the Trivandrum Public Library shall be deemed to be a State Library established by the State Library Council under this clause.

(e) appoint and control such officers and servants as may be necessary for the efficient performance of its duties and functions under this Act and the rules made thereunder;

(f) (i) carry on propaganda on the importance of library development in the State by providing lectures, conferences, etc., and using any media as appropriate from time to time;

(ii) conduct such othér activities as may be conducive to creating favourable atmosphere in the State for the organisation of new libraries and for the better functioning of the existing libraries;

(iii) impart training to librarians;

(iv) organise activities for promoting distant education, adult education and eradication of illiteracy;

(v) establish and conduct shchools for promoting adult education and non-formal education;

(vi) maintain and preserve useful published and other records relevant to the Cultural heritage of the people of the State of Kerala;

(vii) provide in the Trivandrum Public Library or in such other State Libraries, books, periodicals, newspapers, maps, radios, manuscripts, works and specimens of art and science, lantern slides, films, cinema projectors, recorders, television sets and the like:

Provided that the State Library Council may deldgate any of its powers and functions under this clause to the District Library Councils or the Taluk Library Unions;

(g) do any other act that may be conducive to the furtherance of the objects of this Act with the previous sanction of the Government;

(h) exercise such other powers and perform such other duties as are conferred on it by this Act and the rules made thereunder.

(2) The State Library Council may give to the District Library Councils and the Taluk Library Unions directions in the performance of their functions under this Act and the District Library Councils and the Taluk Lirary Unions shall not in the discharge of their functions under this Act depart from the directions given by the said Council.

10. *Secretary of the State Library Council*— (1) The Secretary to the State Library Council shall be the Chief executive authority of the State Library Council.

District Library Councils

11. Constitution of District Library Councils— (1) For the purpose of organising and administering library service at the district level, the Government may, by notification, constitute a District Library Council for each District in the State.

(2) Every District Council shall be a body corporate, by the name of the district for which it is constituted, having perpetual succession and a common seal with power, subject to the provisions of this

Act and the rules made thereunder to acquire, hold and dispose of property, both movable and immovable, to contract and to do all things necessary, proper or expedient for the purpose for which it is constituted and shall, by the said name sue and be sued.

12. Composition of District Library Councils— (1) Every District Library Council shall consist of—

(a) the Presidents and Secretaries of the Taluk Library Unions in the District; and

(b) four persons to be elected by the General Body of the Taluk Library Unions in the district.

(2) The members of every District Library Council shall elect from among themselves a District Executive Committee which shall consist of a President, Vice-President, a Secretary and a Joint Secretary.

(3) The District Educational Officer/or one of the District Educational Officers to be nominated by the Government if there are more than one District Educational Officer shall be an ex-officio member of the District Executive Committee.

(4) The District Executive committee shall exercise such powers and functions as may be prescribed.

Taluk Library Union

19: *Constitution of Taluk Library Union*— (1) For the purpose of organising and administering library service at the taluk level the Government may, by notification, constitute a Taluk Library Union for each Taluk in the State.

(2) Every Taluk Library Union shall be a body corporate by the name of the Taluk for which it is constituted having perpetual succession and a common seal with power, subject to the provisions of this Act and the rules made thereunder, to acquire, hold and dispose of property both movable and immovable, to contract and to do all things necessary, proper or expedient for the purpose for which it is constituted and shall, by the said name sue and be sued.

20. *Composition of Taluk Library Unions*— (1) Every Taluk Library Union shall consist of not less than two representatives of each affiliated library in the Taluk:

(2) Every Taluk Library Union shall elect an Executive Committee of the Union consisting of eight members including a President, a Vice-President, a Secretary and a Joint Secretary.

(3) Every Taluk Library Union shall elect not more than four persons as memebrs to the District Library Council, under clause (b) of sub-section (1) of section 12.

Development Plan and Funds

29. *Library Development Plan*– (1) Subject to the provisions of this Act and the rules made thereunder and any general or special orders of the Government, if any, in this behalf, a District Library Council may, prepare a District Library Development Plan for establishing, co-ordinating and spreading library service within the entire district or part thereof, in such form and manner and containing such particulars as may be prescribed.

(2) The District Library Development Plan shall thereafter be forwarded to the President of the State Library Council who shall submit it to the Goverment with the views of the State Library Council.

(3) The Government may, if they deem fit, sanction the District Library Development Plan with or without alterations.

(4) The Government may, on application by the District Library Council modify any District Library Development Plan sanctioned under sub-section (3).

(5) As soon as may be after the sanctioning of a District Library Development Plan, the Presaident of the State Library Counicl shall, in conformity with the provisions of the said plan, make an order called the District Library Development Order, specifying the extent and nature of the Library service which shall be established and maintained by the District Library Counicl, the measures to be taken by the District Library council for providing adequate library service to the people in the area and the stages in which such measures shall be taken.

(6) Every District Library Council shall give effect to the District Library Development Plan as sanctioned by the Government under sub-section (3) and the District Library Development Order made under sub-section (5).

30. *Government grant to the State Library Council*– (1) The Government may make every year a grant to the State Library Council of a sum which shall not be more than one per cent of the amount allotted for education in the State budget for the year, taking into account the programme and projects of the State Library Council for that year.

(2) The amount of such grant shall be credited to the State Library Fund maintained under section 31 at such times and in such manner as may be prescribed.

31. *State Library Fund*– (1) The State Library Council shall main-

tain a fund called the State Library Fund from which all the Expenses of the State Library Council, District Library Councils and Taluk Library Union shall be met.

(2) The following sums shall be credited to the State Library Fund:-

(a) grants which the State Government or Central government may make to the State Library Council;

(b) Contributions and gifts made to the State Library Council by any other person, body or authority;

(c) Provident Fund, Superannuation Fund, Welfare fund and other funds of the Granthasala Sanghom transferred under subsection (2) of section 37.

32. *Distribution of funds to the District Library Councils and Taluk Library Unions*— The State Library Council shall distribute from the State Library fund such amounts as may be required for each of the District Library Councils and the Taluk Library Unions.

Kerala Granthasala Sanghom

37. *Dissolution of the Kerala Granthasala Sanghom and transfer of its assets and liabilitis*— (1) Notwithstanding anything contained in the Kerala Non-trading Companies Act, 1961 (42 of 1961), with effect on and from the da.e on which this section comes into force the Kerala granthasala Sanghom shall, by virtue of this section, be deemed to have been dissolved.

(2) All properties and all rights of whatever kind used, enjoyed or possessed by and all interests of whatever kind owned or vested or held by the Kerala Granthasala Sanghom and all liabilities legally subsisting against the Kerala Granthasala Sanghom Including the liabilities towards the Employees dues at the commencement of the Kerala Granthasala Sanghom (Taking Over of Management) Act, 1977 (19 of 1977) shall, with effect on and from the commencement of this section and subject to such directions as may be issued by Government in this behalf, vest in the Kerala State Library Council and the State Library Council shall discharge such liabilities in the order of priority specified in the Schedule to this Act.

(3) Every Offcer or other employee employed immediately before the commencement of this section in connection with the affairs of the Kerala Grranthasala Sanghom shall, as from such commencement become an officer or other employee of the State Library Council and shall hold his office by the tenure, remuneration and terms and conditions of employment as may be altered as per the provi-

sions in the Industrial Disputes Act, 1947 and with the same rights and privileges as to pension, gratuity and other matters as he would have held under the Kerala Granthasala Sanghom if this section had not been enacted and shall continue to do so unless and until his employment under the State Library Council is terminated or until his remuneration, terms and conditions are duly altered by the State Library Council:

Provided that if the Alteration so made is not acceptable to any officer or other employee, his employment shall be terminated on payment to him by the State Library Council of an amount equivalent to thee months' remuneration in the case of permanent employees and one month's remuneration in the case of other employees:

Provided further that nothing contained in this sub-section shall apply to any officer or other employee, who has by notice in writing given to the State Library Council within Thirty days from the commencement of this section intimated his intention of not becoming an officer or other employee of the said Council:

Provided also that nothing contained in this sub-section shall apply to an officer or other employee referred to in sub-section (4)

(4) Notwithstanding anything contained in the Industrial dispute Act, 1947 (Central Act 14 of 1947), or in any other law for the time being in force, the transfer of the services of any officer or other employee of the Kerala Granthasala Sanghom to the State Library Council under sub-section (3) shall not entitle any such officer or other employee to any compensation under that Act or other law, and no such claim shall be entertained by any court, Tribunal or authority.

H-438. Haryana Public Libraries Act (1989)

The Haryara Public Libraries Bill was passed in the year 1989 and published in the Haryana Government Gazette (Extraordirory) vide nolification dated 11th sept.1989. Salient features of the Bill, as culled out from the bill document, can be presented as under:

BILL NO 20-HLA of 1989

THE HARYANA PUBLIC LIBRAIES BILL, 1989

A BILL

To provide for the establishment, maintenance and development of Public Libraries in the State of Haryana and for matters ancillary thereto.

Be it enacted by the Legislature of the State of Haryana in the Fortieth Year of the Republic of India as follows.

Short Title, Extent and Commencement

1. (1) This Act may be called the Haryana Public Libraries Act, 1989.

(2) It extends to the whole of the State of Haryana.

(3) It shall come into force on such date as the State Government may, by notification in the Official Gazette appoint.

Constitution and Establishment of Authority

4. (1) With effect from such date as the State Government may, by notification, specify in this behalf, the State Goverment shall establish, for the purpose of this Act, an authority to be known as State Library Authority, with headquarters at such place as the State Government may specify.

(2) The Authority shall consist of–

(i) the following ex-officio members:

(a) the Minister-in-Charge of libraries who shall be the Chairman;

(b) the Secretary, Libraries Department;

(c) the Secretary, Education;

(d) the Secretary, Finance;

(e) the Secretary, Culture;

(f) the Secretary, Local Bodies;

(g) the Secretary, Social Welfare:

(h) the Secretary, State Devepopment and Panchayat Department;

(i) the Director of Public Relations;

(j) the Librarian of the Civil Secretariat, Haryana;

(k) the State Librarian;

(l) the Vice-Chancellors of all universities in the State;

(m) the Chairman or President, State Library Association;

(n) Director, Libraries, who will be the Secretary;

(ii) a member of the State Legislative Assembly interested in library development to be nominated by the State Government;

(iii) not more than four non-official members having special knowledge of libraries to be nominated by the Chairman of the Authority.

(3) The Authority shall advise the State Government on all matters mentioned under Section 3 and also in regard to promotion and development of library service in the State.

(4) The Authority shall meet at least once in a year.

(5) A nominated member of the Authority shall hold office during the pleasure of State Government: provided that his term of office shall not execed four years from the date of his nomination.

(6) Whenever any member dies, resigns, becomes incapable of acting as a member or is otherwise removed, the State Goverment may nominate other member for the un-expired period of the term of such member.

(7) The Authority shall frame regulations for transacting its business and for matters in respect of which regulations are to be framed by it under this Act and may appoint committees.

Standing Advisory Committee

5.(1) Within a month of the constitution of the Authority an eleven members Standing Advisory Committee shall be constituted of which eight members will be nominated by the Chairman of the Authority from amongst the members of the Authority and the Secretary, Department of Libraries the Director, State Library Directorate and the State Librarian shall be *ex-officio* members.

(2) The Chairman of the Authority shall nominate any members of the Standing Advisory Committee to be its Chairman and the Secretary of the Authority shall also be the Secretary of the Standing Advisory Committee.

(3) A member of the Standing Advisory Committee shall cease to hold office when he ceases to be a member of the Authority.

(4) The functions of the Standing Advisory Committee shall be:

(i) to advise the State Library Directorate in all technical matters relating to the library development and organistation.

(ii) to make recommendations to the authority on matters relating to the promotion and development of library service in the State.

State Library Directorate

6.(1) The State Government shall constitute a State Library Directorate which shall be a department of the Government. The functions of the State Library Directorate shall be as follows:

- (a) to prepare the annual as well as short or long term plans for libraries in the State in co-operation with the development and other concerned departments of the State Government and of the Central Government;
- (b) to prepare and publish descriptive and statistical reports on the working of all the Public Libraries;
- (c) to arrange or to secure training of various categories of library employees;
- (d) to conduct inspection of and render advisory service to the district, block and other libraries in the State;
- (e) to administer the system of grant-in aid to the subscriptive libraries, and to undertake their inspection;
- (f) to fix the boundaries of the operation of district libraries in the districts.

(2) The Director of the State Library Directorate (hereinafter called the Director) shall be appointed by the State Government and will have the rank of the Head of a Department.

(3) The State Library Directorate shall have staff with adequate qualifications and training.

(4) The Director shall perform the following duties:

- (a) he shall participate in all meetings of the Authority and the committees which may be set up by the Authority;
- (b) he shall be responsible for carrying out such of the recommendations of the Authority as have been approved by the State Government;
- (c) he shall perform such other duties as may be prescribed in the regulations made by the Authority;
- (d) subject to any rules made by the State government Directorate:
    - (i) shall be responsible for implementing the programme of work for the year as approved by the Authority;
    - (ii) shall administer the grant-in-aid to subscription libraries;
    - (iii) shall decide where district and other libraries in the State are to be set up and approve the constitution byelaws of a Public Library;
    - (iv) may absorb a subscription library into the Public Library of the State.

State Central Library

7. The State Goverenment shall by an order eslatish a State Central Library in the State.

State Librarian

11.(1) The Officer-in-Charge of the State Central Library shall be known, as the State Librarian.

(2) The State Librarian shall be appointed by the State Government.

(3) The State Librarian shall:

(a) be responsible for the management of all the departments of the State Central Library;

(b) maintain the stock of books and conduct all approved activities of the State Central Library.

The District Library

12.(1) There shall be a District Library in each district rendering book service to the residents of a district.

(2) In addition to the District Library under sub-section (1), there shall also be the followint types of libraries, namely;

(a) Municipal/city/Town Library;

(b) Block Library;

(c) Village Library; and

(d) smaller book deposit centres.

District Library Committee

14.(1) There shall be a district library committee for each District Library in the State which shall be constituted in accordance with such regulations as may be framed by the Authority.

(2) The District Library Committee shall, subject to the approval of the authority, frame its rules of business and procedure for carrying out the functions of the Districy Library.

15.(1) There shall be a City Library Committee for each city with a population of over a lakh, and a Town Library Committee for a municipal town with a population of not more than one lakh constituted in accordance with such rules as may be framed by the District Library Committee concerned.

(2) The function of a City or Town Library Committee shall, so far as may be the same as those of the District Library Committee within its jurisdiction.

(3) The City or Town Library Committee shall subject ot the

approval of the District Library Committee concerned frame its rules of business and procedure.

Block Library Committee

16.(1) There shall be Block Library Committee for each Block Library and its constitution and functions shall be such as may be laid down in rules framed by the District Library Committee concerned.

(2) The Block Library Committee shall, subject to the approval of the District Library Committee concerned, frame its rules of business and procedure.

Panchayat Library Committee

17.(1) There shall be a Panchayat Library Committee for each Village Library and its constitution and functions shall be such as may be laid down in rules framed by the District Library Committee concerned.

(2) The Panchayat Library Committee shall, subject to the approval of the district Library Committee concerned, frame its rules of business and procedure.

Employees of the Public Library

18.(1) The State Government shall create cadres for Pul 'ic Library employees similar to those of the employees of Government Departments and lay down the qualifications and the other terms and conditions of service for those caderes.

(2) Within a year of its first constitution, the Authority shall frame service rules for the various categories of library employees.

Public Library Fund

19.(1) There shall be three types of library funds in the State;

(a) The State Library Fund;

(b) The District Library Fund;

(c) The City or Town or Block or Village Library Fund;

(2) There shall be credited into the State Library Fund:

(a) the amount provided by the State Government for development, improvement and maintenance of library service in the State.

(b) the contribution received from the Central Government

(c) any special grant that the Central or a State Government may make for any specific purposes;

(d) the amount received under the library rules of the State Central Library;

(e) any amount received as gift, contribution or endowment for the deveopment of Public Libraries in the State.

(3) There shall be credited into a District Library Fund:

(a) the amount transferred to it from the State Library Fund, the State contribution to the District Library Fund being in no case less than the total amount of liberary cess collected in the district.

(b) any special grant that the Authority may make to the district Library Committee for any specific purpose;

(c) the amount collected under the rules of the District Library;

(d) any amount received as gift, contribution or endowment for the development of libraries in the district;

(e) any loan that the District Library Committee may raise.

Library Cess

20. Every local body in a district may levy in its area a library cess in the form of a surcharge on property tax and house tax at such rate as the Government may decide from time to time.

State Library Assosiation

23.(1) The Athority shall recognise only one State Library Association as co-opraling Institlon the consltutlon of which shall be approved by the Authority.

H-5. CONCLUSION

Owing to S.R. Ranganathan's efforts library legislation was enacted in the four Indian states from 1948 to 1967. After winning these big battles in the history of public library movement in India later it appeared that library movement in the country had been pushed to backward direction. This looked evident from the fact that in 20 years time after Independence, 4 Indian States enacted library legislation but from 1967 to 1979– in thirteen years-only one State (West Bengal) could enact it, though draft library bills were prepared by Ranganathan and various Library Associations for almost every State by 1967. The Position of enactment of library legislation between 79 to 90 was not very satisfactory. Only Kerala, Manipur and Haryana adopted library legislation though provisions of the act are generally yet to be implimented. It is however a matter of great satisfaction for the profession that these three states have taken bold steps in deciding to adopt library legislation.

J

Library Extension Work

J-1. DEFINITION

In the context of libraries, extension work is concerned with two types of activities:

(i) to reach those who cannot (or donot) reach the library, and

(ii) Besides issue and return of books, to perform such other functions as are essential for establishing the library as a social and cultural centre.

J-2. OBJECTIVE

Objectives of extension work is to extend library services by taking documents at the door-steps of the people, to establish the library as the intellectual social and cultural centre and to develop in people interest towards library by making available to them healthy, informative and recreational literature.

A service institution does not serve only those who come to it, it also serves those who do not or cannot come to it. It does so by extending its services and thus by reaching those who cannot or do not reach it. The library is also a service institution and therefore it should also reach people by extending its services. By doing so, the library can convert many non-readers into readers. To take books at the doorsteps of people is not the only objective of extension work. Its second objective is to make the library a social and cultural centre. The Kenyon Committee, in its report (1927) indicates that a public library is the "Centre of intellectual life of the area it serves" [1], and the UNESCO's Public manifesto declares, "It [the library] is concerned with refreshment of man's spirit by the provision of books for relaxation and pleasure with assistance to the student and with provision of upto date technical, scientific and sociological information".[2]. Therefore the fact that the library today should function also as a social centre has already been accepted. By starting extension activities the library can maintain its social character.

J-3. NEED

The following factors emphasise need for starting extension service by libraries:

1. Limitations of would-be readers
2. Expectation of the Third Law
3. Rights of citizen
4. Social Character of the library

J-31. Limitation of the Would be Users

Would be readers are those persons who can be converted into good users of the library, provided some initiative is taken by the library in this direction. Some of such persons have time to come to the library but either due to their indifferent attitude or due to lack of encouragement, they do not come to the library. Such a person can be converted into a good reader with the help of public relation and publicity work. There is another category of people, who do not have time to come to the library. For example, many reside at a distant place, many others have long working hours, and still many others are not in a position to come to the library in spite of their earnest desire to do so: such as the child, the aged, patients, prisoners, etc. Library, being a service institution, should endeavour to serve all these groups by going to their doorsteps. And this is in the interest of the library also. Many of these persons, when converted into readers, will be the vocal admirers of the library, and at the same time will also be better and enlightened citizens.

J-32. Expectation of the Third Law

A proverb says, books are the best friends'. The Fifth Law prescribes, "Library is a growing [hence a living] organism"; the Third Law proclaims, "Every book (should get) its reader". Read together, these convey, that (i) books are living entities and (ii) every book is made for and is eager to meet its reader(s). Therefore sincere efforts should be made to ensure that the existence or availability of the book in the library should be brought to the notice of those readers for whom the book was written or in other words, who may be interested in reading it. On the other hand books, being dumb and deaf cannot on their own, invite reader's attention. Therefore it is essential to make efforts to send books to those who, because of one reason or the other, cannot reach the book. (For details see the Third Law in section). In this connection Dr. Ranganathan writes:

> "The laws of library science walk into the library during the hours of relaxation. They feel happy if reading circles are busy. If there are group discussions, if there are cinema shows...,..and if there is activity everywhere as in the beehive. If books are taken out for service in prison and hospitals the laws bless the library".

J-33. Rights of the Citizen

Public libraries receive finance through public fund which is expended in purchase of books, staff salary, maintenance, etc. Thus, a library is a social organisation run through social fund. This indicates that every citizen has a right to dervie benefit of library service. Therefore, if some citizens cannot reach the library, it becomes the duty of the library to reach them.

J-34. Library: A Social Institution

The library of today is not a study centre alone. It is also social and cultural centre and in order to become a social centre, the library is required to extend its activities. In developed countries libraries "have operated Railway Station, housed Red Cross classes, supplied community meeting rooms, sponsored concerts and dramatic production, operated museums and even planetariums, held art shows, loaned umbrellas on rainy days and furnished high chairs for the infants"[3] In our country libraries are adopting such activities but their rate is to be accelarated.

J-4. MEASURES

It will be of interest to know as to what are the different steps and measures which can be taken for running extension service. We know that extension work is concerned with two things: (i) to take books and other audio visual materials to users; and (ii) to make the library a social and cultural centre.

This can be achieved by adopting the following measures:

1. Opening branch libraries, study centres
2. Starting mobile library services
3. Establishing circulating book deposit centre
4. Providing reading time
5. Providing story time
6. Organising exhibition/competition/contests
7. Conducting lectures
8. Dramatic presentation, film shows, etc.

J-41. Branch Libraries, Study Centres

The main library can open branch libraires or study centres in various localities or places. This way the library can reach that particular locality or place. These branches or centres act as extended service centres, the acquisition and technical processing are done at the main library. An extension library with small collection can be housed in rented accomodation, or else, other organisations in the area, such as school, hospital, municipal committee etc. can be approached for providing accomodation for this noble cause. A small collection of healthy, popular, general and recreational literature is kept in branches. It is essential however to survey the subject interest of the people before starting a branch or centre in a particular area. Normally one staff may suffice for a small centre. These may also be opened on part time basis for two-three hours a day, and a local youth may be given the charge.

J-42. Mobile Library

A mobile library is library on wheels. It moves from one place to other on fixed timings and serves many localities. Therefore, it is one of the most effective and economical extension services. In America, the first mobile library service was started in horse driven carriages. Around 1920s motorcars were employed to serve as mobile library. Around 1950s specially designed motor vans were build up to suit the requirement of a mobile library. The physical appearance and shape of a mobile van has been varying from time to time. It can be a full van, or a trailor attached with wagon. Inside the van or wagon special racks are fitted to house a few thousand books. these are prepared and fitted in such a way that the books may not fall down when the van is in movement. There is space inside for movement of one person, and also for keeping charging trays, membership record and form etc. The driver of the van may also be a semi-professional so that, if need be, he may also issue/return books and enroll new members. The time for each locality is fixed and notified for the information of the residents. Book mobiles may also be run on Rickshaws or Cycles. Raja Ram Mohan Roy Library Foundation has a scheme of financial assistance for running book mobile service in Rickshaws.

J-43. Circulating Book Deposit Centre

Circulating Book Deposit Centres can be set up in various places, such as villages. Each centre has one or two big trunks full of books. The village teacher or mukhia or a person authorised by the mukhia is made incharge of this library and the trunk/s and books are kept in room in the school or at the residence of the incharge which can work as a centre. In the scheme many such centres, located in different villages participate. If there are 50 (fifty) villages in a block villages 1-5 may constitute set I; 6-10 set II; 11-15 set III and so on. After a fixed interval, say three months, the books of Centre 1 are sent (alongwith the trunks) to Centre 2, books of Centre 2 are sent to Centre 3 and so on in a circle. This circle continues until the books of Centre 11 of Set 1 villages reach Centre 5 of the Set I village. The same procedure is followed amongst the libraries of other sets, i.e., Set II, Set III etc. When this circle is completed within the each set of village, the entire collection of Set I villages will be sent to Set II villages, the collection of Set II villages to Set III villages and so on. In this scheme the cooperation of villagers is essential. It is a highly economical and effective means of extension service.

J-44. Reading Time

Under this scheme, the main library or branch libraries can organise reading of newspaper, religious literature, recreational literature, etc. in the premises of the library at a specified time. The person reading the text should have good voice and pronunciation and his presentation should be interesting. Such people are available in every locality and will be pleased to read these material for the society, this programme may look trivial, but is very useful. Neoliterates, semi literates, women and aged people listen to such readings with interest. This programme is also useful in developing reading habit in literates as well as in converting illiterates into literates. Dr. Ranganathan has stressed that this service should be introduced by every public library. In the year 1930 Madras Library Association experimented on this scheme which was welcomed by the citizen. In USSR also such programmes have helped in increasing rate of literacy. There is another benefit of this scheme, though it is not apparent. Persons, requested to 'read' the literature, news, etc. for the citizens also become admirers of the library and persuade others to become the members of the library. If some of such persons are retired people (such as government servants), they also find some opportunity to have some engagement and mental satisfaction that their services are required by the society even after retirement. If need be, such persons can also manage grant, land and other facilities for the library by using their previous contacts in the government and convincing the concerned authority about the utility of the library.

J-45. Story Time

Under this programme stories are recited or told at a specified time. The person reciting or telling story should have good voice, interesting way of presentation and the theme of the story should be of interest to children because this programme is run for children, though neoliterates and semi literates may also find it interesting. Famous fictions, dramas, etc. of foreign countries may also be recited after translating them in local language. Translation of many such works are available in market which may be purchased for the library. It will be better to request lady teachers or ladies of the locality to read the stories etc. because children require the presentation of such things in *'Kantasammat'* way.

J-46. Reading Circle

Reading circle may be constituted by the library by bringing together persons connected with one subject or one profession and providing them a platform for discussion on a theme of their interest. Libraries can encourage persons to form such circles and provide venue to them for discussion.

J-47. Exhibition and Competition

From time to time libraries may also organise exhibition and competition/contests at relevant occasions. For example, exhibition of (i) patriotic books on the eve of Independence Day; (ii)sports books during the days when cricket match is being played, etc.

A few of such exhibitions and competitions may be listed as under:

(i) exhibition of newly acquired books
(ii) exhibition of books on a particular subject
(iii) exhibition of books on a particular incident
(iv) exhibition of books on a particular personality
(v) exhibition of books on a particular festival
(vi) exhibition of books on a particular sports
(vii) exhibition of books on a particular hobby
(viii) exhibition of books on a particular scheme programmes
(ix) exhibition of books on local production
(x) Organisation of healthy child contest
(xi) Organisation of Essay, Declamation, etc. contest
(xii) Organisation of programmes for honouring Regular Readers.
(xiii) Organisation of film shows, dramatic performances, cultural evenings, etc.

These exhibitions and contests increase citizens' interest in library and make the library a social and cultural centre. These can be organised with the help of public relations department, local theatre group, song and drama division, etc. Film shows and dramatic presentations can be organised on library campus. Libraries in developed countries have evinced keen interest in such activities. The American Library Association (ALA) prepared a list of dramas and circulated it amongst its member-libraries so that one or more of these dramas may be staged on library campus for the public. In the year 1926 the Indiana Library Association stage a drama "Exit Miss Lizi Fox" which became very popular and in turn the popularity of the libraries that staged this drama was also enhanced. In India also public libraries can organise such programmes together with such other programmes as puppet show, magic show, etc.

J-5.. CONCLUSION

At first sight many of the programmes included under extension work may not appear to have direct relation with library work. But if we go into depth and consider that the benefits of the library should flow to the society, it will become evident that these are essential elements of library service and should be forcefully adopted so as to make the library a social and cultural organisation.
(See also Library Publicity and Public Relation)

K

Library Publicity and Public Relation

K-1. DEFINITION

Public relation and publicity are concerned with such activities as may be adotped for attracting the attention of masses towards an entity. In context of the library, public relation and publicity are concerned with informing the people, of the activities and services of the library by propagating them. Objectives of these activities is to attract people towards the Library and make them regular and habitual readers. Another objective of public relation and publicity work is self assessment of the library because it also helps the library to know people's opinion about itself.

Publicity and public relation work is comparatively a new concept for libraries. In the early nineteenth century it was felt that public relation and publicity is not a part of library activity because libraries do not have any thing to propagate or publicise. It was then felt that libraries are supposed to perform only two activities:

(i) to maintain an organised collection of books; and

(ii) to make these available to people on demand

This will be evident from a definition of the term library, as given in the New Oxford Dictionary.

"A library is a public institution or establishment charged with the care of a collection of books and the duty of making them accessible to those who require the use of them".

But later, it was felt that libraries should perform another activity also, i.e., 'to tell the people about/and to propagate its activies. Dr. Ranganathan used to compare a library with a business establishment. A business establishment propagates its products or commodities and attracts people by enumerating the qualities, utilities and benefits of their products. Similarly a library should also make necessary efforts to attract people by enumerating the qualities utility and benefits of using a library. Dr. Ranganathan advocated this view in 1933 at the All India Library Conference held at Calcutta. In this conference Dr Ranganathan had delivered a lecture on the topic"Salesmanship and Librarianship". In his lecture he established the importance of public relation and publicity work in a library, and suggested that the definition of the New Oxford Dictionary should be modified as under:

"A library is a public institution or establishment charged with the care of a collection of books, the duty of making them accessible to those who require the use of them and the taste of canvassing every person in its neighbourhood into a habitual library goer and reader of books."

K-2. NEED

Following factors emphasise the need of public relation and publicity by libraires:

1. Demand of the First Law
2. Demand of the Third Law
3. Obligation of the libraries

K-21. Demand of the First Law

The First Law of Library Science prescribes, "Books are for use". This implies that it is the duty of each librry to take necessary steps to increase the use of books.It is an established fact that publicity and public relation are the two principle means for promoting the consumption (i.e.,use) of a commodity. So, by public relation and publicity work more people can be made readers. Some feel that public relation and publicity are costly activities and libraries cannot afford to undertake these activities. However, it should also be considered that small expenditure and some efforts taken for public relation and publicity work can ensure proper utilisation of the money spent on library. When a book is read by more number of readers, the expenditure on the library is divided into many persons. Thus with these activities, on one hand the use of books is increased and on the other hand the average cost of a book is divided into more readers which indirectly ensures economy.

K-22. Demand of the Third Law

The Third Law of library Science prescribes, "EVERY BOOK ITS READER." It implies that every effrots should be made by the library to ensure that the 'would be readers' know of the activities of the library and come to it in search of their books. Would -be-readers are those persons who can become a user of the library but owing to lack of knowledge about the library, or due to their indifferent attitude they do not come to the library. On the other hand, books, being dumb entities, cannot invite readers' attention on their own. These can neither go to the reader or can call them. Added to it, people generally do not have earnest desire to read. Dr. Ranganathan writes in this direction that in a European town, with hundred percent literate adult population, hardly forty percent people used the local library. In our country situation is still grim. Literate population is less in number, people lack reading habit and library awareness is minimum. Therefore in our country library publicity and library public relation are needed the most. If people are told as to how they can become members of the library, what benefits they may derive by becoming members, what type of books they can get, then many of them will like to become library users.

K-23. Obligation of Libraries

Public libraries are financed out of public fund. Therefore it is obligatory for public libraries to acquaint the public about its activities and services. For this reason also, a public library should engage itself in public relation and publicity activity.

As far as other libraries are concerned, these are also opened and run for specific group of users, it is obligatory for these also to bring their services,stock etc. to the notice of the community these are expected to serve.

K-3. SOME IMPORTANT ISSUES

Before starting public relation and publicity activities, following major issues must be taken into consideration:

(i) Public relation and publicity should be envisaged as a continuous activity and it serves no purpose to do it once and then forget later to continue it. These can give desired result only if pursued continuously. Sale of a commodity does not increase by giving advertisement and contacting people only once. It takes time to become popular. Even after becoming popular, publicity work and public relation should not be dispensed with. Any slackness in public relation and publicity is likely to gradually decrease popularity.

(ii) Publicity and Public relation however does not mean presenting an exaggerated picture of the activities of the library. The library must keep in mind that influenced by the publicity and advertisement many people will come to the library with high hope and the library will have to come up to their expectation. Therefore the library should publicise the activities and services actually performed by it.

(iii) Public relation and publicity work are bound to create proper impact and result in increase in number of readers. The library should not then cease its public relation and publicity activity.

K-4 PLANNING

Public relation work and publicity should be started and continued under a well formulated plan. The following activities are to be planned in advance for the whole year either by the librarian, or by the library committee:

(i) to make provision in the budget for necessary finance for public relation and publicity work.

(ii) to decide dates and subjects of exhibitions and contests

(iii) to finalise outline of library publications

(iv) to decide the name of the journals, newspapers, etc. in which advertisement pertaining to the activities of the library will be sent

(v) to decide about the places where poster boards will be pasted/ displayed

(vi) to decide about the theme, text, participants, etc. of dicussions which may be televised or broadcasted

(vii) to decide dates and subjects of exhibitions or contests

(viii) to decide about qestionnaires to be circulated in the local public

(ix) to decide the theme on which lectures are to be organised

(x) to decide as to who will be incharge of publicity and public relation work

K-5. MEASURES TO BE TAKEN

The following are some of the important programmes and activities which when adopted, make the library popular in the society:

1. Extension work
2. Library publications
3. Advertisement
4. Newspaper, Radio, T.V.
5. Posters/Boards
6. Surveys
7. Miscellaneous

K-51. Extension Work

Organising exhibition and contests make the library popular. Book exhibitions can be organised throughout the year on various occasions and the books being exhibited should match the occasion. For example, around children's day, exhibition of children books may be organised. The place of exhibition should be near the entrance, so that it may come to the notice of the readers easily. The theme of the exhibition may be displayed on notice board. Apart from book exhibition, the library can organise contests and competitions also. Thus to make the library popular the following steps may be taken:

(i) to organise exhibition of newly arrived books
(ii) to organise exhibition of books on a particular subject
(iii) to organise exhibition of books on a particular event
(iv) to organise exhibition of books on a particular person
(v) to organise exhibition of books on a particular festival
(vi) to organise exhibition of books on a particular sports
(vii) to organise exhibition of books on a particular hobby
(viii) to organise exhibition of books on a particular scheme
(ix) to organise exhibition of books on a particular occasion
(x) to organise declamation contests, dramatic presentation, film shows, etc.

(For details see chapter-Extension work)

K-52. Library Publications

Library publications are those publications which are published by the Library for informing the users and the public about the activitles, services and collection of the library. Some of the important publications of the library may be as under:

(i) Know your library
(ii) Library bulletin
(iii) List of recent additions
(iv) List of periodical articles
(v) Readers profile

Every library must publish literature like "Know your library, "Your library", etc. This contains general information about the library, such as nature of collection, staff, services, how to become member, etc. This can be placed on circulation counter so that users may collect it from there. It may also be distributed for making the people aware of the services of the library. Other important publications of a library may be in the form of "Library bulletin", Annual Report, News Letter, etc. Annual report may be published periodically and may contain description of the activities of the library including library statistics during the period under report. Another publication of the library may be a periodically published list entitled "List of Additions" containing the list of titles, alongwith bibliographical details, acquired in the library recently. This helps the readers to know about newly acquired books. Similarly the library may also periodically bring out a periodical list of articles culled out from recent journals with or without abstracts. The library may also maintain readers profile for those readers who are interested to know of recent documents appearing in their field of interest. All these activities make the library very popular. Such publication may be in cyclostyled form. With the introduction of computers, it has now become easy to bring out and print these through computer easily in no time.

K53 Advertisement

Advertisement is a forceful and effective instrument of public relation and publicity. Sometimes it is said that good things do not require any advertisement, but it is not true. The text of advertisement should be compact and expressive. Besides getting the advertisement published in newspapers, it may also be sent to Principals of local schools, colleges, postmaster, (Rail) Station Master, Hospital incharge, District Magistrate, etc. with a request to display it at a prominent place. They may also be requested to become a member of the library and if thought appropriate, these people may be approached personally to become a member of the library. Such acts enhance the popularity of the library.

K-54. Interviews etc. on Radio, T.V.

News papers, Radio and T.V. are helpful not only in advertising the activity and services of the library directly. These also project the image of library, indirectly, by publishing and broadcasting writeups and discussions and write-ups concerning the library. Normally, these are accepted without any charge as contrary to advertisement for which the library is charged. Some eminent/popular person may be interested or requested to present their views about the library. Librarian or the Chairman Library Committee may also prepare a write-up which may be got published in local news papers. Similarly discussion may be organised on Radio or T.V. highlighting the major services and collections of the library. Such programmes must be organised during National Book Week (Nov. 14 - 20) every year.

K-55. Posters

Posters may be pasted at prominent places in the area which the library serves. Language of the posters should be such as may invoke interest in the Library. Posters may also contain slogans and quotations highlighting the importance of libraries.

K-56. Survey

Every library should conduct surveys at regular intervals in order to ascertain:

(i) which individual or family in the locality are members of the library;

(ii) those who have become members, what are their reaction or feelings, and

(iii) those who are not members, can become member or not after persuatsion.

Such a survey has many advantages, such as (a) the library comes to know as to upto what extent it is popular in the society, (b) the library comes to know of its limitations and drawbacks of its services, (c) library staff come into the contact of the society and then they can remove the society's misconception, if any, about the library; and (d) it adds to the popularity of the library.

K-6. CONCLUSION

Public relation and publicity work is essential for each library. It increases the popularity of the library, imposes society's confidence in the library and establishes the library as a living organism. Every library must remember the words of James Duff Brown wherein he has emphatically said that librarys have only two ways: either they should propagate their services and importance or be prepared to be perished.

L

Library Building

L-1. INTRODUCTION

If the book is soul of the library, library building is the body in which the soul dwells. Hence it is highly essential to examine all factors before constructing a building for a library. Every building is constructed for a particular purpose and to suit specific requirements. The fact also lays emphasis on taking into account all the concerned factors in minute details before starting construction of the building. Some of the broad points pertinent to library building have been discussed in succeeding section.

L-2. QUALITY OF GOOD LIBRARY BUILDING

A look at some old library buildings will reveal that earlier, elegant and huge construction, fitted with engraved and closed almirahs and high roofed rooms were supposed to be the qualities of a good library building. The reason was that in early days all good buildings were supposed to be elegant and huge. Similarly it was also essential to keep books in closed almirahs, because books were available in manuscript form and were therefore rare commodities. Reproduction and making multiple copies was a very costly affair. But after the popularity of printing press, books were started printing in multiple numbers which made it possible to open more and more libraries for the use of common people. Therefore now a days emphasis is on a building which is useful. There are two different opinions about the location of a library, viz., (i) it should be located at a deserted and distant place so that only those will come there who have real interest in reading, (ii) it should be conveniently and centrally located so that maximum number of people can come there easily. We can make a compromise between the two views by accepting that for a research library distant location can be preferred and for a public library central location preferred. Library buildings should be functional, not ornamental, and the construction should be modular and not fixed. Functional and modular buildings allow flexibility and space adjustment. Library buildig should also be safe for books so as to protect these from their enemies, i.e., dust, moisture, sun and ofcourse, humans. In the building adequate space should be provided for staff, library activities, movement of trolleys, lounge, physical facilities, etc. It should be built in such a way that maintenance may not be very costly. It should have adequate provision for natural and artificial lighting and cooling. however the construction will also depend on the fund available and the services contemplated to be run by the library, number of anticipated members, staff and collection in the coming twenty years, etc. Quality of a good library building can be summed up as under:

(i) Centrally located building
(ii) Modular and functional construction
(iii) Adequate provision for natural and artificial light
(iv) Protection against theft and injury to books
(v) Lounge and other physical facilities
(vi) Adequate space for library staff, collection, movement of trollies and library operations, such as circulation counter, reference desk, check and property counter, etc.
(vii) Connected units should be adjacent to each other, for example Technical section should be adjacent to Acquisition section, and Periodicals section, should be adjacent to Documentation section.

L-3. ORNAMENTAL Vs FUNCTIONAL BUILDING

Buildings with high walls, elegant look and engraved front portion are known as ornamental buildings. In these buildings more attention is paid on decoration and outer attractions. On one hand it increases cost of construction, and on the other it does not aim at optimum utilization of available space. On the contrary a functional building aims at maximum utilization of available space and also on the scientific location of various sections and units of the library based on the work flow. There is no denying the fact that the library building should be good looking and environment around it should be pleasant. But then it should be functional also and should be constructed in such a way as to allow smooth functioning of all library operations.

L-4. FIXED Vs MODULAR CONSTRUCTION

Fixed construction implies constructing separate room (with permanent partition or walls) for separate work. On the contrary in modular construction no room is constructed. In it only main or outer walls of the library are constructed, besides a few rooms for administration, technical work, physical facilities, lift, etc. the space inside is left open in the form of hall/halls. In these halls work area can be created by erecting temporary partitions made of wood, ply, racks, almirahs or even bricks. "Modular construction refers to a system of building construction in which the floor area is divided into equal rectangular unit of space defined by structural columns at the corner instead of overbearing walls". Modular construction ensures flexibility and in case of need new interior compartmentalisation can be done without any tear and wear. Difference between fixed and modular construction is that in the former, construction is done in the form of rooms, such as reading room, stack room, periodicals rooms etc; whereas in the latter, construction is done in the form of areas, such as reading area, stack area, periodicals area etc. by erecting temporary partitions. Main features of modular construction are optimum utilisation of space, flexibility, economy in construction, maximum use of natural light and facility to change the existing arrangement without much tear and wear.

L-5. INTERNAL ARRANGEMENT

Building should be constructed keeping in view the requirements for-the next twenty years. Location of different service points, stack area, etc. should be decided on the basis of workflow. ordinarily, there should be only one main entrance. Circulation counter, and property counter should be near the entrance. Catalogue cabinet should be near stack area. Sufficient space should be provided inside and outside the circulation counter to accomodate required number of seats for staff, charging tray, returned books, etc. If library has a multistoried building, reference and periodicals section should be on the ground floor. About reading area and stack area one of the following arrangements may be followed:

(i) *Centre location:* In this arrangement stack area is surrounded by the reading area, i.e., stack area is in the centre
(ii) *Peripheral location:* In this arrangement reading area is surrounded by stack area, i.e., reading area is in the centre
(iii) *Vertical location:* In this arrangement reading area and stack area are adjacent to each other, i.e., both remain side by side
(iv) *Rear location:* In this arrangement reading area and stack area are separated from each other

However, artificial light through electricity is also essential. In stack area flood light arrangement should be made so that there is sufficient light on the upper and lower position of racks. As far as readers area is concerned, arrangements should be made to ensure that every reader gets sufficient light. Special tables, fitted with tube lights may be made. In the library such bulbs and tubes should be used as do not strain on eyes. Exhaust fans ventilators and airconditioners should be fitted at required places.

L-6. OTHER FACILITES

While planning and construction a library building, many other things which look small but are important should also be kept in view. For example, readers cannot talk in the library. After reading for sometime, many may like to relax by talking, smoking, etc. Therefore, a lounge should be provided for readers. Similarly, for carrying books trollies are useful. There should be sufficient space for movement of trollies. if the library has a multistoried building, it will have lift also. The lift should be big enough to accomodate book trollies. There should also be reprography room and computer room.

L-7. MAINTENANCE

Construction of library building is a costly affair. It is therefore, essential to look after the building and pay attention towards its maintenance. Maintenance demands regular cleaning and sweeping. Polishing of floors is essential. Apart from cleaning, sweeping and polishing floors, it is also essential to clean the racks. Dust blowers and suckers are available in the market which can be used for cleaning racks and books. It is also essential to check the glasses of windows and to replace them if these are broken. Otherwise dust, air and rain may enter and damage books. From time to time face lifting of the library may be required, particularly when the library is housed in an old building.

L-8. LIBRARIAN Vs ARCHITECT

The librarian plays a vital role in planning of the library building. It has been observed that in many cases the Library Building Committees-which have nominees of finance, management and orchitect-are constituted without the Librarian. It is however essential that the architect takes the advice of the Librarian in preparing the blue print of the library building. The advice of Consultant Librarian or a Chartered Librarian may also be taken in this matter. The blue print is preparad by the architect but the librarian's opinion or advice should also be sought. There are many areas in which Librarian's opinion is essential. These are as under.

(i) the number of readers and space requirement per reader
(ii) the number of books and other materials and space requirement per book
(iii) the number of racks and space requirement per rack
(iv) What are the service and what should be their location
(v) What should be the locations at each floor on the basis of flow of work
(vi) The location of the other physical facilites
(viii) Type of lighting
(ix) Space required for future
(x) Special arrangement for safety of books
(xi) Location of carrels, reading area and stack area etc.

Only the Librarian can opine on the above mentioned points. Librarian should obtain the clearance of Library Committee, on these issues if need be. This ensures proper utilisation of available space. Architect engaged for this work should have a local office and should obtain the advice of the Librarian in making arrangements for lighting and ventillation. A building constructed with the joint efforts of the Librarian and the Architect is bound to serve as an ideal library building.

---

* A new concept introduced and discribed by Dr S R Gupta in his book entitled *Stock Verification in Libraries: Problems and Solutions (Delhi, Ken Publications, 1990).*

M

Library Associations

M-1. DEFINITION

The term association is used to denote a group or body of individuals or institutions associated with a common purpose. This common purpose generally revolves round two main types of activities, viz. (i) advancement of service oriented goals of the association and (ii) protection of the members' interests. English history of the term attributes more importance to the latter activity which is evident from the fact that the first voluntary association, receiving legal recognition from the British Parliament (in 1584-85), was formed with the sole purpose to "withstand and revenge" any attempt likely to be made on the life of Queen Elizabeth by the Roman Catholics. A plot to assassinate William III, which was hatched and came to light in the year 1696, also resulted in formation of a similar association by the Parliament. Associations were thus originally formed with the sole purpose of protecting the interests of some individuals or members. The purpose stated under (i) above i.e. advancement of service oriented goals was later included in its activities and in the present day it certainly has a dominance over the activity stated under (ii) above. On the basis of the foregoing a library association may be defined as *a group or body of libraries or librarians and users of libraries formed with the common purpose of advancement of library profession including library service and also for the protection of common interests of the members and Libraries, including raising their standards and capability to serve more effectively and efficiently.*

M-2. LEVEL

Library associations may work at different levels: International,

National, Regional, State, Local etc. For example, IFLA is an international level association, IASLIC etc. are national level associations; U.P. Library Associations is a State level association, and Bombay College Library Association is a local level association. Similarly some associations are affiliating, they affiliate other Library associations. For example, IFLA is an affiliating association. Some library associations are general in nature, such as-ILA, in the sense that they work for all types of libraries, whereas some other Library associations are special in nature (such as IASLIC, ASLIB) in the sense that their activities relate to special libraries and their services.

M3 FEATURES OF A LIVE LIBRARY ASSOCIATION

A live library association possesses the following qualities:

(i) Its membership should be open to all libraries, staff of libraries and other institutions and persons having interest in libraries, (ii) It should be the representative body in its area of work

(iii) It should encourage people from all activities and fields to become members.

(iv) It should work with dedication for the development of library profession.

(v) Its office bearers should be elected by a democratic procedure

(vi) In order to obtain its objectives it should engage itself in various programmes and activities, such as publication, organisation of conferences, seminars, workshops, training etc.

M4 FUNCTIONS

Advisory Committee on Libraries set up by the the Government of India in 1955 under the Chairmanship of Shri K.P. Sinha mentioned following five important functions of a library association:

(i) First, it tries to build up a sense of brotherhood among librarians. Cutting across the boundaries of caste, creed, colour and country it binds men and women in a self concious community devoted to the cultural uplift of their fellow men. This raises the morale of independent librarians and branches then up to their task. Librarians the world over are not distinguished by the lucrativeness of their jobs and yet they have time and again received praise for their zeal and devotion. That is due, in no small measure, to their sense of wide brotherhood of librarians.

(ii) Secondly, library associations, explicitly or implicitly, help to build up and instill into the minds of individual librarians a code, or ethics of conduct vis-a-vis their communities. In a profession such as this, where contact with independent consumers is frequent and sustained, this code helps to place the librarian on a platefrom of respectability in his community.

(iii) Thirdly, library associations make an earnest effort to raise the standards of training of librarians to enable them to perform their tasks with greater competence and for the larger benefit of society

(iv) Fourthly, a library association fights for better conditions of service of librarians

(v) and lastly, it is the standard-bearer of library extension in every country where it exists".

Library associations have played vital role in library movement in their respective countries, states etc. The Advisory Committee has mentioned five functions of a library association which are of general nature and all library associations should strive to fulfil these. Major functions of a library association may be enumerated in detail as follows:

(i) To ascertain the existing state of libraries, librarians and library service in the world (International association) country (national association), region (regional association) state (state association) etc, and to prepare a comprehensive but feasible plan for strengthening library movement in their area (i.e. world, country etc.)

(ii) To bring together persons concerned with and interested in libraries/library service and to create library awareness and consciousness.

(iii) To organise conferences, seminars, training courses, educational programmes and like activities on such topics as may have relevance to libraries, library services, library techniques and users of libraries.

(iv) To work vigourously towards enactment and adoption of library legislation in the country, state etc., and to try for its proper promulgation and implementation after it is enacted.

(v) To protect and promote the common interest of the professionals and to try for enhancement of their status and side by side also to work for the protection of the rights of the users.

(vi) To prepare a code of conduct and ethics for library personnel;

(vii) To prepare standards relating to various areas of library work, library service and library education for ensuring uniformity in library services, techniques and education.

(viii) To make efforts to see that standards of education and training programmes of librarian do not fall below standard so that the profession gets perfectly trained personnel to serve the society.

(ix) To ensure establishment and proper functioning of lower level library associations. For example a national level association may take care of a state level association, a state level association may take care of district level association and so on.

(x) To bring out publications, such as conference proceedings and papers, books, survey reports etc. on topics relevant to the profession, not only for raising finance, but also for educating the members and the professional and to show that the association is working lively.

(xi) To prepare, maintain and update a complete register of chartered/registered/authorised librarians.

(xii) To prepare, maintain, update and publish directory of libraries in the country, state etc.

(xiii) To maintain relation and to coordinate with other library associations of various levels within and outside the country; and last but not the least

(xiv) To promote resource sharing among libraries and also to impress upon the libraries and authorities to boost library extension activities.

It must however be remembered, as pointed out in the Advisory Committee report, that "In all these, the objective of library associations is to strengthen and expand the library movement and not to assist any particular library or section of librarians". Therefore only common cause may be taken up by library associations and not the cause of an individual library or member.

M5 MEMBERSHIP

It is some time advocated that only persons working in libraries, and out of them also, only those who possess some qualification in library science should be allowed to become members of a library association. This is however an orthodox and conservative point-of-view. For a healthy growth of libraries and proper development of the profession, all the persons and institutions interested in the development of libraries, such as a reader or a publisher, should be allowed to become its members. At the most, such persons may be made only associate members, not confering on them right to contest elections of the associations or to cast vote in the elections. But they must get other and entitlements, such as participation in conferences etc.

M6 FINANCE

Sufficient funds are required, in order to run the activities of the association smoothly. An association can get fund mainly through the following sources:

1. Membership
2. Sale of publications
3. Grant
4. Donation
5. Miscellaneous sources

M61 Membership

Every association charges some fee for enrolling persons or institutions as members. This can be in form of annual or life membership fee. It must however be kept in mind that the objective of charging membership fee should not be to earn money. Money received from members should be spent on them in form of sending official journal etc. This enhances the confidence of members in the association and establishes the association as the representative body of the profession.

M62 Sale of Publications

The objective of venturing into publications activity is three fold:

(i) to arrange finance for the association;
(ii) to make the members aware of the programmes and activities of the association and also to inform them of the latest developments in the profession and
(iii) to make the association an active organisation.

Special discount should be allowed to individual members on these publications. Publications should include books, journals, newsletters and proceedings of conferences etc.

M63 Grant and Donation

Governments at Centre, State and local level should be persuaded to give grant to associations for their various activities, such as conferences, publications etc. Donations in the forms of cash or kind may also be obtained from individuals and institutions through persuation

M64 Miscellaneous Sources

Funds can also be arranged through miscellaneous sources, such as, lenting out a portion of the association's building, starting consultancy and councelling service to libraries on technical matters, organising book faires at the time of conferences etc.

M7 LIBRARY ASSOCIATIONS IN INDIA

Development of library associations in India is different from that of development of such associations in other countries. In other countries national level library associations emerged first, but in India we already had some state level associations prior to the formation of the first national level library association namely Indian Library Association. For example Andhra Desa Library Association (1914), Maharashtra Library Association (1921), Bengal Library Association (1925), Madras Library Association (1923), and Punjab Library Association (1929) were formed before the formation of Indian Library Association (1933). A brief study of some of library associations in India has been presented below:

M71 Indian Library Association (ILA)

M711 Description

Full form of ILA is Indian Library Association. It has members from all the parts/states of the country representing all types of libraries. Majority of members belong to library profession including teachers of library science, but there are members belonging to other walks of life also, as ILA contitution allows anyone who has interest in library to become its member.

Indian Library Association was formed on 13th Sept. 1933 at the First All India Library Conference, held in Calcutta with AC Woolner (Vice-chancellor, Punjab University) as Chairman and K.K. Asadullah (Librarian, Imperial Library) as Secretary. It was decided that the Association will work for development of libraries and library movement, improvement of status of librarians and stressing for better training for librarians. Since then ILA is working as a representative body of Indian librarians and of Indian libraries and is dedicated to the cause of libraries.

M712 Objectives

The ILA constitution[1] lays down the following objectives of the Association:

(a) promotion of library movement and improvement in library service in all its aspects in India;

(b) promotion of library science education and the improvement in the training of librarians in India;

(c) promotion of bibliographical study and research in library science;

(d) improvement in the state and conditions of service of librarians;

(e) affiliation of state and other library associations with Indian Library Association and co-operation with international organisations with similar objective;

(f) publication of bulletins, periodicals, books, etc. which will help in the realization of the objectives of the Association;

(g) establishment of libraries, documentation centers and assistance in their establishing and working.

(h) promotion of appropriate library legislation in India;

(i) providing a common forum to all persons engaged or interested in library and information work by holding conferences and meetings for discussion of professional, technical and organisational issues.

(j) accreditation of institutions imparting library and information science education and training;

(k) promotion as well as formulation of standards, norms, guiding for management of library and information systems and service; and

(l) carrying out all such other activities as are incidental or conducive to the attainment of the above mentioned objectives.

The Association has been organising annual conferences, seminars and other such activities since its inception. It is affiliated to IFLA (International Federation of Library Associations) and COMLA (Commonwealth Library Association) and is represented on RRRLF (Raja Rammohun Roy Library Foundation), NBT (National Book Trust), CBT (Childern Book Trust) ISI (Indian Standards Institute) etc. It publishes ILA Bulletin (quarterly) and ILA news leter (quarterly) besides publishing papers of its various conferences. It is considered to be the representative body of library profession in the country and has been functioning to justify its existence.

M-713. Membership

The membership of (ILA) is open to all individuals and institutions who are interested in the development of libraries and library professions, such as library staff, library users, publishers etc. It has following eight categories of membership.

(i) Patron members
(ii) Honorary members
(iii) Foreign members
(iv) Life members
(v) ordinary members
(vi) Institutional members
(vii) Library Associations
(viii) Associate members.

In the year 1933 (i.e. the year of establishment) it had only 70 members. Now it has over 3,000 members.

M-714. Constitution/Composition

All ordinary members, including the life, institutional and library associations members are members of the General Council also. After every two years the members elect the office bearers. Election is held through postal ballots. The association organises its annual conference each year. Before every alternate annual conference the work of elections is completed. Counting of ballot papers is done at the time of the alternate annual conference and results are announced there. Any valid member with continuous membership for the last two years can contest for any position or can cast his votes for any position. Elections are held for President (1), Vice presidents (6), General Secretary (1) and Council Members (14). Public Relation Officer, Librarian and Treasurer are nominated. Besides, the members are also nominated for various sectional Committees, constituted for various type of libraries (such as School Libraries, Agricultural Libraries, Oriental Libraries, Governmental Departmental Libraries etc.

M-715. Publications

Indian Library Association started the publications of Library Bulletin in the year 1942 as its official organ. It was ceased in 1946. In the year 1949 the association started publishing *Abgila*. It had three parts: Annual (A), bulletin (B) and Granthalaya. (G). *Abgila* was the abbreviation used for of annals. bulletin, Granthalaya of Indian Library Association. This also ceased publication in 1953. Since 1955 the association is publishing *ILA Bulletin* as its official organ. The assocation is also regularly bringing out ILA News Letter, besides publishing papers and proceedings of its annual conferences and books on professional topics.

M-716. Activities and Affiliations

The association organises annual conferences each year, besides regularly organising seminar, workshops and training programmes in various parts of the country. It has also started consultancy service and contracts. The two most prestigious of these are the consultancy/contract got by it as for the Lal Bahadur Shastri National Academy of Administration, Musoorie, and Indira Gandhi National Centre for Arts, New Delhi. It is all affiliated to IFLA and is represented in many national level organisations, such as Raja Rammohun Roy Library Foundation, Delhi Public Library, National Book Trust, Bureau of Indian Standards etc.

M-717. List of Annual Conferences

A list of annual conferences organised by ILA is given below:-

	Day	Month	Year	Place	Organiser
First	12-14	09	1933	Calcutta	Imperial Library
Second	19-22	04	1935	Lucknow	Lucknow University
Third	22-24	12	1937	Delhi	Delhi University

Fourth	13-14	04	1940	Patna	Patna University
Fifth	04-06	04	1942	Bombay	Bombay University
Sixth	07-10	04	1944	Jaipur	Jaipur
Seventh	25-28	01	1946	Baroda	Baroda State Library Association & Baroda Central Library.
Eigth	19-21	01	1949	Nagpur	Nagpur University.
Ninth	11-15	05	1951	Indore	Indore Central Library
Tenth	01-06	06	1953	Hyderabad	Osmania University
Eeleventh	07-11	04	1956	Calcutta	Calcutta University
Twelvth	17-18	04	1960	Calcutta	Indian Library Association
Thirteenth	10-12	02	1962	Calcutta	Indian Library Association
Fourteenth	10-15	04	1964	Patna	Patna University
Fifteenth	17-19	06	1965	Mysore	Mysore University
Sixteenth	26-28	11	1966	Chandigarh	Punjab University
Seventeenth	27-28	11	1968	Indore	Indore University
Eighteenth	29-31	12	1969	Tirupati	Shri Venkateshwar University.
Nineteenth	24-26	03	1972	Delhi	Indian Library Association and National Book Trust
Twentieth	09-12	07	1973	Hyderabad	Academy of Library Science and Documentation
Twenty-First	13-16	01	1975	Bhuvaneshwar	Utkal Library Association Orissa Agricultural and Technical University
Twenty-Second	17-20	01	1076	Delhi	Delhi University
Twenty-Third	06-11	10	1976	Shrinagar	Indian Library Association and Jammu & Kasmir State
Twenty-Fourth	29Jan-1Feb		1978	Bangalore	
Twenty-Fifth	14-18	05	1979	Trivendrum	Indian Library Association, Kerala State and Trivendrum Public Library

	Day	Month	Year	Place	Organiser
Twenty-Sixth	06-09	03	1980	Delhi	Indian Library Association and National
Twenty-Seventh	09-12	01	1981	Hyderabad	Academy of Library Science and Documentation
Twenty-Eighth	20-23	10	1982	Lucknow	U.P. Library Association and U.P.Govt
Twenty-Ninth		11	1983	Mysore	Mysore University
Thirteith	28-31	01	1985	Jaipur	Rajasthan Library Association, Rajasthan University Library
Thirty-First	01-04	11	1985	Baroda	
Thirty-Second	03-06	01	1987	Anantpur	Shri Krishnadevaraya University
Thirty-Third	28-31	12	1987	Tiruchirapalli	
Thirty-Fourth	20-23	12	1988	Calcutta	Bengal Library Association
Thirty-Fifth		12	1989	Pune	University of Poona
Thirty-Sixth			1990	Jodhpur	University of Jodhpur

M-72 IASLIC

Full form of IASLIC is "Association of Special Libraries and Information Centres". It came into being on Sept. 3, 1955. With good number of decidated members, IASLIC is functioning with zeal for the realisation of following objectives,

1. To encourage and promote the systematic acquisition, organisation and dissemination of knowledge;
2. to improve the quality of library and information service and documentation work;
3. to co-ordinate the activities of and to forster mutual co-operation and assistance among special libraries
4. to serve as a field of active contact for libraries, information bureaues
5. to improve technical efficiency of the workers in special libraries;
6. to act as a centre of research in special library and documentation techniques;
7. to act as a centre of information in scientific, technical and other fields.
8. to take such action as may be incidental or conducive to the

attainment of the objects of the association;

9. to act as a nucleus for research in special librarianship and documentation techniques.

M-722. Constitution/Composition

The General Body is the collective form of all the members, individual as well as institutional. The General Boady elects the members of the 'Council' which has 34 members out of which 14 are office bearers and 20 are general members. Council is the highest body to look after the affairs of the association. The Council constitutes 'Executive Committee' and finance Committee to help it.

The association has different divisions, such as Documentation Services Division, Publication Division etc. Each division has one Secretary and four members.

M-723. Activities & Programmes

The main activities and programmes of the Association are as under:

1. Publication
2. Document Reproduction Service
3. Training
4. Study Circle
5. Conferences, Seminars etc.

M-7231. Publication

The Association has been issuing quality publications in form of books, seminar paper, conference proceedings, monographs, pamphlets etc. Besides, it is publishing the below named journals which have received appreciation of professionals.

(i) *IASLIC Bulletin:* This is a quarterly journal in which papers relating to library and information science are published. It is sent free of charge to the members of the IASLIC. Others can subscribe to it.

(ii) *IASLIC Newsletter:* Contains news partaining to persons, places and institutions and development in the field of library and information science.

(iii) *ILSA:* Its full forms is Indian Library Science Abstract. It contains abstracts of articles published in selected library science journals. It is a priced publication even for members.

M-7233. Document Reproduction Service

The association is running this service for researchers and teachers.

M-7233. Training

The association has been conducting short term courses on the topics relevent for the current needs of libraries, such as computer applications, presentation and conservation of documents, indexing techniques, bibliographic control etc.

M-7234. Study Circle

The association has been organising since 1965 study circles in different parts of the country. In these study circles lectures are organised on the subjects of professional interest.

M-7235. Seminars/Conferences

The Association has been organising two seminars and one conference each year in different parts of the country on the topics concerning the profession and the professionals.

M-73. AGLIS

M-731. Desprıption

Full forms of AGLIS is Association of Government Librarians and Information Scientists which is its current name: The need for organising association of the Government libraries was felt fairly early but it was in May 1933 that some librarians working in the then Imperial Secretariat sat at Simla and laid the foundation of the Association. It was named as "Government of India Libraries Association." In 1970s it changed its name to "Government of India Library Association." At the time of its registration in 1975, under the Society Registration Act, its name had to be changed as "Government of India Libraries Association" at the instance of the Registrar of Societies, Delhi. The founders of the Association in 1933 included Shri A.M.R. Montagu, a young Engineer and S-Shri Madan Gopal, R. Gopalan, Mohd. Shafi and Brij Bhushan, all librarians. Shri Montagu was the first president and Shri Gopalan the first Secretary. The association received a great impetus when Sir John Sargent, the first Education Commissioner (and also Education Adviser to the Government of India) became its president in 1940. The other landmark in the history of the Association came in the year 1952 when, vide letter number D-251-52-B, I dated 18th Nov. 1952 of the Ministry of Education, Government of India, it recieved the recognition of the Government. The names of its some of the Presidents are: Sir John Sargent (the first Education Commissioner and later Education Adviser to Government of India), Prof. Humayun Kabir (the then Cabinet Minister and Scholar), Dr. P.N. Kirpal (the then Secretary, Ministry of Education), Dr. K.L. Joshi (formerly Secretary, U.G.C. and Vice Chancellor, Indore University), Dr. S.R. Ranganathan (needs no introduction to librarians), S. Sohan Singh (the then Deputy Education Adviser) etc.

M-732. Objectives

The objectives of the Association, as listed in its constitution and Memorandum of Association are as under:-

(i) Consistent with the objectives of the libraries set up by the Government of India, this Association aims at the building up of a body of a professional experts to be utilised in the smooth and efficient functioning of these libraries;

(ii) to help libraries provide effective service to the planners, policy-makers and administrators in the Government of India;

(iii) to evolve methods and techniques for the continuos improvement of the Libraries and the qualities of information and documentation services, in the Government of India;

(iv) to forster mutual cooperation and assistance among the various libraries of the Government of India and the library personnel working therein;

(v) to serve as an institution for the exchange of professional knowledge and experience by organising training courses, seminars, symposia, confornces, lectures, etc. and by publishing reports, monographs, bulletins, catalogues, bibliographies, journals etc. and to promote the interests of the Government libraries and librarianship;

(vi) to co-operate with approved institutions and interested bodies, national and international, in the furtherenece of its said objectives;

(vii) to issue appeals and applications for money and funds in the furtherence of the said objectives and to accept gifts, donations, subscriptions of cash and securities and of any property movable or immovable;

4. The association shall do all such things and perform all such

acts as may be necessary or proper for the achievement of all or any of the aims and objectives either by itself or in association and co-operation with other organisations.

5. For the effective carrying out of the aims and objectives of the association to acquire, receive and hold property of any kind including cash and other contributions, securities and negotiable instruments, to construct and maintain building, to alter or improve them and to equip them suitably, to manage, transfer or otherwise dispose of or deal with property of any kind belonging to the Association, to enter into contracts for and in connection with any of the purposes of the Association, to raise money in such manner as may be deemed fit, for and on behalf of the Association.

M-8. LIBRARY ASSOCIATIONS ABROAD

M-81. American Library Association (ALA)

The American Library Association was formed in Oct 1876 with the assent of a large gathering of librarians from U.S., Canada and U.K. who had assembled at philadelphia. Its first President was Justin Winsor and Melvil Dewey was its first Secretary. It is the oldest and the largest national library association in the world. Its ambitious objective is "to extend and improve library service and librarianship in the United states and throughout the World."[2] It is composed of type of library division (eg. of college and reaearch libraries, public libraries etc.) type-of-activies (e.g. children service division, adult service division, technical service division etc.), state, regional etc. chapters (based an geographical division), and more than a dozen affiliated library associations. The association admits three types of members: personal and special membership is open to any person or organisation interested in the development of library and library service. Its range of activities are very wide and diverse. It is an accreding assocation.[3] It also formulates standards of various aspects of librarianship with a view to raising standards of service. It has also spelt out and established privileges to guide professionals in performing their duties. For example, the association formulated and adopted as early as in 1938 the "code of ethics for Librarians" It also takes care of readers which will be evident from "ALA Bill of Rights" which bestows upon the readers the right to read by adopting "The freedom to read is essential to our democracy."

M 82 Library Association (LA)

The Library Association (LA) is an organisation of librarians in United Kingdom of Great Britain and Northern Ireland. It is chartered professional organisation[4]. It was founded in Oct. 1877 at the first international conference of librarians in London as "Library Association of United Kingdom" (LAUK). Till 1896 it was known by this name. In 1896 it changed its name by retaning only "Library Association" (LA). In 1898 it was granted by the Queen Victoria a Royal Charter of incorporation, which defined its objectives as under:

> "to unite all persons engaged or interested in library work, by holding conferences and meeting for discussion of bibliographical question and matters affecting library or their regulation, or management, or otherwise; to promote whatever may tend to the improvement of the position and qualification of librarians; to hold examination in librarianship and to issue certificate of efficiency, to promote the esteblishment of reference and lending library for use by the public, to promote and encourage bibliographical study by research".[5]

Its membership is open to every one who is interested in libraries. Library Association Record is its official journal. Besides, it also publishes Journal of Librarianship, Library and Information Science Abstract (LISA) and has published over hundred titles.

M 83 ASLIB

Full form of ASLIB is Association of Special Libraries and Information Bureau. As is evident from its name, ASLIB is an association with members runing in thousands from the fiels of business, commerce, learned societies, government departments. Technical institutions and even universities and individual specialists. It was started in 1924 and registered in 1926 with a view to "facilitate the coordination and systematic use of sources of knowledge and information in all public affairs and in industry and commerce and in all the arts and sciences". It runs course in special librarianship and documentation, maintains a register of translators in specialised fields and publishes books and periodicals of repute. Its important publications are Journal of Documentation (monthly) ASLIB Book

List (monthly), Hand book of Special Lihrarianship etc.

M 85 IFLA

M-851. Introduction

Discussion on library associations will remain incomplete without dwelling upon IFLA, which in a federation of international nature and its members are library associations, libraries and other organised groups of similar nature belonging to about one hundred countries. Full form of IFLA is International Federation of Library Associations. It was founded in 1927 during the 50th annual conference of British Library Association in the presence and gathering of librarians from about fifteen countries. This gathering decided to set up an international library and bibliographic committee, which later changed its name as IFLA in 1929.

M 852 Objectives and Functions

Basic objectives of IFLA are as under:

(i) to promote international understanding and cooperation in the field of library science and bibliography;

(ii) to carry out investigation and research for the development of library and information service;

(iii) to promote the discussion over matters relating to international relation betwen libraries, library associations and organised groups with similar purpose; and

(iv) to provide the libraries, lbrarians and library associations a platform for international representation of the matters relating to the development of library and information sicence, library service and library profession.

M 853 Membership

IFLA has two types of memberships

(i) Full membership and (ii) associated membership. National or international library associations and other organisations interested in the development of librarianship may become full members. Full membership is admitted by the Executive Board of IFLA. Associate membership is open for libraries and bibligophic centres and institutions with similar objectives. It is admitted by the Secretary. IFLA now has about 100 full and 300 associate membership from 100 countries.

IFLA has provided an international forum for libraries and librarians. Its two major programmes are the talk of the day. These are Universal Availabilitiy of Publications (UAP) and Universal Bibliographic Control (UBC). The UAP aims at providing access to the published information throughout the world by each and every individual. The UBC aims at producing one such bibliographic record for each publication which may be internationally standardised, compatible and available.

M 9 CONCLUSION

Library associations throughout the world have been playing important role in promotion of library service, raising the standards of the profession and the professionals and also in creating public interst in libraries. Their exstence has benefited not only the profession and professionals but also the society as a whole.

REFERENCES

1. Modified upto and effective from Jan, 5, 1987 (New Delhi, ILA, nd.)
2. Allen Kent: Enclopedia etc., op. cit.
3. Accredition means recognition accorded to an academic institution which meets the precribed standard laid down by the competent agency. The competent agency is known as accrediting agency. Such an agency (i) lays down minimum standard which an institution in supposed to meet in teaching a course (ii) examining whether the academic institution is capable of meeting the laid down standards. ALA is such an (accrediting) agency accrediting institutions teaching library and information science coureses.
4. A chartered professional organisation maintains registers of qualified personal membres or fellows or associates.
5. As quoted in Encyclopedia of Lib. & Inf. Sc. etc., op. cit. v. 12, p. 312.

N

Library Organisations & Systems

There are organisations in India and abroad that are engaged in the promotion of library and documentation services. Such organisations are many. A few of these have earned high reputation due to their wide range and qualitaitve activities. Description of some of library organisations including systems has been presented in succeeding pages.

1. FID
2. UNESCO
3. UNISIST
4. NISSAT
5. NASSDOC
6. INSDOC
7. RRRLF

N 1 FID

N 11 History

Full form of FID is Federation Internationale de Documentation. Or International Federation of Documentation. Historically, this organisation was established in 1895 at the Conference Bibliographique Internationale, at Brussels (Belgium) with the efforts of two jurists, namely Henri La Fontaine and paul Otlet. It was named as Institute International de Bibliographie (IIB) and was established with the objective and aim to organise and publish and update a bibloigraphical World Catalogue and to study matters related with bibliography. In 1931 the 'Institut' changed its name as Institut International de Documentation (IID). This change in name reveals shift of emphasis from bibliography to documentation, such as reporgraphic service. In 1938 the organisation adopted Federation Internationale de Documentation (FID) as its name and since then it has been functioning with this name. By 1955 it had 25 national and 2 international members. Its present central office is located at the Hague (Netherland). As stated above, the Federation has national and international documentation centres as its constituent members.

N-12. Aim

Helmut Arntz has discussed the activities, aims and objectives of FID in detail. These were adopted by the council of the General Assembly in 1970 with a view to give FID a broader outlook. It has been stated that the aim of FID is (i) to promote, through international co-operation, research in and development of documentation which includes, inter alia, the organisation, storage,retrieval, dissemination and evaluation of information wherever recorded, in the fields of science, technology, social sciences, arts and humanities" and for this purpose to increase substantially the effectivencess of documentation efforts, (ii) to develop means of information storage, retrieval and dissemination, and (iii) to develop, set up created and form linkage of national regional and mission oriented system of information storage, retrieval, and dissemination centers throughout the world.

N-13. Field of Tasks/Activities

Arntz has enumerated the field of tasks or activities of FID (in Ibid) under two major heads, namely methodological tasks, and applied tasks. Methodological tasks include (i) study various methods and means of communication and suggest ways for their imporovement; (ii) make efforts to ensure increased use of new technology such as computer, reprography etc. in dissemination of information; (iii) to assess information needs of users and to develop programmes to suit their information needs; (iv) to make continued efforts to improve UDC for its aplication and use in documentation work; (v) to undertake detailed study of principle of compilation, processing, storage, search, retrieval and transmission of ideas; (vi) decide the theoretical methods and methodological base for documentation and define its principal terminology; (vii) identify research trends in the field of documentation and promote them etc. Arntz enumerates the following applied tasks which are aimed at productivity in programmes:

> "Help in setting up information activities and establishing documentation centres in countries where they do not exist and assisting in the developent of existing centres.
>
> "Encourage the establishment of information analysis centres especially, in the fields of science and technology.
>
> "Promote the training of documentalist
>
> "Promote the eduction of documentation users in the efficient utilization of documentation services.
>
> "Publish and promote the publication of manuals, text books, for general and specialized training of documentalists and users of documentation.

N 2 UNESCO

Full form of UNESCO is United Nations Educational Scientific and Cultural Organization which is an organ of United Nation (A body set up by 50 nations in 1945). It (UNESCO) was set up in Nov. 1945 at a conference in London attended by 44 nations on the invitation of British Government. Basic objectives of Unesco is to promote education, culture, and sicence. Since very beginning Unesco realised the role libraries could play in providing education and information. It therefore, has been working for development of library facilities and services. As early as in 1949 Unesco issued its famous manifesto for public libraries which recommended that opening free libraries for all is the responsibility of the government. The manifesto proclaims, "the public library is practical demonstration of democracy 's faith in universal education as a continuing and life long process. It is the principal means whereby the records of man's thoughts and ideas are made freely available to all... It is concerned with the refreshment of man's spirit by provision of books for relaxation and pleasure with assistance to the students and provision of up date technical, scientific and specialized information'.

This statement reveals Unesco's intesrest in development of libraries and library service with reference to libraries and library services. Unesco is responsible for setting up many institutions through out the world for providing educational, cultural and scientific information to people. In early 50s with the help of Unesco many under developed/ developing countries started model libraries as pilot project of Unesco. As a result we have Delhi Public Library in India. Unesco continued to open such libraries in other countries too. In addition to supporting public libraries it also supported academic libraries and special libraries including documentation centres. INSDOC (Indian national Scientific and Documentation Centre) may be named here as an example.

Unesco is known for its efforts to provide avenues and opportunities for international cooperation and coordination in the field of library and documentation services. From the very beginning Unesco has been organising (and rendering financial assistance towards) seminars and conferences in the field of library and documentation including stndaradisation of library techniques.

N 3 UNISIST

Unisist, which is a joint project of ICSU* and UNESCO is fully known as 'Intergovernmental Programme for Co-operation in the field of Scientific and Technological Information.' It aims at universal control of scientific (including social science) information through the cooperation of existing and future informaton centers throughout the World. Need for such a programme was felt much earlier. Organising and putting together the ocean of information available in the field of science and technology in particular is its concern. New researches and finding are vital only when these are known to the world at right time. Coordinated handling of scientific and other information checks duplication, saves wastage and ensures progress of research in right direction. UNESCO and ICSU realised the need for launching such a programme and set up a joint committee in 1967 under the chairmanship of Harris Brown to study the feasibility of a world science information system. The committee in its report submitted in 1970 strongly recommended launching of such programme and as a result UNISIST came into being with an objective to bring cooperation among scientific and technical information services and centers at national, regional and global level. UNISIST's activities are based on following eleven principles.[2]

(i) The unimpeded exchange of published and publishable scientific information and data among scientists of all countries.

* International Council of Scientific Unions.

(ii) Hospitality to the diversity of disciplines-as well as to diversity of languages used for international exchange of scieentific information.

(iii) promotion of the interchange of published information and data among the systems for the use of scientists and engineers.

(iv) Maintenance of technical standards on cooperative basis with a view to facilitate international interchange of scientific information and data among systems.

(v) to make efforts to ensure uniformity and compatibility among information processing systems developed in different countries in different fields.

(vi) Promotion of cooperative arrangements among the information processing systems developed in different countries with a view to sharing work load and making available the needed product at any place.

(vii) To assist any country in finding contemporary or future information service.

(viii) To develop trained manpower and resources of published information for the utilisation of machine systems.

(ix) Increased participation of scientists in the development and use of information system.

(x) To involve coming generation of scientists in the planning of scientific information system of the future.

(xi) To reduce administrative and legal barrier in the flow of scientific information between and among countries.

UNISIST is not expected to act as a centralised but as coordinating agency. It coordinates the activities of different Governments and agencies. The General Conference of UNESCO held in Nairobi in 1976 launched a new programme know a General Information Programme (PGI). The aims and objectives of this programme were similar to UNISIST: So UNISIST has become entegral part of PGI programme which is also known as UNISIST-II.

N4 NISSAT

N 41 Description and Objectives

Full form of NISSAT is National Information System for Science and Technology. It was established by Government of India, under Department of Science and Technology in 1977. The purpose for which NISSAT was formed is clear from its name. Its broad objectives are as under:

(i) To take steps for making provision for information in the fields of science and technology to meet the present and future needs.
(ii) To develop mechanism for locating the information.
(iii) To ensure maximum utilisation of available information in the field.
(iv) Coordination between and among national scientific information centres and promotion of exchange of scientific information at national and international level.
(v) To encourage participation in educational training and research programmes relating to management of scientific and technical information in the country.
(vi) Support, promotion, and encouragement of research and development in the field of information technology.
(vii) To identify potential scientific and technological users working in public or private sector and to disseminate the information useful to them.

N 42 Sectoral Information Centres

Under the NISSAT Programme the major instrument for information resources development and dissemination is a sectoral information centre which provides bibliographic as well as factual and numeric information on a product, discipline or mission. The Sectoral Centres established under the NISSAT Programme are given in the Table 1 at next page.

The Centres were built around the existing information resources and facilities. They were, however, provided with a wide range of documents, sophisticated equipments and manpower so that they could provide information services on a national scale. They maintain an extensive collection of published and unpublished documents in the form of books, periodicals, research reports, development of trade reports etc., pertaining to the relevant subject area. Regular monthly technical publications from these centres include Current Indian literature, Patents highlights and Industry highlights in respective sectors and also semitechnical and popular ones in the form of digests. Besides, the centres have also brought out ad hoc publications like Buyers Guides, Directories of Agents, Research, Foreign Collaborations, etc. The Centres have also developed information management tools.

Table 1: NISSAT Sectoral Centres

	Sector	Institution
i)	Leather Technology (NICFOS)	Central leather Research Institute, Madras
ii)	Food Technology (NICFOS)	Central Food Technoological Research Institute, Mysore
iii)	Machine Tools (NICMAP)	Central Machine Tools Institute, Bangalore
iv)	Drugs and Pharmaceuticals (NICDAP)	Central Drugs Research Institute, Lucknow
v)	Textiles and Allied subjects (NICTAAS)	Ahmedabad Textile Industry's Research Association, Amedabad
vi)	Chemicals (NICHEM)	National Chemical Laboratory, Pune
vii)	Compact-Disk (NICDROM)	National Aeronautical Laboratory, Bangalore
viii)	Bibliometrics (NCB)	Indian National Scientific and Documentation Centre, New Delhi

The sectoral centres have created and are maintaining several databases to cater to different information requirements of their clientele. For example, NICMAP maintains Bibliographical Database, Patent Database, World machine Tools Statistics, Indian Machine Tool Production Statistics Database & Import/Export Statistics Database; NICDROM has Library & Information Science Abstracts (LISA) database on CD-ROM etc. Services provided by these centres also include document supply, compilation of special bibliographies, publication, patents search, reprography, micrography, translation and industrial enquiry services.

NISSAT has plans to establish more sectoral information centres in addition to the eight already existing. New activities will be in the form of database development rather than information centre development. NISSAT is the agency authorised by UNESCO to distribute CDS/ISIS free to libraries in India.

N 43 Online and SDI Services

In order to bring the Information support services available to the scientists and technologists in India at par with those available to their counterparts in the developed countries. NISSAT has taken up the establishment of online search facilities on permanent basis in the country. Five regional access centres (called NACII) have been established (Table 3).

Table 3: NISSAT Access Facilities to International Datacentres

	Place	Institution
i)	New Delhi	Indian National Scientific Documentation Centre (INSDOC)
ii)	Pune	National Chemical Laboratory (NCL)
iii)	Bangalore	National Aeronautical Laboratory (NAL)
iv)	Madras	Central Leather Research Institute (CLRI)
v)	Calcutta	Indian Association for Cultivation of Science (ICS)

N 44 Library Networking

NISSAT took the initiative for the development of metropolitan networks to ensure better utilisation of S&T information resources through resource sharing, to moderate functional load of information centre management and to take care of communication. CMC Limited, Calcutta has completed the feasibility study for CALIBNET. Divided in two phases; phase-I of the network would include Indian Association for Cultivation of Science (IACS). Central Glass & Ceramics Research Institute (CGCRI), Jadavpur University Central Library

(JU), Indian Institute of Chemical Biology (IICB), Institute of Radio Physics & Electronics (IRPE), General Library of Calcutta University (at old Saha Institute location), Bose Institute (BI). Indian National Scientific Documentation Centre (INSDOC) Regional Centre Calcutta will act as the Network Services Centre and Regional Computer Centre would host the Union of databases.

On similar lines, the establishment of DELNET was conceived for about 30 libraries in Delhi and has started functioning (For details see, DELNET in Chapter S).

NISSAT has also been organizing sponsoring computer courses for librarians and information scientists.

The need for computerisation is felt at all levels and in all activities. The nature of activities which demand use of computers may vary from automation of routine management function in libraries to information retrieval or analysis of global databases. Unfortunately, application of this tool is still not significant in India. Realising this, NISSAT accorded high priority to all aspects of computer based bibliographic information processing. NISSAT acquired a proven software pckage "CDS/ISIS–Micro–version 2.3" from UNESCO. Official distribution rights in India were also obtained for UNESCO.

N 45 Conclusion

The last few years have witnessed a sea change in the S&T information scenario in the country. Easy and quick access to information through organized information centres integrated into a network is one manifestation of this change.

Promoting and supporting this process is the objective of NISSAT, the apex information coordinating agency under the Department of Scientific and Industrial Research. By establishing sectoral centres in different S&T areas and running a series of programmes for education and training of those responsible for manning the centres, NISSAT has spearheaded the development of indogenous capabilities to meet the fast growing appetite of scientific and technological community for information in diverse areas.
(Based on NISSAT Newsletter (90/2), April-June 1990.

N5 NASSDOC

The National Social Science Documentation Centre (NASSDOC) was earlier known as Social Science Documentation Centre (SSDC). It was set up in 1970 by Indian Council of Social Science Research (ICSSR). Its major activities, as contained in a brochure (mimeographed) circulated by the organisation are as under:

(i) To build up a collection of reference materials including unpublished doctoral theses approved by Indian universities and research reports and periodicals.

(ii) To provide duplicating and reprographic services.

(iii) To work for bibliographic control over social science materials by bringing out various documents (42 titles have so for been brought out).

(iv) To compile and make available bibliographies on demand.

(v) To provide bibliographic information about Indian publications in social science discipline to international documentation agencies.

(vi) To provide study grants to scholars for working at libraries of their interest.

(vii) To provide consultancy to social science institutions in setting up documentation and inormation centres.

(viii) To provide activities or staff participation in professional seminars and conferences though contributing papers as well as taking active part in their deliberation.

(ix) To organise B. Lib. & Information Science classes for Andhra Pradesh open University students in capacity of Northern Regional Coordination Centre of the university.

(x) To process project proposals and finance for the consideration of ICSSR Committee on Documentation.

(xi) To strive for exchange arrangement with national and international organisations for their publication.

The centre has a rich library which remains open from 9.30 A.M. to 5.30 P.M. throughout the year except the three national holidays. Its documentation programmes and publications include Union List of Social Science periodicals, Union Catalogue of Social Science Periodicals, Directory of Social Science Research Institution in India etc.

N 6 INSDOC

N 61. Description

Indian National Scientific and Documentation Cente (INSDOC) was established in 1952 with technical assistance from UNESCO with the aim to provide a wide range of documentation services to scientists and scientific and technological researchers. For about a decade from its establishment it worked under the administrative control of the National physical Laboratory (NPL). Now it is functioning as an independent unit of Council of Scientific and Industrial Research (CSIR). It has three regional centres at Banglore, Calcutta, and Madras, beside the main centre at New Delhi.

N 62 Obectives

INSDOC has following major objectives:

(i) To receive and retain all scientific periodicals which may be of use to the country.

(ii) To inform scientists and engineers of articles which may be of value to them.

(iii) To answer specific enquiries from information available in the centre.

(iv) To be a national repository for reports of the scientific works of the nation both published and unpublished, and

(v) To be a channel through which the scientific work of the nation is made known and available to the rest of the world.

N 63 Functions

INSDOC divides its work in various sections, such as bibliography and information, document copy supply, translation, reprography, printing, Indian Science Abstracts, Union Catalogue, information retrieval including SDI, Russian Science Digest service, Russian Science Information centre, Library publicity and sales, translation bank, Training, Planning and Coordination, Administration and accounts.[3] That INSDOC provides wide range of services will be evident form the enumeration of its various sections. Some of the major activities of Insdoc have been described below in brief.[4]

N 631 Biblioography and Information Service

Scientists and Scientific researchers before proceeding to do some research work are keen to know about previously published literature in their topic of research work. On request INSDOC compiles bibliography of literture and supplies to the scientists. Besides, it also answers scientific enquires.

N 632 Document Copy Supply Service

Supply of copies of documents to interested users has been a popular and useful service of INSDOC. These documents may be procured from other libraries. For example, the patent collection available in microfilm in the National Information Centre New Delhi is being made use of for meeting the requirements for copies of foreign patents. Many libraries from Delhi, Banglore, Madras and Calcutta cooperate with INSDOC in providing this service. Some time documents are procured from abroad also to meet the needs of Indian scientists and scientific researchers.

N 633 Reprography Service

Delhi office and Bangalore regional centre have facilities for microfilming, photocopying, xerox copying and slide making and Madras and Calcutta centres have facilities for xerox copying.

N 634 Information Dissemination & Retrieval of Information

INSDOC disseminates information through Indian science Abstracts, Russian science Digest, science, National Index translation, Ntional Union Catalogue of scientific serials. Its other important publications are Annals of library Science and Documentation, Current Research projects in CSIR laboratories, Directory of Indian scientific periodicals etc.

N 635 Education & Training

INSDOC have been organising regular and short term courses since long. It has been conducting a regular course on "Associateship in Information Science" since 1964. Students for the course are selected through written test and interview held at several places in India. Minimum qualification for applying to the course is Master degree in a subject, or a four year plus degre such as B.E., MBBS etc. or post-graduate degree in library science with three years' working exprience. Form and prospects for admission to this course is normally availble in April each year and the course starts around August each year.

In addition, INSDOC have also been conducting since 1989 short Term courses in computer basics and computer application to libraries in collaboration with NISSAT. These coures include training in MS-DOS, CDS/ISIS, dBase, Lotus, Data Base Management. etc. These are normally of 4-5 weeks duration.

N 635 Networking

INSDOC have also launched programmes and projects in computrised networking.

N 7 RRRLF

N 71 Description

Full form of RRRLF is Raja Ramohun Roy Library Foundation. It is an autonomous organisation under the Department of Culture, Ministry of Human Resources Development, Government of India. It was set up in the year 1972 in the memory of Raja Rammohun Roy, who, born in 1872, devoted himself for the cuase of adult education and social well being. Its central office is located at Calcutta at DD 34, Salt lake, Sector I, Calcutta. The Foundation is registered under the West Bengal Societies Registration Act and is fully financed by the Government of India.

N 72 Constitution/Composition

The Minister of Human Resource Development or his/her nominee is the Chairman of the Foundation. The Foundation is governed by its Executive Committee which is constituted by the Chairman, the Director (full time), eminent Librarians and representatives of the Ministry of Human Resources Development.

N 73 Activities & Programmes

Activities and programmes of the Foundation are as under:

(i) Financial assistance to libraries
(ii) Grant to Library Associations
(iii) Efforts for enactment of library legislation
(iv) National Library Policy
(v) Publications

N 731 Financial Assistance to Libraries

The Foundation has implemented many programmes for financial assistance to libraries. These include hundred percent assistance, and matching assistance as under:

1. Hundred percent assistance

(a) Distribution of books to State Central and District libraries through Central Selection scheme.
(b) Assistance to centrally sponsored libraries, such Balbhawans and Nehru Yuvak Kendras.
(c) Opening children's libraries either independently or as a part of a bigger public library.
(d) Assistance to voluntary organisations for running libraries.

N 732 Matching Assistance

(i) For purchase of books and other audio visual material
(ii) For opening and running Rural Book Deposit Centre and mobile library service
(iii) For storage of books and display of books including book exhibitions
(iv) For organising conferences, seminars etc.
(v) For extension of building to libraries below district level
(vi) For purchase of vedio and television to district and state central libraries

N 74 Publications

Details of the activities and programmes of the Foundation are available in one of its publications, entitled "Books for the Millions at their Doorstep". Its other publications include "Indian libraries: trends and perspectives (published by some other publisher in agrrement with the Foundation), being a series of lectures organised by the Foundation; 'Directories of Public Libraries in India', being a directory of libraries assisted by the Foundation so far; 'Granthna' - being a journal in the field of library and information science, and 'Newsletter' carrying news relating to the recent activities of the Foundation as well as recent developments in the field of library and information science.

N 75 National Library Policy

In the year 1981 the Foundation constituted a working group for preparing a draft National Library Policy. The draft was ready by 1983 on the basis of which the Government of India, Department of Culture issued a 'Draft Policy Statement' and constituted a Committee under the Chairmanship of Prof. D.P. Chattopadhyay. In May 1986 this committee submitted its recommendations to the Department of Culture. The Department again constituted an "Empowered Committee" the reports of which was also submitted long back. Further development in the matter is not known.

On the basis of the foregoing it can be said that the Foundation is doing appreciable work in its field.

REFERENCES

1. Kent: *Encyclopedia of Library and Information Science, op. cit.* v. 12.
2. Sarab, Veena, In S.M. Agarwal etc. *ed.: Prospective in Library and Information Science*, v. 1. pp. 382-83 (Lucknow, Print House, 1983).
3. INSDOC, Annual Report 1984-85, p-2.
4. From ibid.

P

User Education

P-1. INTRODUCTION

User education is concerned with educating the users in use of the library with a view to enable them to derive maximum benefit from the materials kept in the library. It consists of familiarising the user with all those techniques and tools which lead them to the treasure of knowledge hidden in books and other reading materials. In short, it involves helping the reader to find his information himself. The concept of helping the reader is not very new. It is backbone of reference work. The concept of 'reference work' and readers' help was discussed with vivid details by S.S. Green in 1876 at the first conference of American Library Association. While defining reference service as "a process of establishing contact between the reader and his book in a personal way", Ranganathan also has laid marked emphasis on 'helping readers'. The seeds of user education were, therefore sown in 1876 with the emergence of the concept of reference work and service. It is however to be borne in mind that readers' education is not a part of reference service. It differs distinctly from reference service, though both strive to attain common goals. Reference service presupposses personalised service and help to the user *when he needs;* on the other hand user education presupposes personalised training and orientation of the user with the presumption that *he needs it.* Secondly, in reference service the user is *helped* in finding information : rather he in taken to the document of his interest; but in users' education the user is trained in use of the library so that he could search the document of his interest *without any body's help.* Thirdly, reference service normally does not require a course related planned programme whereas user education does. Summarily, user education aims at making user self-dependent.

It may therefore be said that the concept of user education was present in reference service in non-systematic state of exposition. Systematic use of the concept of user education is the contribution of Patricia B. Knapp. In the year 1964 she brought out a project report concerning "student use of university library resources".[1] The project was undertaken at Monteith College of Wayne State University. Later Earlha College also stressed on user education programme. It may thereforre be said that user-education is course-based instruction in use of the library, and the concept is the contribution of Patricia B. Knapp and forged by her in 1964.

P2 DEFINITION

There are numerous words that convey meaning analogous to the terms 'users education'. Some of such terrms may be enumerated as, user or reader orientation, instruction, assistance, guiding, library-instruction, bibliographic instruction etc. etc. The term 'user-education' however connotes broader meaning and encompasses all analogous terms which will be evident from the definition of the term. Some of the most widely quoted definitions of user education have been cited below:

> "...instruction given to readers to help them to make best use of the library".[2]
>
> —H. Mews
>
> "User education is concerned with the whole information and communication process and one part of this involves the total interaction of the user with the library. This should be continuous process starting with school and public libraries and with possibility of extension into academic and specialised libraries".[3]
>
> —Fjallbrant and Malley
>
> "User education is to include any effort or programme which will guide and instruct existing and potential users in the recognition and formulation of their information needs, in the effective and efficient use of information services and in their assessment".
>
> —Jacques Tacatlian

On the basis of the definitions cited above, it may be said that the concept of user education includes the concepts like orientation, initiation etc. As a matter fact these are aspects of user educations.

P3 NEED

An user is the centre round which all the activities of librarry revolve. Any library is set up for users. Each and every document in a librarry is processed, organised and maintained only to serve the needs and requirements of users. It is therefore necessary to ensure that a contact is made between document and the reader or user. User education not only ensures it, but is also the most effective way of making the contact self generating and spontaneous. Discussed below are some of the major factors that make user education necessary in any library in general and in academic and research libraries in particular:

P31 Literature Explosion

There has taken place enormous growth of information in all fields of human knowledge. This is known as literature explosion. As a result, production of documents has heavily increased. These documents are of complex nature. There are various types of documents and their scope is not known to all the users. At the same time titles of some of the books do not reveal their contents. Information sources are so many in quantity and have assumed such complex character that it is beyond the comprehension of an average user to extract information contained in these sources unless they are taught to do so. As a result the user is unable to tap informtion contained in books, and therefore, needs to be educated in search and use of information and information sources.

P32 Changed Nature of Education

User education has become more necessary in academic institutions due to emphasis on library oriented education. During the past formal education was based on dictation. Teachers used to dictate and speak, and the students used to listen to. This system of education has already been done away with in western universities and in India also we are adopting new methods with appreciable speed and success. The present day education lays marked emphasis on use of libraries. Parry Committee (UK) revealed in its report[4] of 1967, "lecture and text book method is no longer remained as the sole method for teaching" and stressed that "reading by students must be preferable to attendance at a lecture unless the lecture is superior in presentation or contents to the available literature." Students of today are supposed to devote more time in the library than in the class room. They must therefore, be taught the use of librarry. Cyril Norwood[5] has rightly said that it was a better proof of education to know how to use a library than to possess a university degree.

P33 Library Techniques and Users' Psychology

Libraries adopt specialised techniques of classification, cataloguing, classified arrangement, create special collections and use latest techniques of information storge and dissemination. Without having an introductory and working knowledge of such techniques a user may not find for himself the information needed by him. On the other hand an average reader, and particularly a freshman is normally a shy person. He hesitates in asking the library staff about such techniques. Some users who may not be shy also do not care for such things, as Ranganathan has said "readers do not take to books easily." This is the psychology of an user, not only in India but also in developed and advnced countries. For example, Parry Committee (U K), after a survey of use of library by undergraduate students reported in 1967[6] that (i) 22 per cent of the students were not aware whether or not author catalogue existed in the library, (ii) 28 per cent of the students were not aware whetherr or not the library had subject catalogue, and (iii) 63 per cent of the students did not know what is an abstracting journal. It is therefore, an established fact that users are ignorant of library techniques. Particularly library catalogue is key to the collection of the library. An user who is ignorant of the type of catalogue, arrangement of entries in it and types of entries it contains, may not be able to locate a document. In short it will have to be accepted that the complex nature of library techniques coupled with the fact that the users do not take to books easily, make it essential that user education is imparted.

P4 ADVANTAGES

Main advantages of user education programme may be enumerated as under:

1. It ensures greater use of library's material.

2. It saves the time of users as after becoming acquainted with library's techniques, information sources and literature search skills, they take less time in searching information for them.
3. User becomes able to search material without anybody's help which gives him immense pleasure. At the same time it makes the user self-dependant.
4. It also saves the time of library staff as each and every time the user will not require their help. The library staff can utilise the time saved thus, in some other service or work.

P5 PLANNING

Programming and planning of user education programme is very important particularly in academic and research libraries. It needs a careful planning. According to Thomas G. Kirk[7] planning of user education programme requires four things, namely (i) orientation, (ii) bibliographic instruction, (iii) course in literature search, and (iv) seminar. Kirk has also mentioned about acquaintance with six skills, viz., (i) reference sources, (ii) indexing and abstracting periodicals, (iii) library catalogue, (iv) organisation of knowledge, (v) search strategy, and (vi) subject analysis. As a matter of fact many library scientists have suggested many methods for planning of user education. All these may conveniently be grouped in following broad groups:

1. Guiding by signs & boards.
2. orientation.
   (a) Introduction to the library;
   (b) Introduction to techniques;
   (c) Introduction to information sources.
3. Literature search techniques.
4. Evaluation of users.

P51 Guiding by Signs & Boards

Signs and Boards are the most potent medium of instruction. A board of reasonable size, with the world 'LIBRARY' written on it should be affixed on the top of librrary building in such a manner as it is visible from a reasonable distance.

On the gate of the library a board should be displayed containing information about opening hours, as under:

UNIVERSITY LIBRARY: OPENING HOURS

Week days:	.... am. to .... pm.
Sunday and Holidays	.... am. to .... pm.

The library remains closed on ....

Similarly single line boards for shelf guide, section guides sould be displayed at appropriate places. Samples of some signs. and boards are given below:

CHARGING COUNTER

PERIODICALS

REFERENCE BOOKS

HOW TO USE THIS CATALOGUE	CLASSIFICATION SCHEME	
•	000	.-
•	100	.-
•	200	.-
•	300	.-
•	400	.-
•	500	.-
•	600	.-
•	700	.-
•	800	.-
•	900	.-

Numerous signs and boards etc. are readily available in market.

P52 Orientaion

Orientation programme includes imparting education or instruction to the users in (i) introduction to library, introduction to library techniques and introduction to information sources. Education of these is imparted by senior library staff or teachers of library science. Duration of classes may be short i.e. of about 25-30 minutes. Course contents in each of the three areas may be as under:

P521 Introduction to the Library

(i) Library timing: opening and closing hours on week days and holidays, closed days, timing for issue and return of books;
(ii) Layout of library building, floors, areas, collection etc. location of various sections, services;
(iii) Library rules: number of books to be issued according to category of borrowers; types of books, loan period for reference books, periodicals, general books and other categories of books, overdue charges, reservation of books;
(iv) Staff: Introduction with the incharges of each section;
(v) Procedures: Membership and registration, borrowing procedures;
(vii) Other things.

P522 Introduction to Library Techniques

(i) Scheme of classification: its features, class numbers representing broad subjects, arrangement of subjects;
(ii) Catalogue: inner form, author, title, subject etc. of the catalogue, how to use catalogue, how to find book with the use of catalogue;
(iii) Shelf arrangement, special collection;
(iv) Facilities, security etc.

P523 Introduction to Information Sources

(i) Types of reference books and information contained in these, e.g., dictionaries, encyclopaedias, dictionary of quotations, biographical dictionaries, gazetteers, almanacs, subject encyclopaedias, subject bibliographies, abstracts, indexes, serial publications, demographic sources, year books, patents, standards, primary and secondary information sources, use of non-traditional sources.

P53 Literature search techniques

(i) use of indexing and abstracting periodicals, thesaurus, citation indexes, style manuals, how to use citation, prepare bibliographies etc. Introduction to audio visual methods.

P54 Evaluation of users

In the last, users are examined whether they have assimilated the instructions imparted to them. During the course of evaluation they may be asked to locate a document, find a particular information and put to other such tests.

REFERENCES

1. Knapp, Patricia B.: An Experiment in coordination between teaching and library staff for changing student use of university library resources. Mimeograhed. (Detroit, Monteith College, 1964).
2. Mews, H.: *Reader Instruction in College and University ; introductory handbook*. (London, Clive Bingley, 1972).
3. Fjallbrant, Nancy and Mallay, Ian: User Education in Libraries. 2nd ed. (London, Clive Bingley, 1984). p. 11.
4. *Op. cit.*
5. *Op. cit.*
6. *Op. cit.*
7. A comparison of two methods of library instruction for students in introductory biology; In Coll. Res. Library, 32 (6), 1971. pp. 465-66.

R

Library Science Education

R1 NEED

A library is an important institution. Special type of manpower is required to manage it. This manpower can be prepared by imparting specialized professional education in the field of Library and Information Science. Library Science is a technical subject and library profession is a service oriented profession. Therefore, Library science education must combine technical as well as service aspects. B.S. Keshwan had rightly pointed out that the professional education and training should ensure two fundemental elements: (i) the trained students wil be useful to the society and (ii) the training will make them able to run their profession.

R2 OBJECTIVES

Objective of Library and Information Science education can broadly be categorised in two groups viz. (i) General objectives; and (ii) course based objectives.

R21 General Objectives

The objectives enumerated below may be considered to be general objectives i.e., objectives to be fulfilled by all levels of courses:

- (i) to prepare sufficient and appropriate manpower for the management of libraries at all levels;
- (ii) to teach and train students in techniques concerning management and housekeeping of libraries
- (iii) to acquaint the students with the major branches, concepts, pratices and information services in different disciplines

(iv) to train working librarians

(v) to inculcate in the students the quality of public relation, liason, and service mindedness

R22 Course Based Objectives

In our country Library and Information Science education is imparted mainly at three levels *viz.* Certificate, Bachelor, and Master level, besides M. Phil and Ph.D. Level. Some institutions and organizations, mainly polytecnics are conduting Diploma level courses. It is higher than Certificate level course but the present Diploma can not be equated with B. Lib. & I. Sc. The reason being that minimum qualification for admission to present diploma course (and certificate course too) is 10th or 10+2, whereas for admission to Bachelor degree course it is graduation. In other words certificates and diplomas are post matric courses whereas Bachelor of Lib. Sc. course is a post-graduate course. Objectives of these three levels of courses, as suggested by the Review Committee. (Ranganathan Committee) set up by the University Grants Commission (UGC) is as under

R221 Certificate Course

R2211 Objectives

(i) To give the student knowledge of the elements of Library Science.

(ii) To train the student in library routine.

R2211 Scheme of Papers

(i) Library routine

(ii) Library service and organization

(iii) Library classification

(iv) Library cataloguing

(v) Record of practical work

R222 B LIB SC Course

The following provisions of the B Lib Sc course form a core showing the necessary items of curriculum for the course. It is possible to have different grouping by different departments in the light of the needs or special facilities available to them. Such a change should always be commensurate with the general standards suggested here.

R2221 Objectives

(i) To give the student an understanding of the basic principles and fundamental laws of library science.

(ii) To enable the student to understand and appreciate the functions and purposes of library in the changing social and academic set up of the society.

(iii) To train the student in the techniques of librarianship and management of libraries.

R2222 Scheme of Papers

(i) Library Organization
(ii) Library Administration
(iii) Physical Bibliography and Book Selection
(iv) Document Bibliography and Reference Service
(v) Library Classification (Theory)
(vi) Library Classification (Practice)
(vii) Library Catalogue (Theory)
(viii) Library Catalogue (Practice)
(ix) Record of Practical Work

R223 M LIB SC Course

The following provisions of the M Lib Sc syllabus are based on the present practice in the departments of library science conducting the course. These will have to be reviewed in future as and when other departments begin to conduct the course and prefer other kinds of specialization or emphasis.

R2231 Objectives

(i) To acquaint the student with
 (a) the organization and development of the universe of knowledge
 (b) research organization and research methods.

(ii) To give the student specialised knowledge in respect of
 (a) kinds of reading and kindred materials, and of documentation lists
 (b) different types of libraries

(iii) To make the student proficient in
 (a) advanced library techniques in the methodology of documentation; and
 (b) advanced management and administration of selected types of libraries.

R2232 Scheme of Papers

(i) Universe of Knowlede. Its development and structure
(ii) Depth Classification (Theory)
(iii) Depth Classification (Practice)
(iv) Advanced Library Catalogue
(v) Any one of the following:
  (a) Public Library System
  (b) Academic Library System
  (c) Research and Technical Library System
  (d) Documentation
(vi) project during term time
  Any one of the following projects:
  (a) Preparation of a project on an approved topic falling within the area of any one of the subjects offered as an optional paper under (v) above.
  (b) preparation of a documentation list on a approved topic on the basis of a set of approved periodicals for one year.
(vii) Literature survey in one of the following fields:
  (a) Indology
  (b) A subject in Humanities, e.g.,
    (1) Literature
    (2) Linguistics
    (3) Religion
    (4) Philosophy
    (5) Psychology
  (c) A subject in Social Sciences, e.g., Geography, History, Political Science, Sociology, Law etc.,
  (d) One of the Pure Sciences
  (e) One of the Applied Sciences, e.g., Civil Engineering, Electrical Engineering, Nuclear Engineering, Mechanical Engineering, production Engineering, Chemical Engineering, Technology, Agriculture, Forestry, Animal Husbandry, Medicine, Pharmacology, etc.,

It will also be completely essential, in changed circumstances to include in B.Lib. Sc. and M.Lib. Sc. Syllabus modern concepts like computer application, CD-ROMS, Networks and like concepts.

R3 HISTORICAL ACCOUNT

In nineteenth century, it was realised in America that any type of manpower can not manage library appropirately, and therefore there was a need for specialised education and training in library science. The first person to advocate, on record, the need for library science education for preparing manpower to manage growing number of libraries in America was Justine Winsor. However, the first library science school was started in America by Melvil Dewey in Columbia College in the year 1887. This was also the first library school in the World. It was named as "School of Library Economy." The course laid equal emphasis on library techniques and practical aspects of library service. In England the first library school was 'London School of Librarianship' Library and Imformation Science education in India can be discussed under the following four heads:

1. Stray efforts
2. Organised efforts
3. Higher education
4. Present trends

R31 Stray Attempts

History of library science education in India has its traces in the year 1911 when education and training in library science was started in the earstwhile state of Baroda. The then ruler of Baroda State, Sayaji Rao Gaekwad (III) was a great lover of books, admirer of libraries and advocate of essential education. As early as in 1907 he declared that elementary education was essential and compulsory for all in his state. He was of the firm believe that libraries are essential for education and for all round development. He, therefore, invited William Allenson Borden, a deciple of Melvil Dewey, to Baroda for organising a well knit library system in his State. By 1910 Borden was able to set up chain of libraries, including mobile libraries, film libraries, special libraries for women etc. In the state Lib. Sc. education was started in the year 1911 but later on it was stopped. Second attempt to start library science course was successfully made in India in 1915 by Punjab Unitversity at Lahore with the efforts of Asa Don Dickinson. The course was conducted upto 1947 by the Punjab University. Here Bengal Library Association also deserves a mention: it started a library training course in 1935 and continued it upto 1945.

R32 Organised Education

Padmashree Dr. S.R. Ranganathan, who is known as father of library science in India, started library science education in India in an organised manner. With the efforts of Dr. Ranganathan, Madras library Association (Dr. Ranganathan was then its Secretary) started imparting training in library science since 1929 with the help of Madras University. From 1931 Madras University took over this course and conducted it during summer vacations. In the year 1937 Madras University upgraded this course to post graduate Diploma level with one year duration. Admission to this course was open only for working librarians, and minimum qualification for admission was graduate in any discipline. The second post-graduate Diploma in Lib. Sc. was started by B.H.U. in the year 1941. Later, other Universities also started Library Science courses, such as: Bombay University (1944), Calcutta University (1946), University of Delhi (1947), Aligarh Muslim University (1951) Baroda University (1956), Nagpur University (1957) etc. Most of these schools were opened with the efforts and support of Dr. Ranganathan. In 1960's award of post graduate diploma in Library Science was stopped and it was converted into B. Lib. Science Course, which, in 1970's was named as B. Lib. & Inf. Sc. Course. Certificate and Diploma level education in library science is being imparted by Library Associations or State Governments. Universities are imparting library science education at B.L. I.Sc., M.L. I.Sc. and Research level (M. Phil, Ph.D.). Higher education in library science in India (M.Lib.Sc. and Ph.D.) was started for the first time in University of Delhi. Master degree course was started in university of Delhi in 1948 and upto 1964 this was the only university to conduct M. Lib. Sc. and Ph.D. Courses in the Deptt. of Library Science. The first Ph.D. degree to a candidate enroled with a Deptt. of Library Science in India was awarded in the year 1957 to D.B. Krishnarao by Delhi University. After a gap of 20 years, the second Ph.D. degree to a candidate enroled in a Deptt. of Library Science in India was awarded in the year 1977 to Dr. Pandey S.K. Sharma, the author of this book by Punjab Univserity.

At the present, library science education is being imparted in the country at large scale. Certificate and Diploma level courses are being conducted by State Governments, Polytechnics, library associations, and also by some colleges. These are of normally 6 months duration but at places diplomas are of 1-2 years duration also. Minimum qualification for admission to these course is secondary or Senior secondary. There are hundreds of places where these courses are being conducted. B.Lib.Sc. education is being conducted in about 70 universities. This is of 1 year duration and minimum qualification for admission is graduation in a subject. Master degree level education in library science is being imparted in over 40 universities. It is one year course and minimum qualification for admission is B.Lib. Sc. University of Bombay is conducting integrated two years course leading to M. Lib. Sc. degree. M.Phil, and Ph.D. programmes are also being run in many universities. Majority of the universities have a seperate department of library science but at some places library science departments are attached to the university library. At these and some other places, the staff of library also teach on part-time basis. An alphabetical list of Universities imparting library science education at various levels is given on next page.

R4 PREREQUISITIES

The Report of the Review Committee of U.G.C. (Ranganathan Committee) recommends the following minimum prerequisites for starting a department of Library Science.

R41 Staff Requirement

"In the present circumstances, we consider a staff-student ratio of 1:10 at the B Lib Sc level and of 1 : 5 at the M Lib Sc level as reasonable. Here staff means full-time staff. In our view, a department of library science conducting the B. Lib Sc course should have a minimum staff of one reader and two lecturers and a department conducting M.Lib Sc course should have a minimum staff consisting of one professor, two readers and four lecturers. The old practice of employing the university library staff as part-time teachers should be discontinued as early as possible.

R42 Physical Facilities

A department of library science should generally provide for accommodation to meet the following requirements :

(a) Two lecture rooms
(b) One practical or laboratory room
(c) One reading room
(d) Staff room for individual teachers
(e) One seminar room
(f) One room for demonstration and use of library equipment
(g) One office room.

R43 Books

We consider a lump initial provision Rs. 50,000 for basic books and a recurring provision of Rs. 8,000 per annum as the minimum requirement for a department of library science."[11]

R5 CONCLUSIONS

It is hightime now for educational planners to modify the library science syllabi of various universities to include in it new areas, such as computer application, netwrok, database management and latest technologies, devices and systems in the field of information storage, organisation and retrieval, etc.

S.No	University	Place	PIN	Course
(1)	Agra	Agra	282004	B.LIB. Sc. and Manuscriptology
(2)	Aligarh Muslim	Aligarh	202001	B. LIB. S.C.
(3)	Andhra Pradesh Open	Somajiguda	500483	B.L.I. Sc. (Correspondence)
(4)	Andhra	Valteyer	530002	M.L.I.S.C.
(5)	Annamalai	Annamalai Nagar	608002	C.LIB. Sc. certificate In Repography, non book material Andhra
(6)	Avdhesh Pratap Singh	Riva	486003	B.L.I. Sc. M. LIB. Sc.
(7)	Banglore	Banglore	560056	B.LIB. Sc. M. LIB Sc.
(9)	Banaras Hindu	Varanasi	221005	B. LIB. Sc. M. LIB. Sc.
(10)	M.S.	Baroda	390002	B.L.I. Sc. B. LIB. Sc.
(11)	Behrampur	Bahrampur	760007	C. LIB. Sc. B. LIB. Sc.
(12)	Bhagalpur	Bhagalpur	812007	B.LIB. I. Sc. M. LIB. I. Sc.
(13)	Bhavnagar	Bhavnagar	364002	
(14)	Bombay	Bombay	400032	B.LIB. Sc. M. LIB. Sc.
(15)	Bardwan	Bardwan	713104	B.L. I. Sc. M.L. I. Sc.
(16)	Calcutta	College Street, Calcutta	700073	B. LIB. Sc. M. LIB. Sc.
(17)	Calicut	Calicut	673635	B. LIB. Sc.
(18)	Delhi	Delhi	110007	B. LIB. I.Sc. M. LIB. I. Sc.; M. FIL.
(19)	Dr. Hari Singh Gaur	Sagar	470003	B. LIB. I. Sc. M. LIB. I. Sc.
(20)	Guvahati	Guvahati	781014	B.L. I. Sc. M.L. I. Sc.
(21)	Gujrat	Ahmadabad	380009	B. LIB. Sc.
(22)	Gulbarga	Gulbarg	585106	B.L.I. Sc. M. L. I. Sc.
(23)	Guru Nanak Dev	Amritsar	143005	B. LIB. Sc. M. LIB. Sc.
(24)	Indira Gandhi National Open, New Delhi-110001			

S.No	University	Place	PIN	Course
(25)	Indian Stastical Institute, DRTC	Bangalore	560059	Associatship In Documentation and Information Science
(26)	Jadavpur	Jadavpur, Calcutta	700032	B. LIB. I.S.C. M. LIB. I.Sc.
(27)	Jamia Milia Islamia	New Delhi	110025	B.LIB. Sc. (Evening)
(28)	Jammu	Jammu	180001	B. LIB. Sc. M. LIB. Sc.
(29)	Jivaji	Gwalior	474002	B.L. I.S.C. M.I. S.C., Ph.D,
(30)	K.P. Gurubhasha Bharati	Jabalpur		B.L.I.S.C.,
(31)	Kalyani	Kalyani	741235	B.L.I. Sc.
(32)	Karnataka	Dharwad	580003	B.L.I. Sc. M.L.I. Sc., Ph.D.
(33)	Kashi Vidyapeeth	Varanasi	22100	B.L.I. Sc.
(34)	Kashmir	Shrinagar	190006	B.L. Sc. M. LIB. Sc.
(35)	Keral	Trivendrum	695034	B.L.I. Sc. M.L.I. Sc.
(36)	Kurukshetra	Kurukshetra	132119	B. LIB. Sc.
(37)	L.N. Mithila	Darbhanga		B. LIB. SC
(38)	Lucknow	Lucknow	226007	B. LIB. SC
(39)	M.S.	Baroda	390002	B.L.I. Sc. M.L.I. Sc.
(40)	Madras	Chepak, Madras	600005	B.L.I.Sc. M.L.I.Sc. Both these syllabus are also carried on by correspondence.
(41)	Magadh	Patna	824234	B. LIB. Sc.
(42)	Marathawada	Aurangabad	431004	B. LIB. Sc. M. LIB. Sc.
(43)	Mohanlal Sukhadia	Udaipur	313001	B.LIB. Sc.
(44)	Mysore	Mansagagotri, Mysore	570005	B.L.I.Sc. M.L.I. Sc.
(45)	Nagpur	Nagpur	440001	B.L.I.Sc. ML.I. SC
(46)	North Hill Eastern	Shillong	793001	B. LIB. Sc. M. LIB. Sc.
(47)	Osmania	Hyderabad	500007	B.L.I.Sc. M.L.I. Sc.

S.No	University	Place	PIN	Course
(48)	Panjab	Chandigarh	160016	B. LIB. Sc. M.LIB. Sc.
(49)	Patna	Patna	800005	B.LIB.I. SC
(50)	Poona	Pune	411007	B. LIB. I.Sc. M. LIB.I. Sc.
(51)	Punjabi	Patiala	147002	B.L. I. SC
(52)	Rajasthan	Jaipur	302004	B. LIB. Sc. B. LIB. Sc. and Documentation in LIB. Sc. and Documentation
(53)	Rani Durgavati	Jabalpur	482001	B. LIB. Sc.
(54)	Ravi Shankar	Raipur	492002	B. LIB. Sc.
(55)	Sambalpur	Sambalpur	768019	B. LJB. L. I. Sc. M. LIB. and I.Sc.
(56)	Sardar Patel	Anand	388120	B. LIB. Sc.
(57)	Saurashtra	Rajkot	360005	B.L.I. Sc. M.L.I. SC
(58)	Shivaji	Kolhapur	416004	B.L. and I. Sc.
(59)	Smt. Nathibai Damodar Thakerse, Mahila	Bombay	400020	B. LIB. Sc. M. LIB. Sc.
(60)	South Gujrat	Surat	395007	B. LIB. Sc.
(61)	Udaypur	Udaipur		B. LIB. Sc. B. LIB. Sc.
(62)	Sri Venkateshwar	Tirupati	517502	B.L.I.Sc. M.L.I. Sc.
(63)	Vikram	Ujjain	450010	B.LIB. and I.Sc. M. LIB. and I. Sc.

S

Network

S1 INTRODUCTION

With the application of computers to libraries, the concept of library networking has gained wide popularity, but it does not mean that before the advent of computers on library scene library network, or atleast its concept, did not exist. Dr. Ranganathan times and again advocated for establishing a network of libraries in which the libraries at block level are linked to the libraries at district level, dstrict level libraries are linked to State level libraries and the State level libraries are linked to the regional or national library. And, computers had not entered library scene when Dr. Ranganathan had conceived the idea of library networking. As a matter of fact he very emphatically said that library movement does not imply opening of libraries hither and thither, but to establish a well knit network among libraries.

It may therefore be said that the concept of library network existed before computers envaded libraries, but after the application of computers it has certainly become easier to transmit required information to any part of the world almost simultaneously at a very less cost without any difficulty and that also without parting with the document phisically.

It is for these reasons that computerised netwroks continue to attract the attention of libraries and information systemsh.

S2 DEFINITION

By computer network is meant inter-connected and interlinked computer system. In other words, a system in which many computer points and terminals, stretching over a room or building or city, or state, or nation or the world, are connected or linked with each other for information communication. Likewise, by Library network is meant inter-linked Libraries, or a system in which many library points, stretching from a locality, city, state, region, nation and the world, are linked with each other for information communication.

S3 TYPES

Computerized Network may be of two types, viz. Local Area network (LAN) and Wide Area network (WAN).

S31 LAN

LAN is a facility that provides data communication, video or voice, within a single building or among closely situated buildings. it consists of a number of micro-computers or terminals and peripherals linked to the central processor kept at the work station (central place). This is known as LAN because all the terminals and peripherals ies are located in one room or building or complex. In this system input of data and access to data is possible through any of the terminals or computers linked with the central computer processor, but the storage and processing of information is done only by the central processor. This system is highly suited for offices, libraries, educational institutions, departmental shops, factories etc. Hence it is a local network, local meaniny a room, building, office or complex.

S32 WAN

It is a network system which operates in a wider area stretching from a city, state, region, nation and the world. The terminals, computers and peripherals of a LAN system can be linked to WAN system with the help of another types of computers known as 'gateway'. In WAN system, therefore every participating LAN is capable of its own input, processing, output, and time sharing, but at the same time it permits a user at any LAN terminal to communicate to and from any of the other participating LAN or central station by giving a password.

S4 ADVANTAGES AND NEED

(i) *Optimum utilization of Hardware and Software:* Networking facilitates optimum utilisation of hardware and software. Hardware and software and computer peripherals are costly things to buy and maintain. In case of networking, one main processor computer the desired software may be installed and then many terminals can be connected to it and all the terminal will work efficiently. There is no need to install main computer processor at many places and to install software in each. This saves lot of money. This is one of the major advantages of LAN.

(ii) *Information transfer and sharing:* Through networking information available on computer anywhere in world can be accessed (input or output), transferred, stored and printed at any place in no time. This is one of he major advantages of LAN & WAN.

(iii) *Knowledge transfer:* Likewise, through network knowledge can also be transferred or transmitted. A class can be run over terminals to kept at any place in a building, city, state, nation, or at any place in the world.

S5 DEVICES AND OPERATION

A network operates through telecommunication device, A communication device which is capable of disseminating information or communicating at a distance (Tele=at a distance) is a telecommunication device, such as telephone, telegraph, radio and television. A telecommunications system, or a networking system, requires the following basic devices and operatons for transmission of information:

1. Transmitter
2. Transmission media

In a computerised network, data transmission is done through cable-wires, transmission media, satelite etc. The transmission can be in two forms of signals, analogue and or digital. with the help of modulators (which converts digital computer code into analogue form), demodulator (which converts analogue code into digital form), and Modem (which does the both)*.

---

* For description of terms see the author's book entifled *Concise Computer Encyclopaedia For L & IS* (In press-New Delhi, Ess Ess).

Any type of communication link can be used for computer network, such as the following:

1. Satellite channel
2. Microwave Radio link
3. electrical wiring or cabling
4. Fiber optics in which data is transmitted as pulses of light beam etc.

S6 TOPOLOGY

By topology is meant the network's blue print or structure, or the mapping or the pattern in which the different units within the network are connected with each other. Topology may be of different types, important of which are described below:

1. Star Network
2. Mesh Network
3. Bus Network
4. Ring Network
5. Fully connected Network.

S61 Star Network

Star Network consists of one central node or point and a number of other subscriber terminals connected to the Central point using a single line for each connection. Since in it a single central computer system serves a number of users, the user or subscriber terminals are dependent upon the reliability and loading of the central system.

STAR NETWORK

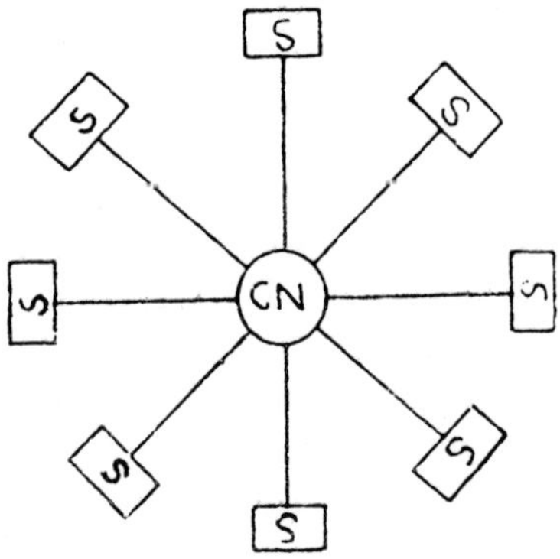

C. = Central Node
S. = Subscriber Node

Features, advantages, and disadvantages of Star Network topology are as under:

(i) All the stations are connected to a Central node and all message-routing and decision are made in the central node.

(ii) Each node in the system is connected independently with the central node which requires large length of Cables.

(iii) The entire network is down if the central node is down.

S62 Mesh Network

It consists of a number of nodes linked together in such a way that sometimes data from one has to pass the third party to reach the destination

MESH NETWORK

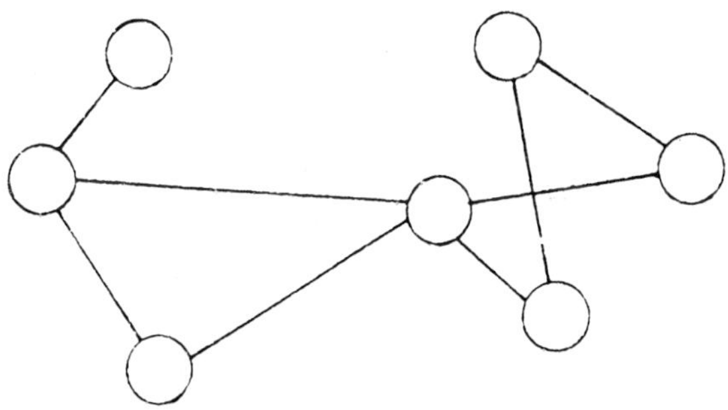

S63 Bus Network

It consists of a number of nodes linked to a 'Central Communication Highway' or bus in such a way that every node has a single bi-directional connection to a shared cable which enables each node to be directly connected to each of the rest of the nodes over this shared cable. Thus any node can directly transmit data to every other attached node.

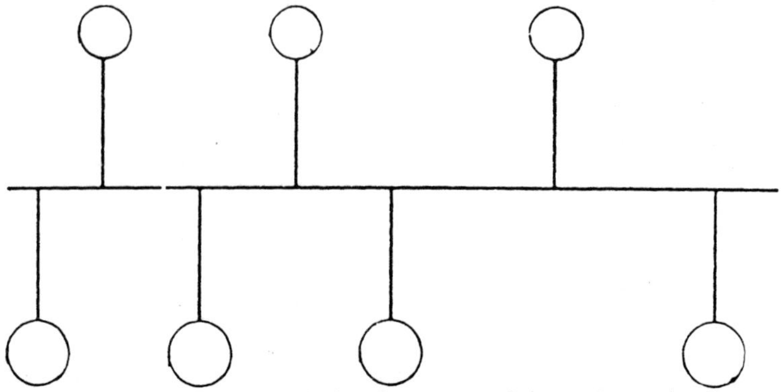

Features, Advangates and disadvantges of Bus Network are as under:

(i) All nodes in the network are connected to a common communication medium

(ii) The transmitted messages are heard by all nodes and it is for the particular node to recognise the messages indended for it and accept these

(iii) Failure of a single node does not affect the network because each node is passive and, unlike star and ring topologies, messages are not transmitted or received by intermediatory nodes.

S64 Ring Network

Ring Network consists of a number of nodes inter-connected with each other in the form of a ring and transmission is in one direction. In such a system data is communicated very speedily from the monitor station and can be accessed at any ring station by giving destination address with the appropriate device. Since the transmission of data is in loop form, this is also referred to as

RING NETWORK

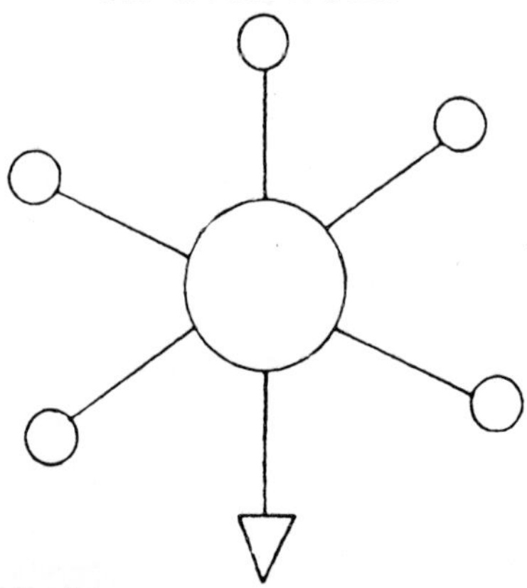

loop network. In this topology, each node is connected directly to two other nodes. "Packet of data are inserted into the ring by user terminals attached to the repeater stations; these packets traverse the ring with all nodes examining the address space of the packet to select packets addressed to them.... Ring networks are generally disigned so that a node which fails can be easily by-passed". (Nissat Newsletter, 90/2)

Features, advantages, and disadvantages of Ring Network topology are as under:

(i) All the nodes are arranged in such a way as the entire collection of nodes form a ring or circle.
(ii) Each node is connected to two other nodes. Messages travel around the circle from node to node
(iii) Each node must recognise its own address and must be able to retransmit message, to the next node.
(iv) Failure of one node or a break in the ring configuration causes the network to fail. Therefore provisions must be made to ensure that the message is by passed in the event of failure of a component.[9]

S65 Fully connected network

Fully connected Network consists of a number of nodes directly connected to each other.

FULLY CONNECTED NETWORK

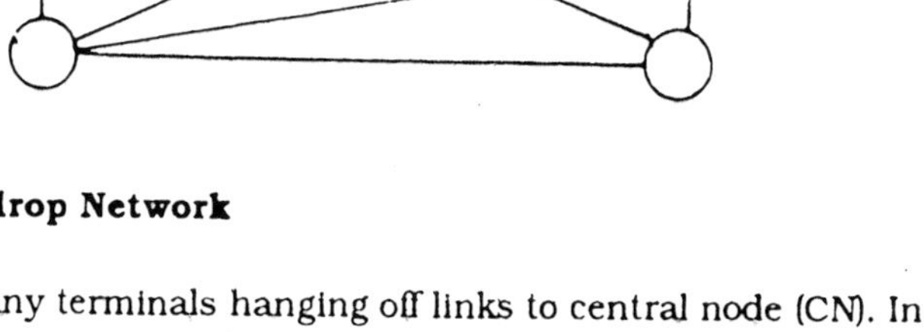

S66 Multidrop Network

It has many terminals hanging off links to central node (CN). In it more than one networks are connected with a Gateway.

MULTIDROP NETWORK

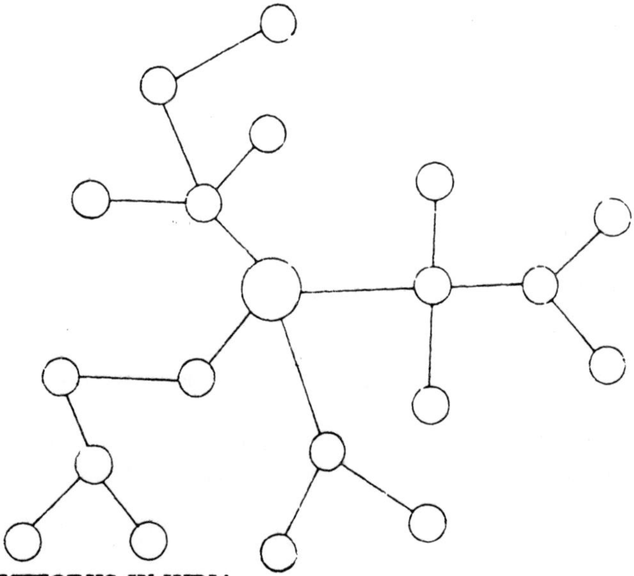

S7 NETWORKS IN INDIA

S71 CALIBNET

Abbreviation for Calcutta Libraries Network. As is evident from its name, it is an ambitious project to connect libraries of calcutta.

S72 DELNET

It is a computerised networking project for resource sharing among Delhi based libraries. In January, 1988 the India International Centre, New Delhi, organised a panel discusson on 'sharing of Resources in Delhi Libraries': Network and Technological Challenges. In this meeting it was decided to establish DELNET with the financial support of NISSAT. On the advice of NISSAT the CMC prepared a Feasibility Study Report of DELNET. Many libraries were surveyed and expressed their willingness to take part in DELNET. The standardization Committee of DELNET after continued meetings decided that a participating library must do data entry is following standard manner:

(i) Key words/subject headings may be given by the individual libraries based on some standard thesaurus/subject heading lists. Later, a thesaurus for DELNET will eventually get created autometically.

(ii) All the participating libraries should follow CCF for giving Tags No. to each field.

(iii) CDS/ISIS will be used as software, to start with, by the participating libraries.

(iv) Libraries may follow/continue to follow a scheme of classification chosen by them.

In March, 1990 the DELNET has started E-Mail through which 10 libraries of Delhi are being connected electronically to the network.

S73 ERNET

Abbreviation for Educaton and Research Network, being a project of the Department of Electronics (DOE) of the Government of India.

S74 INDONET

A project of the Computer Maintenance Corporation of India (CMC), was proposed as the first commercial computer network for an intelligent information management and distributed data processing facilitaing distributed data. In the first phase it was proposed to set up a computer network with five nodes, each at Bombay, Calcutta, Delhi, Hyderabad and Madras and to make these accessible from all parts of the country.

S75 NICNET

Acronym for National Informatics Centre Network, or simply NIC Network. The NIC— conceived in 1973 nucleated in 1975 and set up in March 1977 by Government of India— has now acquired international repute. The primary objective behind its establishment was to demonstrate to the Government the benefits that accrue frm computerization, and to put to use the new technology of computerization and computer networking for ensuring efficient change of information between the Centre and the States, between districts and various Ministries/Departments and between them and the public. The principal objectives of NIC include:

1. Development of Computer-based information systems in various sectors of the economy for planning, project monitoring and decision support.
2. Promotion of informatics culture at district, state and national levels.
3. Improvement of the analytical capability and presentation of statistics utilised for national, state-level and district planning.
4. Development of modelling, forecasting and simulation techniques that are required for planning and decision support.
5. Establishment of a computer network with necessary communication equipment for ensuring easy access of information across the nation and ensuring reliable fast and optimal use of resources.
6. Evolving standards for the data collection, compilation and dissemination, with the cooperation of related agencies at district, state and central levels.
7. Creating a dedicated training school with branches in all parts of the country for extensive training retraining of personnel in public service and users of NICNET.
8. Providing gateways for accessing International Databases for those working in district/states/centre.

The NICNET, which was conceived in 1973 is a practical demonstration of the fact that the NIC has achieved its basic objectives stated above. NICNET is a satelite based computerised information system to provide data-communication, send messages and receive replies between the districts, states regional centres, Ministries, Departments etc. at central level and the central headquarters at NIC, New Delhi. Messages are sent and replies are received on line. NICMAIL facility available on NICNET through which about 500 nodes, geographically distriputed in the country, interact with one other. It is nation-wide network which enables communication with any district, state or regional NIC Centre for interactive communication and on line information retrieval

The other very prestigious network launched by NIC is named as District Information System (DISNIC). It is a data bank, incorporating a number of data-bases which contain statistical information on variety of subjects and geographical area, such as village, districts, agriculture, education, health, employment, administration etc. Some of the data-bases available under DISNIC are Administration Data-base (ADB) and Socio-economic Data-base (SDB). It will also be of interest to know in brief as to how DISNIC came into being. On the initiative the then Prime Minister Shri Rajiv Gandhi, a number of workshops of District Magistrates/District Collectors were conducted during 1987-88 for achieving 'responsive administration.' The nucleus of DISNIC emanated from this forum, as it was felt that for better planning and efficient decision making it is essential to have data from the district and see the latest position on-line at any disired/required time at any place in the country. Objectives of DISNIC are as under:

(i) develop the necessary information system data-bases in various sectors of the economy for planning and decision making at the district level.
(ii) promote informations, at the district level.
(iii) improve the analysis capacity and the presentation of the statistics to be utilized for national regional and district planning.
(iv) develop modelling and forecasting techniques that are required for decision making for socio-economic development.

S76 RAILNET

Abbreviation of Railway Network (Indian) with the Central Computer at new Delhi, connected to nodes at Bombay, Calcutta, Madras and Delhi which are in turn connected to around 700 terminals at various stations in the entire country.

S77 SIRNET

"Acronym for 'Scientific and Industrial Research Network' is a computer communication network for the CSIR laboratories. At present SIRNET has only one mail node known as CSIRD, signifying the CSIR mail node in Delhi. It is connected to a large network ERNET (Education and Research Network) set up by the DOE with financial assistance from UNDP. ERNET in tern is connected to the international network, UUNET (Unix User Network) through which international network like BITNET, CSNET and JANET are accessible. In addition to acting as intra-city node for other CSIR laboratories, CSIRD also acts as a gateway to ERNET and through ERNET to international network"

— from NISSAT, Newsletter, 97/1, Jan-Mar. 1991.

S78 INFLIBNET

S7931 Introduction

Full form of INFLIBNET is Information and Library Network. It is an ambitious project initiated by University Grants Commission which aims at building up a computer communication network of libraries and bibliographical Information centres in Institutions of higher learning (such as Universities) and R&D institutions and national organisations such as CSIR, ICAR, DRDO, ICMR, ICSSR, IC HR, DAE, DOE, DOT etc.

S7932 The Background

The University Grants Commission constituted a Committee on National Network System for university/libraries to suggest measures to network libraries in the country, so as to share the literature-resources for their optimum utilisation and to avoid duplication in holdings, to the extent possible. Professor Yash Pal, the then Chairman, UGC has been the Chairman of the Committee. The first meeting of the Committee was held on 22nd April, 1988.

The Committee, in the meeting, decided on constituting a Working Group on Information and Library Network (INFLIBNET) to prepare a project report within 3 months for consideration and further action.

The Working Group on INFLIBNET took due note of (a) Scientific Policy Resolution and Technology Policy Statement, (b) National policy on Education and (c) proposed Natioal Policy on Library and Information System, and submitted its report. The Executive summeary of the report of the inter agencies working Groups as under:

- INFLIBNET is a computer–communication network of libraries and bibliographical information centres.
- It is a major national effort to improve capability in information transfer and access, that provide support to scholarship, learning, research and academic pursuits.

- Institutions of higher learing covering all disciplines, R&D institutions and national organisations like CSIR, ICAR, DRDO, ICMR, ICSSR, ICHR, AICTE, DAE, DOT, DOE, Indira Gandhi National Centre for Arts, etc., participate in the INFLIBNET.

S7933 What is INFLIBNET

- INFLIBNET is a cooperative network and will contribute to pooling, sharing and optimisation of resources, facilities and services of libraries and information centres in the university system as well as in the R&D complexes

– It is a major programme towards modernisation of libraries and information centres in the country, with application of computer and communication technologies.

– INFLIBNET is a multiple function/service network. It will offer catalogue based services, database services, document supply services, collection development and communication based services.

S7934 Why INFLIBNET?

– Approximately a total sum of Rs. 150 crores/annum is spent towards books and journals by all the libraries concerned with higher education.

– Still a researcher/faculty in any institution is handicapped due to paucity of resources and services offered by his library. It is neither possible nor feasible to fund all the libraries in the country so as to be self-sufficient in meeting fully the needs of their users.

– Instead, if users are enabled to have access to holdings of each other library, the total national resources could be utilised optimally by everyone. This will also ensure that the libraries avoid, to a great extent, duplication in procuring costly books/journals and aim at developing more unique collection.

– Overall economy and improvement of efficiency as well as minimising the incidence of financial and other constraints faced at the level of individual libraries are expected to accrue from the network. apart from this, the academic communities could, through the network, establish instant contact with their counterparts in any part of the country for academic conversation.

S7935 How INFLIBNET will function?

– INFLIBNET is a versatile, integrated library and information system; yet, it operates at different levels-national, regional, sectoral and local.

– The catalogue of libraries will be aggregated bottom-upwards i.e., from college/department to university library and to regional centre. Secondary information/database maintenance and services wili be taken care of by sectoral information centre.

– End users will be served mainly at local level such as college, department, university and R&D institution. About 400 nodes are planned initially for this purpose.

– There will be a national centre for managing, overseeing and coordinating the affairs of the network and four regional centres (North, East, West and South) which will maintain union catalogue of holdings of libraries in the regions and database of projects, institutions and specialists.

– At the sectoral levell, UGC information centes-present (3) and proposed, NISSAT sectoral information centres and other centres which perform national level functions and services in specific subjects/-disciplines/missions are included.

– The sectoral centres will acquire, create and access retrospective and current bibliographic databases and offer a variety of modern information services.

– As many as 100 university and R&D institutional libraries will be designated and equipped to serve as document resource centres for purpose of document delivery service.

S7936 Objectives A INFLIBNET are as under

INFLIBNET is to be a computer-communication network for linking libraries and information centres in universities, deemed universities, institutions of national importance, UGC information centres, R&D institutions and colleges. The main objectives of INFLIBNET are

(a) to evolve a national network, interconnecting various libraries and information centres in the country and to improve capability in information handling and service;

(b) to provide reliable access to document collection of libraries by creating online union catalogue of monographs, serials and non-book materials (manuscripts, audio-visuals, computer media, etc.) in various libraries in India;

(c) to provide better access to worthwhile bibliographic information sources, with citations and abstracts, such as periodical articles, conference papers, preprints, technical reports, standards and specifications, patents, monographs, etc. through indigenously created databases of the Sectoral Information Centres of NISSAT and UGC Information Centres and such others and by establishing gateways for online accessing of international databases held by international information networks and centres;

(d) to provide document delivery service by establishing resource centres around libraries having a rich collection of documents;

(e) to optimise information resource utilization through shared cataloguing, inter-library loan service, catalogue production, collection development and avoiding duplication in acquisition to the extent possible;

(f) to implement computerisation of operations and services in the libraries and information centres of the country, following a uniform standard;

(g) to facilitate scientific communication amongst scientists, engineers, researchers, social scientists, academics, faculties and students through electronic mail, bulletin board, file transfer, computer/audio/video conferencing, etc;

(h) to enable the users disbursed all over the country, irrespective of location and distance, to have access to information regarding books, monographs, serials and non-book materials by locating the sources whereform available and to obtain it through the facilities of new communication technologies and union catalogue of documents;

(i) to create database of projects, institutions and specialists for providing online information service;

(j) to encourage co-operation among libraries, documentation centes and infomration centres in the country, so that the resources can be pooled for the benefit of helping the weaker resource centres by stronger ones;

(k) to develop suitable professional manpower of appropriate quality to establish, manage and sustain the INFLIBNET; and

(l) to evolve standards uniform guidelines in techniques, methods, procedures, hardwares and softwares, services and so on and promote adoption in acutal practice by all libraries, in order to facilitate pooling sharing and exchanging resources and facilities towards optimisation.

(From INFLIBNET document brought out by UGC)

Computer is an imprtant tool for transfer of information. With the advent and availability of bulkwise smaller and costwise chaper computers, now cmputers have even entered homes to set and manage one's day-to-day affairs. India was a bit late in adopting computerzation. by 1964 there were only 16 computers in India. During 1965-72 we had 170 computer systems in the country. After the establishming of Department of Electronics (DOE) in 1975 and NIC in 1977 computer culture has sprouted and the demand and growth of computer has been so much that number of computers in the country are can not be counted.

Bibliography

Agarwal, S.N. and others, ed: Prospectives in Library and Information Science, 2 v. (Lucknow, Print House, 1983).

Alexander Kern: College and University Library (Chartollesville, Michie Co., 1972).

American Library Association: *Bulletin*, Feb. 1966.

Atherton Pauline A.: Putting Knowledge to Work (New Delhi, Vikas, 1978).

Bowker's Library and Trade Annual (New York, R.R. Bowker 1979).

Davies, W.D.: Public Library as Cultural and Social Centres (Mituchen, Scarecrow Press, 1974).

Encyclopedia of Library and Information Science. Ed. by allen Kent and Harold Lancour (New York, Marcel Dekker, 1972-).

Fjallbrant, Nancy and Malley, I an: User Education in Libraries: 2nd ed (London, Clive Bingley, 1984).

Gerad, David: *Library and Society*, (London, Clive Bingle, 1978).

Gupta, S.R.: *Stock Verification in Libraries: Problems and Solutions* (Delhi, Ken Publications, 1990).

Hutchings, F.G.B. : Librarianship etc. (Kuala Lumpur, Oxford University Press, 1969).

India, Education Commission 1964-65, Chairman, L.S. Kothari: Report (New Delhi, Publication Division, 1968).

Jast, L.S.: The Library and Community.

Knapp, Patricia B.: An Experience in coordination between teaching and library staff ...Mimeographed. (Detroit, Monteith College, 1964).

The Kerala public Libraries Bill, 1989, (Trivendrum, Government of Kerala, 1989.)

Kesawan, B.S.: *India's National Library* (Calcutta, National Library, 1961).

The Library as a Community Information Centre: papers presented at an Institute by University of Illinois (Illinois, Onion Book Store, 1959).

McColvin, L.R.: Public Library System of Great Britain.

Mews, H.: Reader Instruction in College and University: Introductory Handbook. (London Clive Bingley, 1972).

Mohanrajan, P.A., ed.: New Trends in International Librarianship (New Delhi, 1984).

Mukherjee, A.K. : Fundamentals of Special Librarianship and Documentation (Calcutta , IASLIC, 1969).

Nagarajan, S. and other, Ed.: Distributed Data-bases; plan for interaction and on-line search (New Delhi Informatics Publication, 1989).

National Informatics Centre: District Information System of National Informatics Centre (New Delhi, The Auther nd.)

National Library Review Committee, Chairman: V.S. Jha: Report 1968.

The New Universal Encyclopedia Ed. by John Hammerlon (London, Educational Books).

Price, D.J. Desola: Science since Babylon (Connecticut, Yalle University Press, 1961).

Ranganathan, S.R: Five Laws of Library Science (Madras, Madras Library Assoication 1939 and later by Asia Publishing House, Bombay, 1963).

Ranganathan, S.R.: Preface to Library Science (Delhi, University of Delhi, 1948).

Rose, Emestine: The Public Library in American Life (New York, Columbiia University Press 1955).

The Shorter Oxford English Dictionary. Ed. by C.T. Onions' 2 v. 3d. ed. (Calcutta Standard Literture Company, 1968).

Snenn, Robert: *Test Questions* for School Library (London, 1958).

Wallace, Sarah Leslie: *So you want to be a Librarian* (New York, Harper and Row, 1962).

Wilson, Louis R. and Tauber, Maurice F.: *University Library*. 2nd Ed (New York, columbia University Press, 1956).

U.K. Board of Education, Committee on Public Libraries in England and Wales: Chairman, Sydney Roberts: *Report* (London, Her Majesty's Stationary Office, 1959).

Unesco: *Manifests for Public Libraries* (The Author, 1949, rev. in 1972).

University Grants Committee (U.K.); Report 1921.
University Grants Commissions, on Revision of Pay Scales of Teachers in University and Colleges, popularly known as Melhotra Committee: *Report* (New Delhi, U.G.C., 1986, mimeographed).

Index